IMAGES
of America

Cincinnati Radio

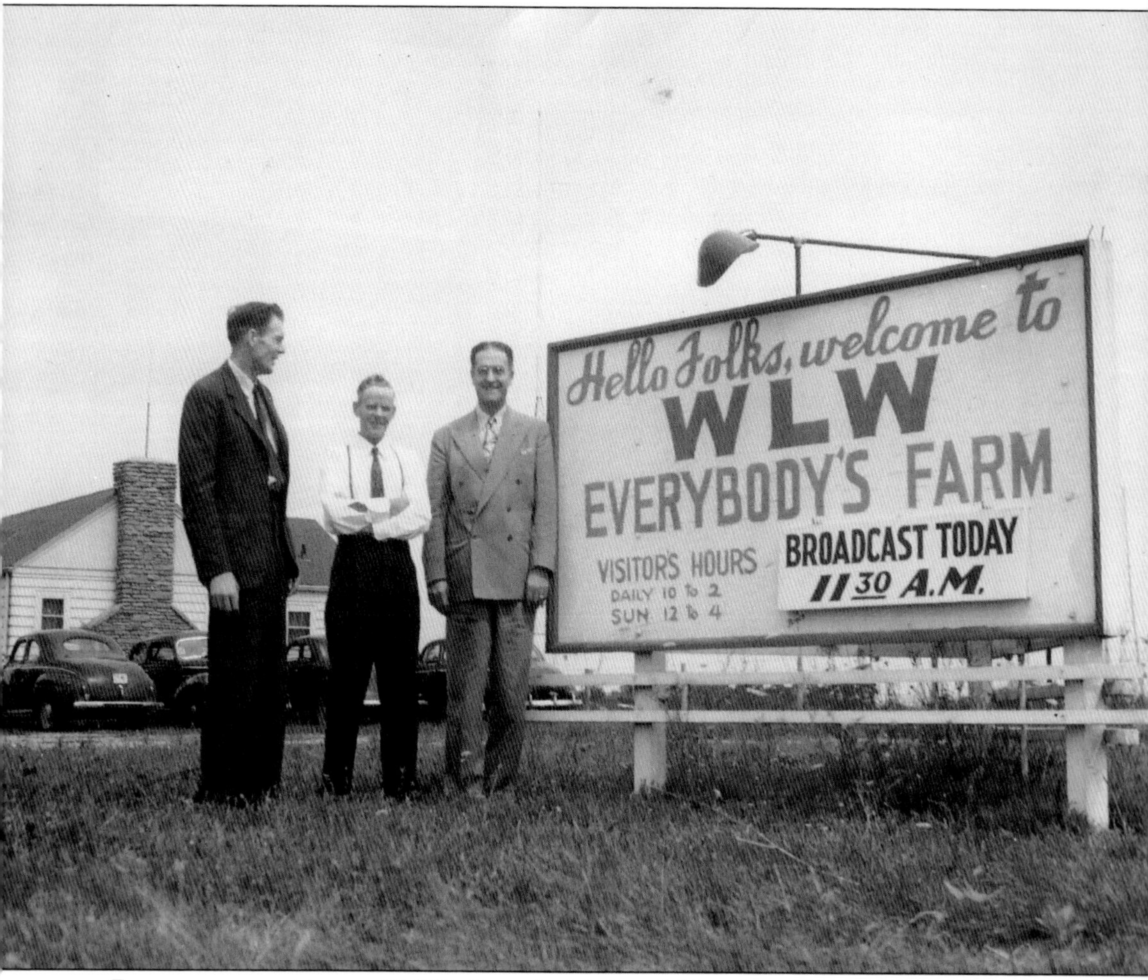

For many years, visitors to WLW's "Everybody's Farm" felt welcomed, in person and over the air. Indeed, there is a friendly tradition in radio to welcome listeners and to express appreciation for being permitted into listener homes and automobiles. From "Howdy folks . . ." to "Good evening and welcome . . .," radio hosts and announcers over the years have extended their greetings. Roy Battles (left) and Earl Neal (center) are seen in this image from around 1945. (Media Heritage archives, Robert and Dorothy Miller collection.)

On the Cover: Created by Fred Smith in the 1920s, the Crosley Players were the first organized dramatic ensemble at WLW. The Crosley Players handled a variety of dramatic scripts and featured, among others, Charles Egleston and Virginia Payne in its ranks. The announcer to the right is Harry Holcomb, who would go on to Chicago and a successful career as a producer (*Curtain Time*) and advertising executive, and later enjoy a career as a Hollywood character actor. (Media Heritage archives, Ed Dooley/Clyde Haehnle collection.)

IMAGES
of America

CINCINNATI RADIO

Michael A. Martini

ARCADIA
PUBLISHING

ISBN 978-0-7385-8864-3

Published by Arcadia Publishing
Charleston, South Carolina

Printed in the United States of America

Library of Congress Control Number: 2011939101

For all general information, please contact Arcadia Publishing:
Telephone 843-853-2070
Fax 843-853-0044
E-mail sales@arcadiapublishing.com
For customer service and orders:
Toll-Free 1-888-313-2665

Visit us on the Internet at www.arcadiapublishing.com

Contents

Acknowledgments		6
Introduction		7
1.	Early Years and Pioneers: The Early Development of Radio	9
2.	Behind the Microphone: The Announcers, Actors, and Newscasters of Cincinnati Radio	35
3.	Music to the Ears: The Bands, Vocalists, and Musical Acts of Cincinnati Radio	63
4.	Rural Radio: Broadcasting Cincinnati Sounds to the Farm Folk of the Country	83
5.	Radio Reinvents Itself: World War II and the Postwar Era of Cincinnati Radio	103
Epilogue		127

ACKNOWLEDGMENTS

There is a lot of love and support behind this book, and many kind people assisted in its creation and production. Seeds for a project like this were planted over a decade ago under the guiding hands of Dr. James C. King at Xavier University and George Zahn and Mark Magistrelli, my co-conspirators over the years who all have a few drops of blood in this work. Incidentally, 89.3 WMKV-FM deserves a shameless plug for allowing me to pursue the "harvest."

A special thanks goes to Dave Burns and Barry Mishkind for their encouragement and to Arcadia Publishing and their wonderful editors Melissa Basilone, Jim Kempert, and Sandy Shalton, who have been nothing short of delightful, helpful, and patient.

This book celebrates Cincinnati broadcasting legends, and I was fortunate to have two legends help edit, double-check facts, and offer suggestions: Clyde Haehnle and Bill Myers. Bill, in particular, was ever so accommodating despite deadlines, vacations, and my penchant for misusing commas, apostrophes, and dashes.

Special thanks to Arlene and Larry Smith, as well as Maureen Jacques, who perhaps helped more than they realize in this book's production, and to my lovely wife, Sue, and my boys Gabe, Tony, Theo, and Dom, who had to share daddy and part of vacation with a laptop, stacks of papers, and a grumbling temper. Gabe, in particular, deserves praise as my personal IT guy who was always willing to help me overcome any computer issues.

Mom and dad, also known as Carole and Ron Martini, contributed more than they know . . . dad as a lifelong lover of radio and mom, the history maven, who purchased Luke Feck's *Yesterday's Cincinnati* for me when I was 11 and got me hooked.

The stars of the book are, of course, the photographs. The majority of the images were taken from, and copyrighted by, the Media Heritage, Inc. archives and collected over the previous two decades. The photograph credits are listed in parentheses at the end of each description and are credited to collections in the Media Heritage archives: Robert and Dorothy Miller collection (RDM), Ed Dooley/Clyde Haehnle collection (EDCH), Jim Ranney collection (JR), Charlie Guffin collection (CG), Eugene Patterson collection (EP), George Bryant collection (GB), Will Warren collection (WW), Jerry Thomas collection (JT), Luise Reszke collection (LR), Minabelle Abbott Hutchins collection (MA), Frederic W. Ziv collection (FZ), Dave Burns collection (DB), Henry Thies family collection (TF), Marian Spelman collection (MS), Boss Johnston collection (BS), Carrol McConaha Rhodes collection (CMR), Lloyd Baldwin collection (LB), the Schulkers family collection (SFC), the Media Heritage general collection (MH), and on loan, the Mike Martini collection (MM).

Other photographs came from the following sources: Charlie Stinger (CS), the Cincinnati Historical Society Library at Cincinnati Museum Center (CHSL), the Gray History of Wireless Museum (GHW), the Kenton County Public Library (KCL), Maya DeBus (MD), Debby Delmore (DD), Judy Perkins Sinclair (JPS), Janet Jones (JJ), Wray Jean Braun (WJB), Jim Scott (JS), Carol Dunevant and the Frank Simon Band (FSB), Barbara Cameron (BC), Leona Atkins family (LA), Dusty Rhodes (DR), Ron Case (RC), Barbara Stough (BS), Walter Rogers (WR), and Kathleen O'Neill (KO). Thanks to Judy Schultz, Bill and Marianne Myers, Linda Bailey, and Bridget Kaiser.

Above all, I would like to thank all Cincinnati radio broadcasters, those I have known and those I was never fortunate enough to meet, for laying the foundation for my career and the careers of all who are in radio today. This book falls well short of giving credit to *all* who deserve it. But each of you *is* in this book, whether mentioned specifically or not.

INTRODUCTION

It is a fairly strong statement to place Cincinnati radio history above the radio traditions in other similarly sized cities. Pittsburgh's KDKA is credited as the birthplace of commercial broadcasting, and St. Louis's legacy is tied closely to the traditions of the legendary KMOX. Great radio has come from Cleveland too, and one should not forget the fantastic productions from Detroit's WXYZ. Indeed, it would be an even greater stretch to have the audacity to compare the radio history of Cincinnati to even larger cities like New York, Chicago, and Los Angeles and all of the amazing achievements "on the coasts." Audacity aside, however, Cincinnati was a pretty important place in terms of the development of radio broadcasting. Perhaps Cincinnati radio was often considered a stepping-stone on the career paths of many famous performers, but the fact that this so-called stepping-stone was so universally recognized and sought out is, in itself, a credit to its power and potential. Technology certainly had something to do with it . . . some of the greatest technical achievements in the history of broadcasting originated in the engineering laboratories of Cincinnati radio and television. But beyond the blueprints and signal test reports were the people—the talented men and women who actually stood in front of and in some cases behind the microphone and were responsible for the broadcasts that connected with listeners around Cincinnati, the Midwest, and beyond.

Beginning in radio's earliest days, pioneer broadcasters managed to put on the air some of the country's first radio stations: WMH, WRK, and WLW. This last station quickly became a national standard bearer in hiring one of the first program directors in the country, which helped forward the business from strict amateurism into a true profession. In doing so, WLW pioneered the development of original radio drama and news reenactments and expanded the programming options to reflect the interests and tastes of the listener. It developed some of the first soap operas and acquired such a following as to attract talented acts from all around the country through a nationwide talent search. Meanwhile, WLW balanced its on-air advancements with technological achievements so amazing the rest of the world stood in awe. WLW started using the slogan "the Nation's Station" as early as 1928 when it became one of the first clear channel, 50,000-watt radio stations. In 1934, when it became the nation's only superpower broadcaster with an output of a half million watts, the massive, gym-sized transmitter beamed its bold, brilliant signal over most of the continental United States. Led by founder and owner Powel Crosley Jr., WLW and its parent Crosley Radio also helped develop the most powerful shortwave transmission plant for the Voice of America, pioneered in the refinement of television and later color television, and developed one of the first high-fidelity radio transmitters. Well into the television age, Crosley developed a regional network of television stations and featured a stock company of talented performers who offered no rival in terms of popularity anywhere in the country.

The unique contributions of Cincinnati broadcasting were not limited to Powel Crosley's enterprise either. WKRC, for example, was a CBS-owned-and-operated network station that featured one of the country's first female program directors. WCKY, under the direction of a master showman named L.B. Wilson, was a leader in the field of self-promotion and boasted aggressive growth by developing a signal that dominated the nighttime South. Even tiny WCPO, the runt of the Cincinnati radio litter in terms of power output, offered the nation's top baseball announcer—twice—and was a leader in the development of radio news that set the standards of broadcast journalism as newscasting moved into television in the 1960s.

There is a popular old adage that radio is show business, except with a steady paycheck. Nearly all radio broadcasters—from the general manager, to the sales person, to the continuity writer, to the traffic person, to the on-air talent—have at least a little showbiz in them. How else could one explain a willingness to tolerate odd work schedules, less-than-munificent salaries, and fierce competition for too few jobs in the industry? Egos and an eye toward public attention notwithstanding, it takes only a glimmer of showbiz within one's soul to drive nearly all radio broadcasters. Still, there is also a sense of camaraderie in the business of radio. Even seemingly cold and blood-thirsty rivals, otherwise willing to do anything to get that extra Arbitron ratings point, are nonetheless willing to, perhaps secretly, acknowledge that deep down, fellow broadcasters are brothers and sisters in the show business family.

Therefore, this book is more of a family photograph album than the detailed and scholarly history Cincinnati radio deserves. The images of the men and women of the first 50 years of Cincinnati radio are the "great aunts" and "forgotten uncles" of a sometimes dysfunctional but mostly loving broadcasting family. The family is not limited to those actually working in the profession—every listener who turned a radio dial and spent any amount of time enjoying a program from a local station is also considered a member of the family. The individual listener is every bit as important—and perhaps even more so—as any announcer, vocalist, or sound technician. All it takes is one listener to complete the communications process, and although participation might be a chuckle, or a tear, or even some companionship for a lonely soul, the connection between family members through the ether is usually heartfelt, sincere, and very real. Like most family photograph albums, though, not every face or name is immediately recognized, and sadly, some names have been entirely forgotten. Nor is every family member represented as they should be because, as fate would have it, some stories have been lost permanently to time. But perhaps as you glance through the pages of time in this album, you will be introduced or reintroduced to some "kinfolk" who have brightened lives, informed and entertained masses, and helped set apart Cincinnati from the rest of the nation in terms of its many contributions to the development of radio broadcasting in this country.

One final note—to some degree, this book is the product of the mission of Media Heritage, Inc., a nonprofit archive and museum of Cincinnati radio and television history. A portion of the proceeds of the sale of this book benefits the preservation of that history. Information about Media Heritage and its programs and membership opportunities are available at www.historyofbroadcasting.com. For more information about the performers, announcers, and technicians mentioned in this book, as well as many others who are not mentioned, readers are invited to visit www.cincinnatiradiohistory.com.

One

Early Years and Pioneers
The Early Development of Radio

The concept of radio broadcasting was not an immediate revelation to the inventors of wireless communications in the 19th century. Those brilliant minds—and there were many who contributed to the invention of radio—primarily conceived of a means of person-to-person communication. They envisioned a series of wireless channels connecting people to people, people to ships, and country to country. Both sender and receiver of the communicated message would be well aware of the other. Both would be active participants in the process, and wireless would be the channel.

While many credit NBC's David Sarnoff, clearly, someone had to consider the concept of broadcasting as it applied to wireless communications. In broadcasting, one still has a sender and a message, but the capabilities and limitations of the receiver are not known. Like a farmer who tosses a handful of corn kernels into a strong wind, the spreader is not exactly sure where the seed will land or if it will actually take root. All he knows for certain is that the seed was tossed.

Radio broadcasters "toss a lot of seed" and many other things as well. Except for an occasional complaint or letter, though, there is virtually no knowledge that anyone actually received or understood the message. Without feedback, the limitations of radio broadcasting are such that the communications event is incomplete. Despite this fact, however, there is still an unexplainable level of intimacy between sender and receiver. The illusion of a one-to-one communication is still there, and many radio listeners feel as though the broadcaster is speaking directly to them.

Those fortunate enough to have the proper equipment with which to experiment in early wireless technology of the 1920s struggled with rudimentary apparatus to overcome basic problems. Radio was largely the toy of the amateur and the hobbyist. Camped out in the back of the garage, one envisions young "radio bugs" sifting the ether for signals from Pittsburgh, New York, and St. Louis. It was not until the development of the proper magnetic loud speaker that radio joined the family together in the living room.

Like the young "computer bug" fanatics of today, early radio was advanced by trial and error through brilliant minds dedicated to the advancement and the seemingly unlimited possibilities of the technology. The contributions of the countless professional and amateur enthusiasts who labored behind the scenes endure while they themselves have faded from memory. However, were it not for these progressive thinkers who were so entirely dedicated to advancing all the aspects of radio broadcasting, the shape and nature of the business here in Cincinnati would not have been the same.

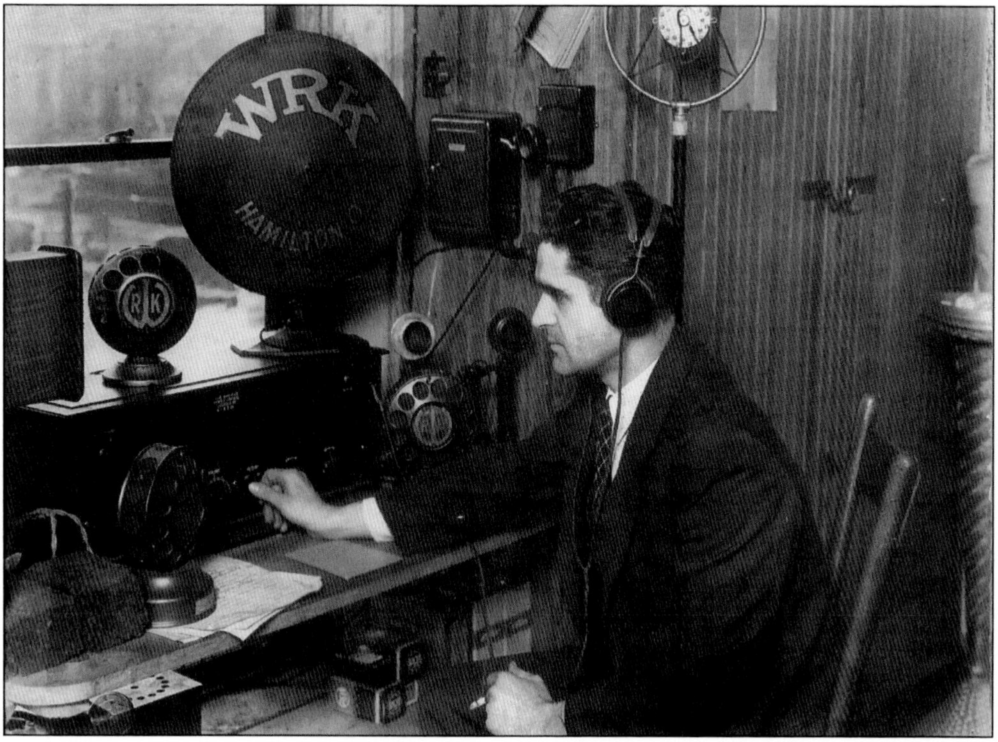

One of the first radio stations in southwestern Ohio was Hamilton's WRK. As early as 1915, brothers Shuler and Joseph Doron, with the encouragement of their father, Joseph Sr., were experimenting in amateur radio with the call letters 8ZU. After service in World War I, the Dorons went back on the air and in February 1922, put WRK on the air using their large home atop a hill overlooking downtown Hamilton. The Doron brothers also manufactured radios and parts, but the economic downturn ended both factory and radio station in 1930. In this image, announcer Tom C. Smith is posed in the rustic WRK radio studio. (CS.)

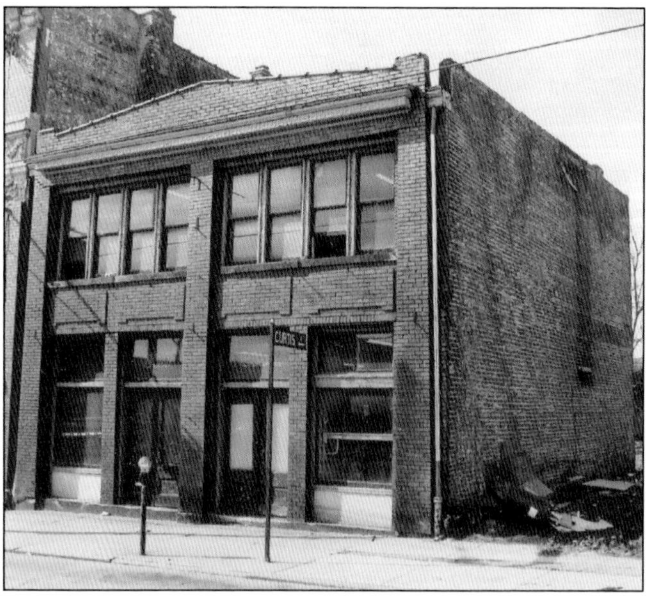
Cincinnati's first radio station grew out of experimental broadcasts dating back to 1919 on the second floor of this nondescript building near Peebles Corner at 2437–2439 Gilbert Avenue. The Precision Equipment Company was granted one of the first commercial broadcast licenses, and WMH went on the air on December 30, 1921. Precision manufactured the ACE radio, a competitor to Crosley. Because Crosley wanted an important patent that Precision owned, Crosley purchased Precision in 1923 and turned the license back to the government. (MM.)

In February 1921, as the story goes, Cincinnati entrepreneur Powel Crosley Jr. (right) went to purchase a "radio toy" for his son Powel III (standing). Rather than pay the exorbitant price of the day, Crosley instead built one himself from parts and then started manufacturing them through his company. By 1924, Crosley was the largest radio manufacturer in the world. Pictured with his father, Powel Sr. (left), Powel Jr. began experimentally radio broadcasting immediately in 1921 and had WLW on the air on March 2, 1922. (EDCH.)

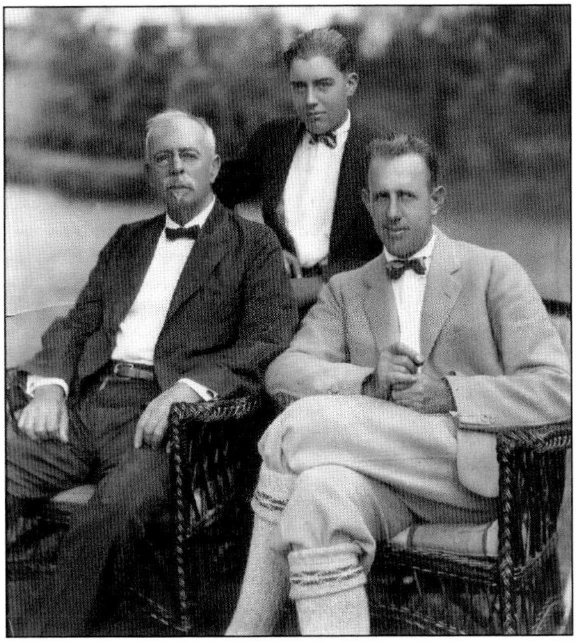

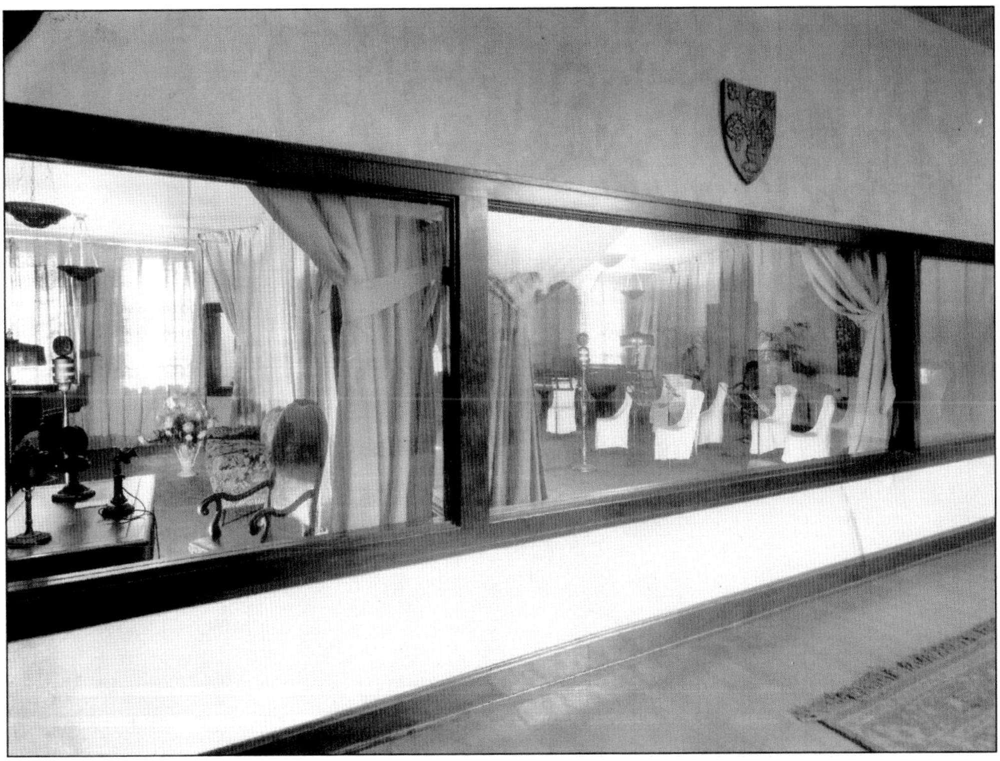

After being temporarily located in a corner of one of Powel Crosley's manufacturing plants, WLW's first permanent radio studios were constructed in a Crosley-owned building at Colerain and Alfred Streets near Northside. The studios featured long windows through which guests could observe programs being broadcast. Ignored, however, was the fact that the building was located next to a railroad siding, and the rumble of trains could be heard during certain broadcasts. (EDCH.)

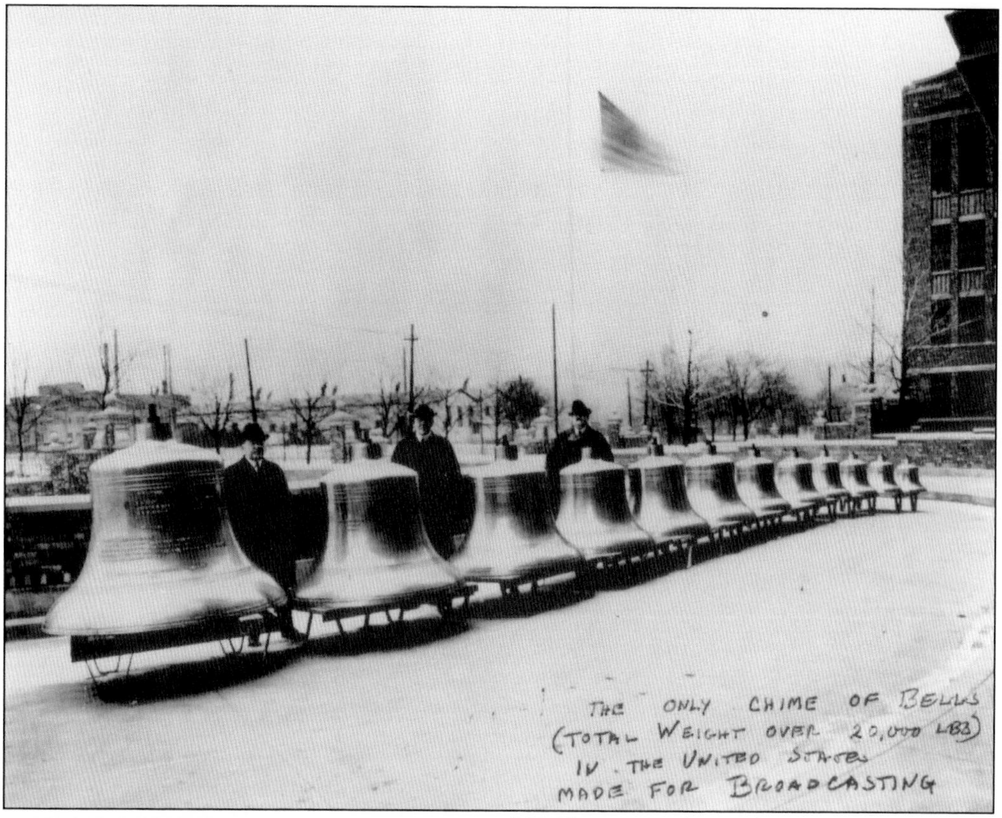

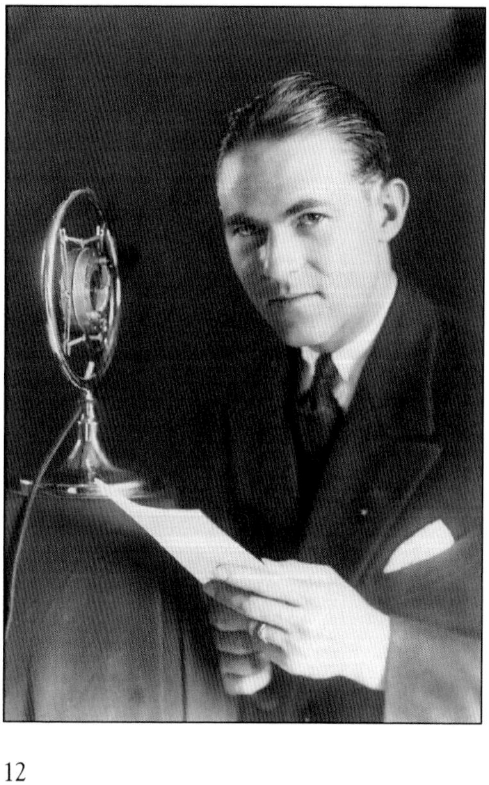

US Playing Card president John Omwake purchased an expensive set of carillon bells for the central bell tower at his sprawling factory in suburban Norwood. Omwake had learned about radio and thought it could be used to broadcast the music of his new carillon bells and at other times to chime each quarter hour. It was not until after the radio station was completed that Omwake accepted Paul Greene's suggestion to offer programming other than bells. (MM.)

To build a radio studio at the US Playing Card factory, company president John Omwake gave Bell Laboratories engineer Paul Greene pretty much free rein to complete the task. Greene spared no expense in creating what some termed the greatest radio studios anywhere. He also applied a little "reverse engineering logic" to choose a rural cornfield in Mason as the remote transmitter location. As a reward for his work, Omwake named Greene the station's first manager, announcer, salesman, and chief engineer, among other titles. (MM.)

In the mid-1920s, most radio stations placed their tower and transmitter near the studios for convenience. But with improvements in dedicated program lines, the transmitter could be located practically anywhere. Using a receiver to pick up distant radio stations as well as a map of various soil types, Paul Greene drove around the area until he determined that the Mason site had the best reception and thus would originate the best signal. Because of this and despite output power of just 500 watts, WSAI was heard at night all around the Eastern United States, and other stations quickly took note. (EDCH.)

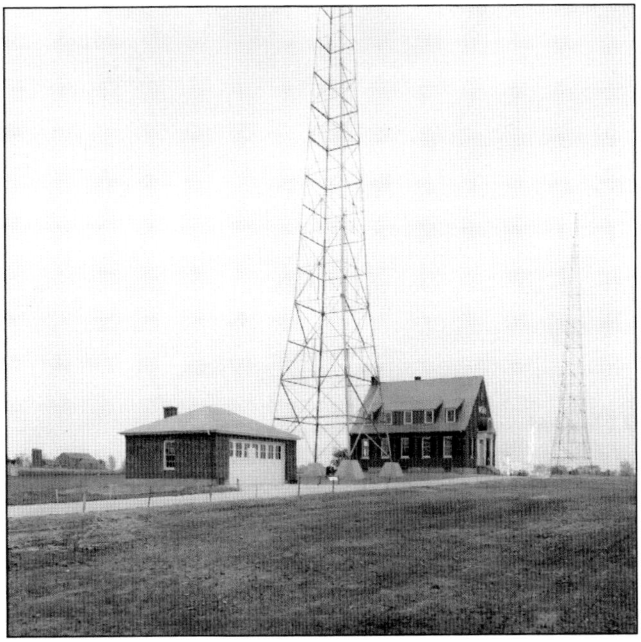

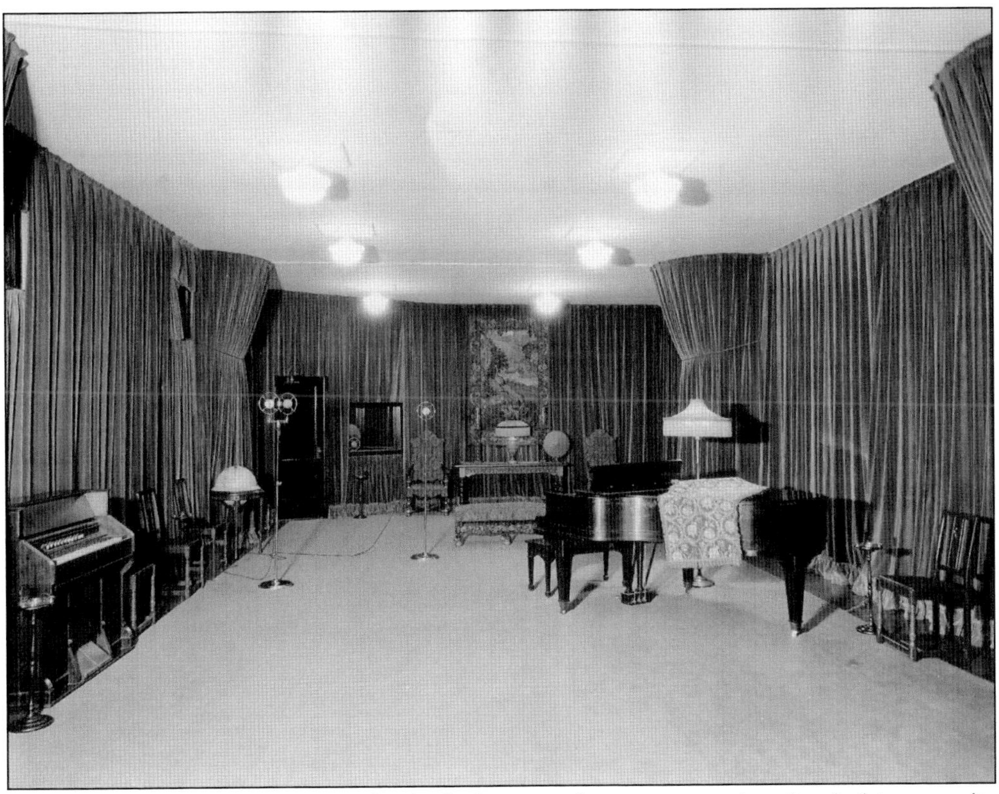

WSAI owner John Omwake wanted only the best sound equipment and studios for his new radio station. No expense was spared in finding just the right chandelier or antique furniture accent. Like most studios of the era, the walls and ceilings were draped in monk's cloth to deaden the sound. WSAI featured an "ensemble studio" and this larger "performance studio." (MM.)

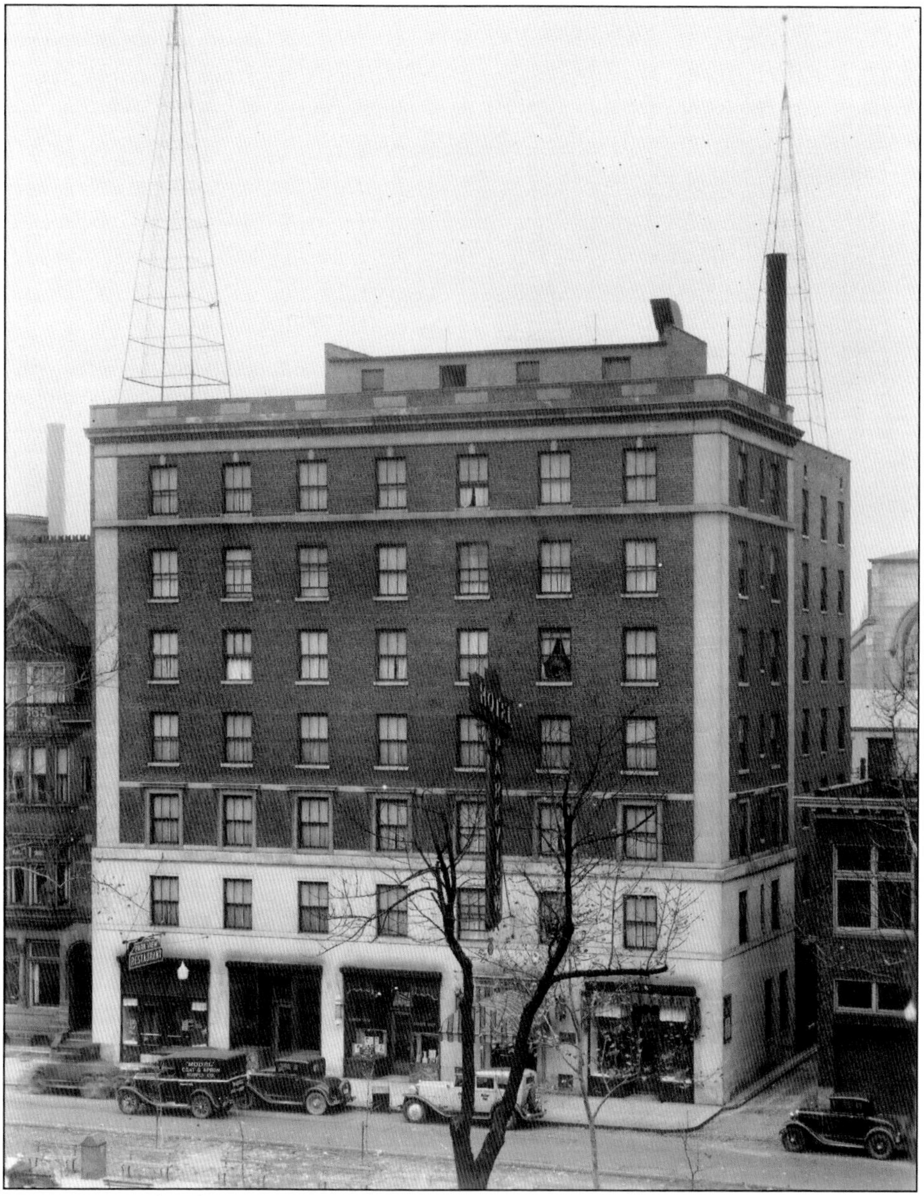

There were several radio stations in Cincinnati in the early to mid-1920s that did not survive the decade. WAAD, WLAZ, WIZ, WILG, and WHBR all were licensed in Cincinnati and did not last more than a year or two. An exception was WFBE, which was located in the basement of the old Parkview Hotel on the north side of Garfield Place in downtown Cincinnati. At 250 watts, WFBE was the smallest of the original five surviving stations. When the hotel was sold in 1930, the new owners did not know that the radio license was part of the sale. Despite its small size and low power, WFBE became very successful, emphasizing sports, including boxing and baseball broadcasts. Actor Bob Bentley led a small but enthusiastic dramatics department, Harry Hartman sold airtime and announced sports, and Deke Moffitt's orchestra provided music. The transmitter was located on the roof of the hotel, and the studios occupied a suite of small storage rooms in the basement. Eventually, WFBE was moved to the Keith's Theater and became WCPO. (CHSL.)

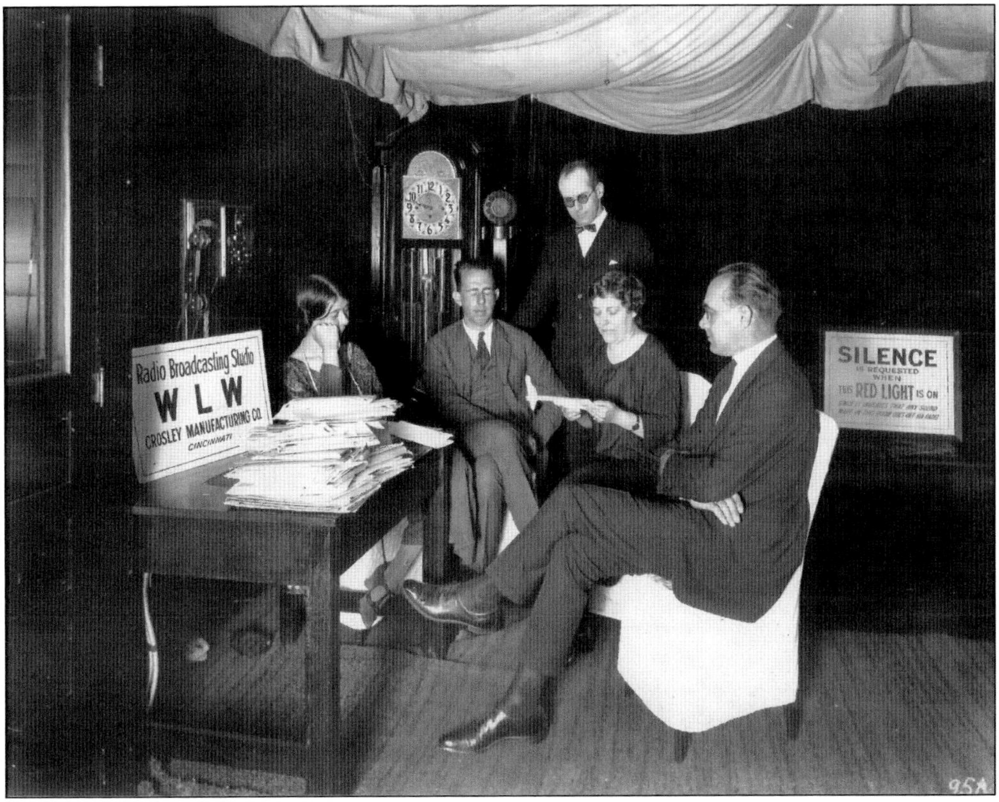

When WLW went on the air March 2, 1922, Powel Crosley thought of broadcasting as an adjunct to the sale of radio receiving sets. But Crosley had long been interested in promotion and advertising and was quickly amazed by the scope and scale of broadcasting—reaching thousands of people with a directed, personalized message at the same time. WLW's "Lightning Bugs"—the name given to the listeners' fan club—soon flooded the station with letters, praise, and requests, which often were bound in book form and given to guest performers, like opera star Mabel Garrison (seated third from left). (EDCH.)

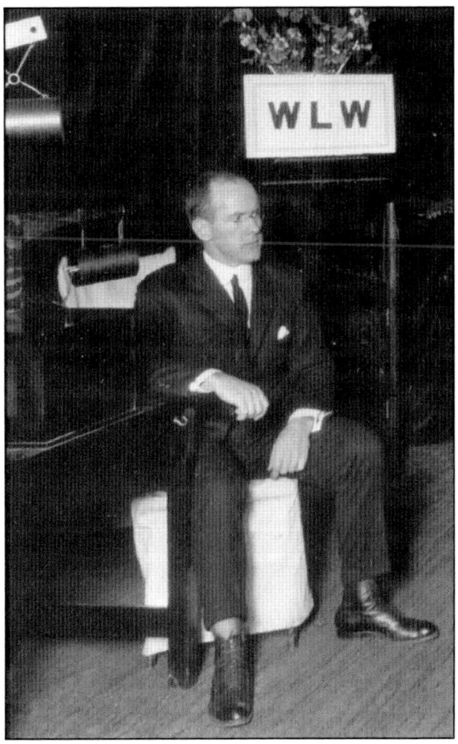

Among early Cincinnati radio broadcasters, Fred Smith was a truly innovative pioneer. Smith approached Powel Crosley in 1924 with the then unheard of concept of a regular daily program schedule while most stations' programming was haphazard and spontaneous. Thus Smith became, perhaps, radio's first official program director, as well as promoter, dramatist, creator of the drama-news hybrid *The March of Time*, and later the board of trustees executive manager at the College of Music. (EDCH.)

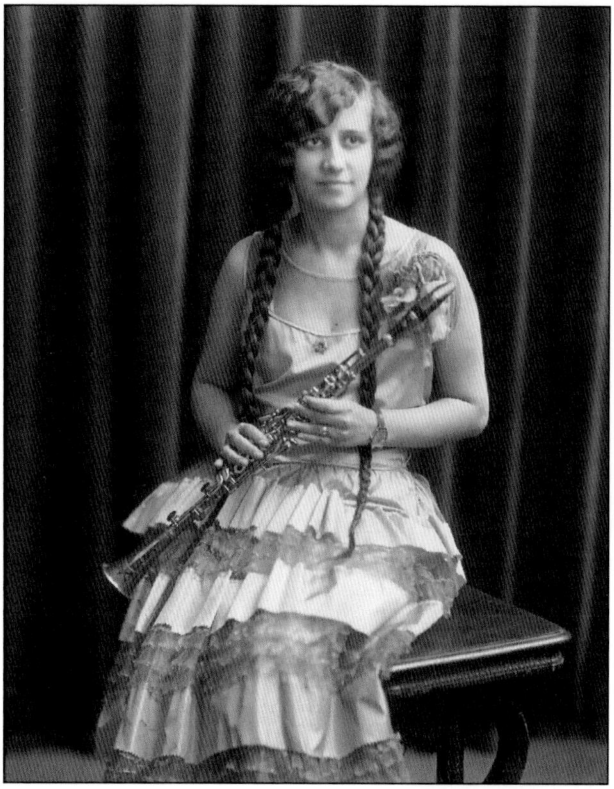

One of the best examples of WLW program director Fred Smith's innovations occurred in 1926 when he discovered a pretty and talented teenage clarinet prodigy named Luise Reszke. Smith featured her performances on the air but kept her identity secret, referring to her as the Phantom Clarinetist. Soon, the mystery was turned into a contest where people would write letters with their best guess about the age and appearance of the musician. The publicity stunt—perhaps one of radio's first—generated thousands of guesses before Reszke's identity was finally revealed in December. (LR.)

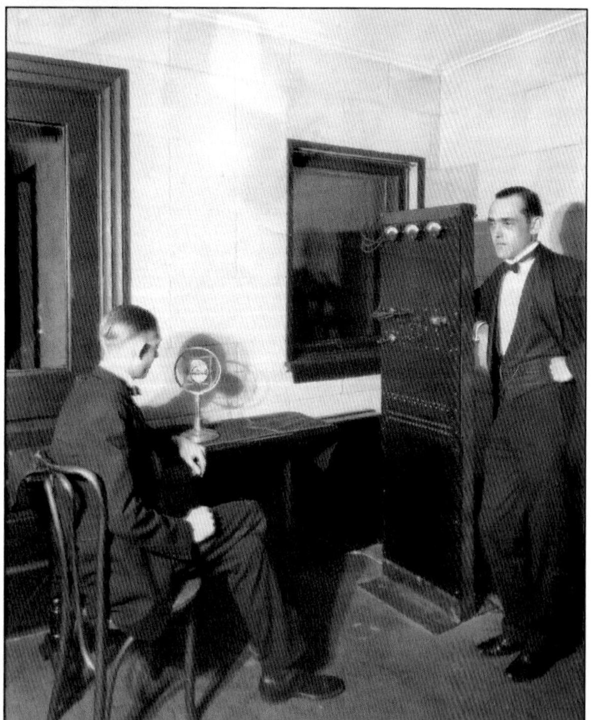

The WMH call letters returned to Cincinnati in 1924, and in April 1925, radio entrepreneur Clarence Ogden purchased the license. Ogden manufactured radios under the Kodel nameplate, so he changed the call letters to WKRC (for Kodel Radio Corporation) and built new studios in the Hotel Alms in Walnut Hills. Among the early employees at WKRC were announcer and manager Eugene Mittendorf and technician John Church, seen seated here in the WKRC announcers' studio. (MM.)

Harry Hartman was easily the first big star of WFBE. Pulled out of the audience to announce a boxing match when the scheduled announcer became ill, Hartman left his job as a tailor to become a full-time announcer and salesman for WFBE in 1929. He is pictured here (at left) in front of the WFBE microphone with comedian Ben Bernie. Another early WFBE hire was announcer and actor Bob Bentley, who produced several original dramas and comedies at the tiny 250-watt station and later joined WLW as a writer. (MM.)

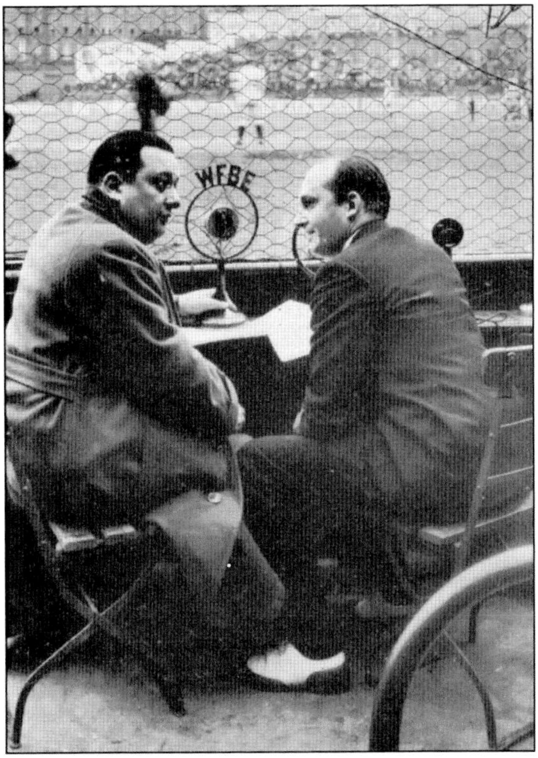

By 1932, and thanks to Harry Hartman, WCPO had gained such a reputation for its baseball broadcasts that the station was granted permission to construct a permanent broadcast booth at old Crosley Field. In this image is a "Wheaties Day" promotion at Crosley, and it is assumed these fans were granted entrance to the game for bringing a box of Hartman's longtime sponsoring cereal. (MM.)

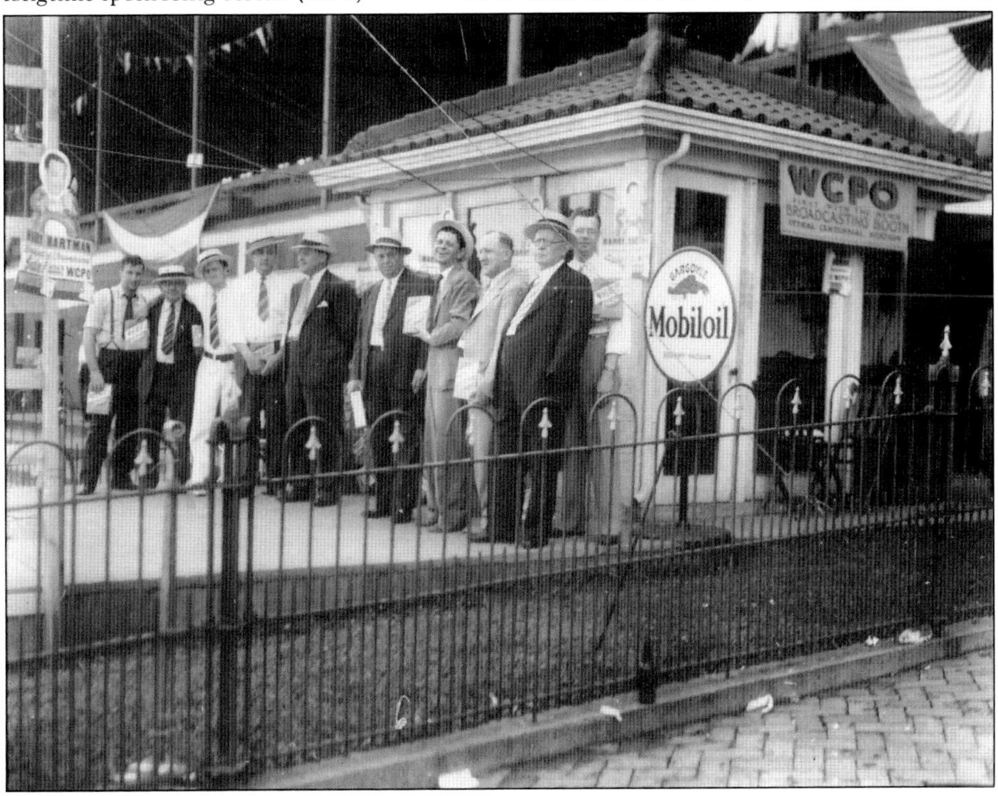

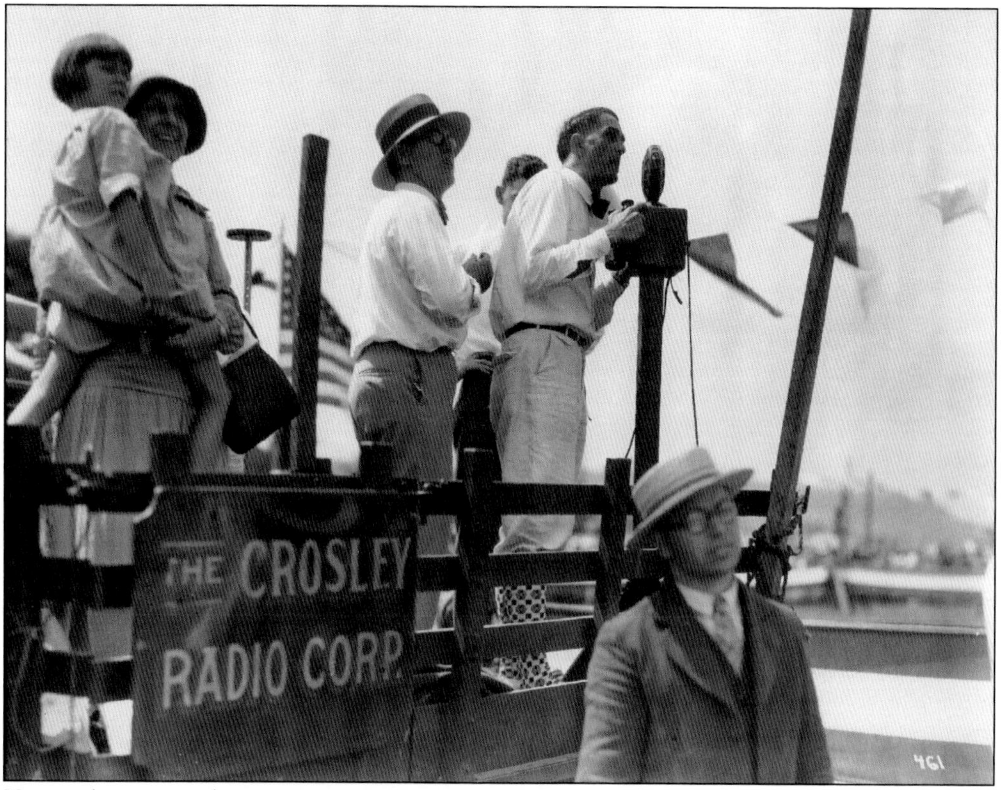

Having his own radio station provided several opportunities for a sportsman as diverse and multifaceted as Powel Crosley Jr. Crosley, who loved terrapin fishing, once did a live broadcast from a boat during a fishing derby in Sarasota. Crosley's radio stations also originated reports from the Black Powder Rifle Championships in Friendship, Indiana. Crosley loved airplanes and had several Crosley-sponsored planes in air contests, which he occasionally would broadcast on his radio station, shown above in 1928. A baseball fan, Crosley himself would help announce an occasional opening day at Redland Field, shown below with announcers Ford Rush (left) and Glenn Rowell, long before Crosley purchased the team. (CMR.)

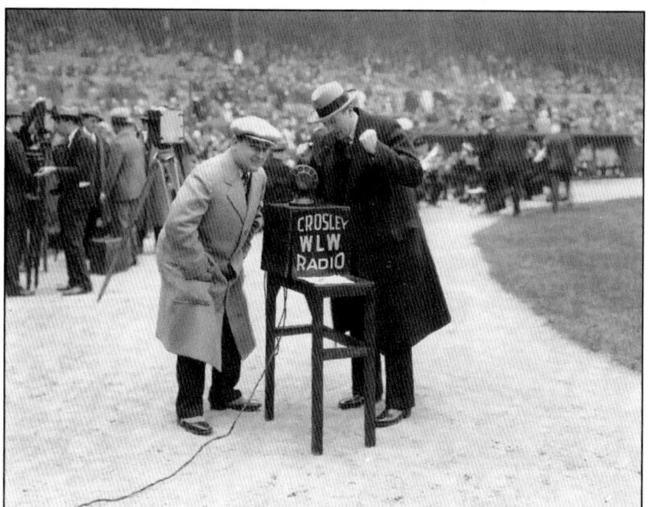

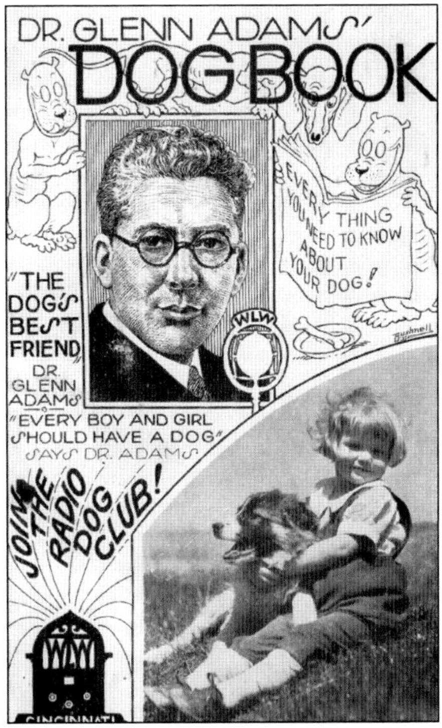

Until the rise of the networks and the introduction of advertising dollars in the late 1920s, radio was primarily an amateur operation. Radio "talent" could range from volunteer vocalists to local amateur bands, which would perform on air simply for the opportunity to promote an upcoming live appearance. US Playing Card–owned WSAI had a radio bridge card game program, and WLW featured programs teaching swimming and in the case of Dr. Glenn Adams, a program devoted to dog training. (MM.)

WLW musical director William Stoess and his players might have felt uncomfortable dressed in costume in a non-air-conditioned 1920s studio, but dressing up for broadcasts at that time was the norm rather than the exception. Tuxedos were common attire for announcers, and even transmitter and studio technicians would wear a coat and tie. If a sponsor, such as the Clicquot Club Eskimos or the A&P Gypsies, requested a costume for a performance, radio performers complied. (EDCH.)

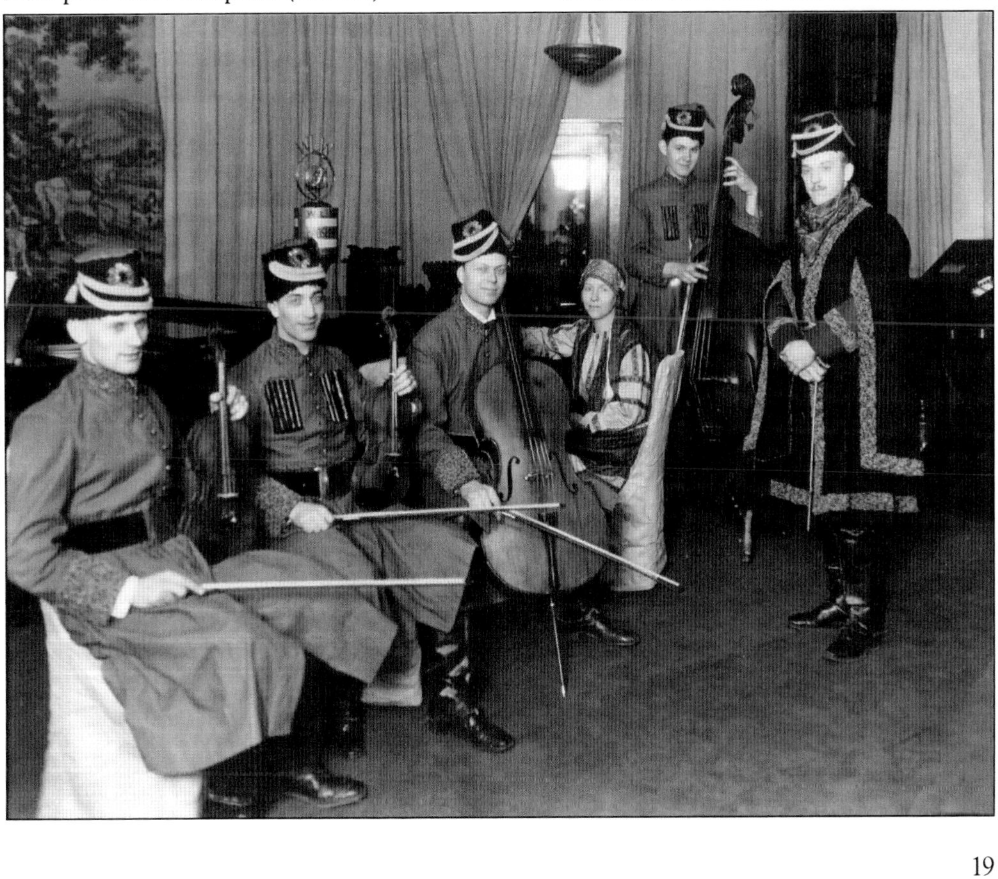

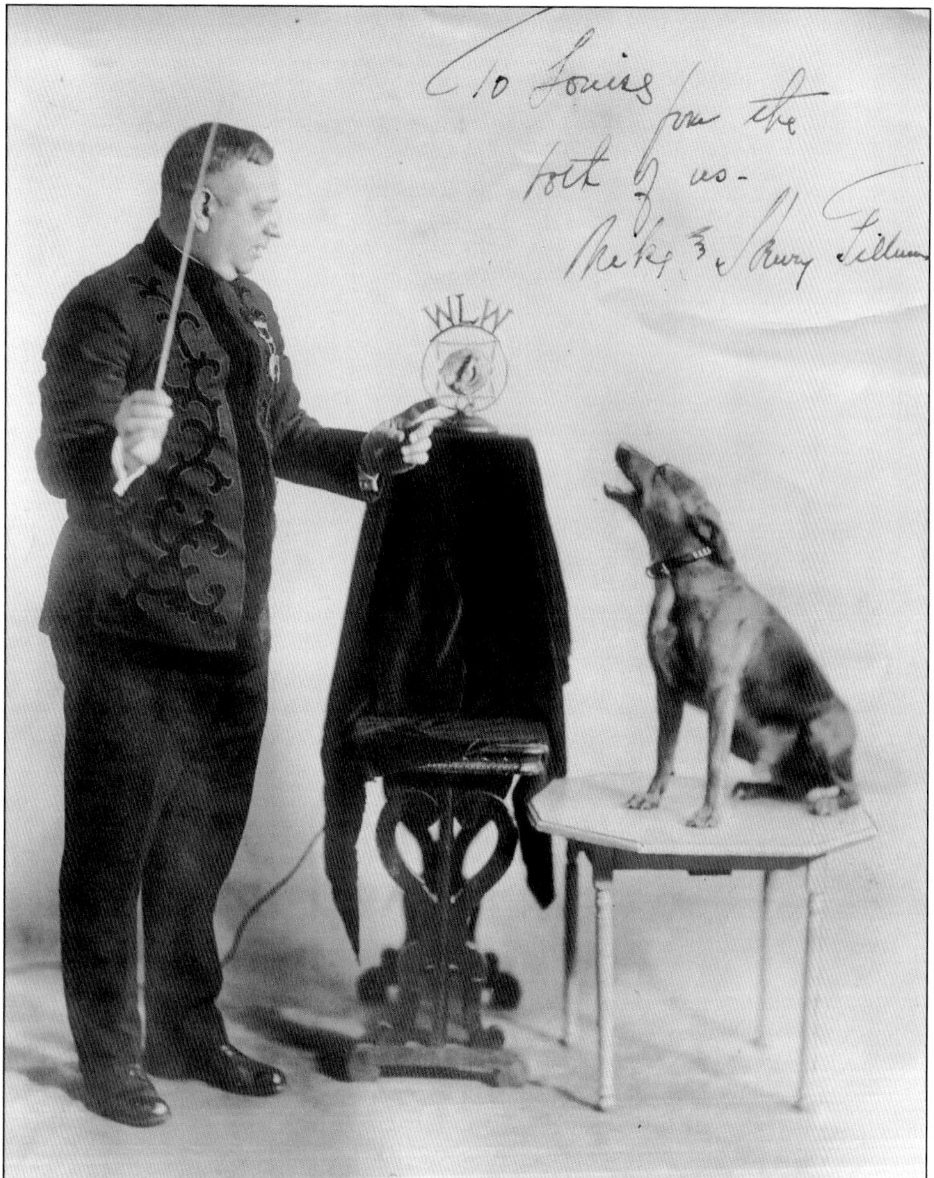

Aside from John Philip Sousa, few American march music composers hold the regard of Henry Fillmore. Fillmore's family owned a music publishing business in Cincinnati, and surrounded by music, Henry demonstrated his proficiency by composing such greats as the "Americans We" march and "Lassus Trombone." Beginning in April 1924, WLW began featuring Fillmore's band and eventually gave him his own program. Sometime in 1925, Fillmore adopted a shaggy, sickly puppy, which he named Mike. It was not long before Fillmore discovered Mike's talent: he would bark on cue when Fillmore raised his arms a certain way. Mike was also willing to come on stage, sit facing the audience, and perform with the band. Fillmore eagerly included Mike in the act, even composing songs featuring his barking solos. Suddenly, "Mike the Radio Hound" was a fan favorite, receiving bags of fan mail each week and touring and recording with Fillmore's band. Mike died unexpectedly in 1932, and Fillmore never really recovered from the loss of his companion, retiring to Florida for the remaining years of his life. (LR.)

In 1918, newspaper serial writer Robert Franc Schulkers had already established a popular following with several series of children's stories—most notably, those centering around a chubby, fictional child scribe named Seckatary Hawkins. As early as 1922, Schulkers was bringing those stories to WLW radio, performing all roles himself. In 1926, Seck moved to WSAI but returned to WLW in 1928 when Crosley purchased the former. In 1933, with Ralston as sponsor, *Seckatary Hawkins* was moved to Chicago where it gained a cast of juvenile actors and found a national radio audience for several years. (SFC.)

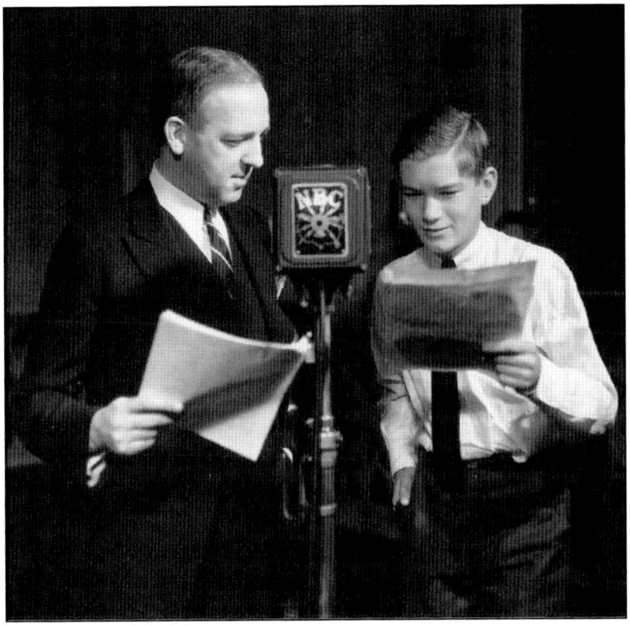

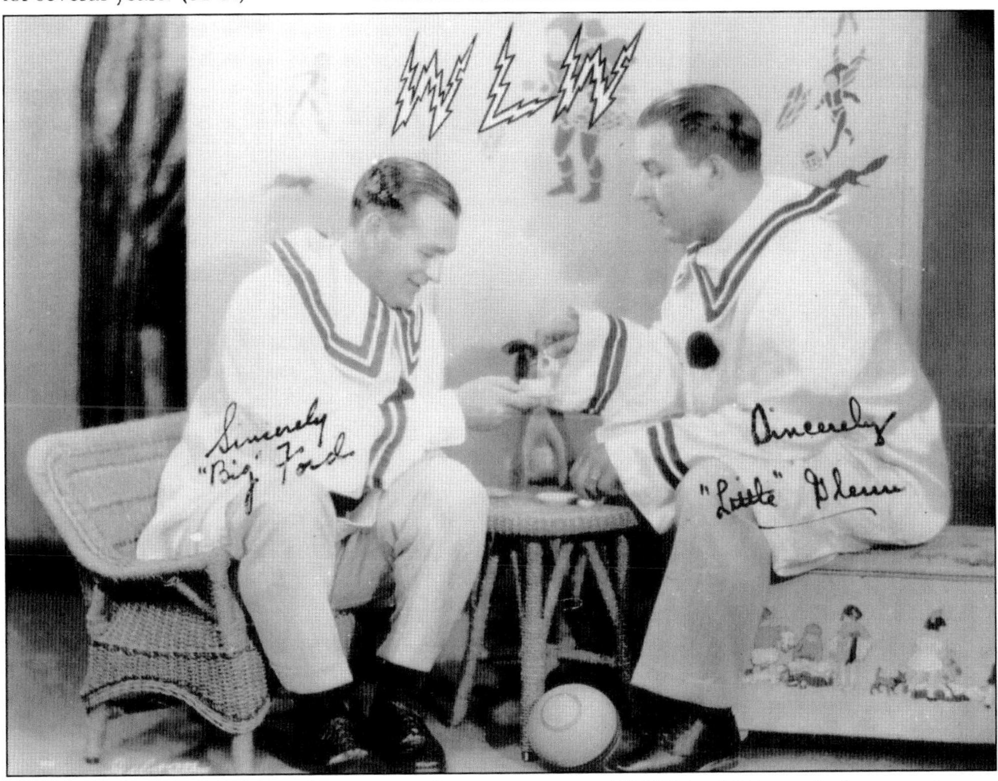

Ford Rush had been a popular song-and-patter man on WGN in Chicago before coming to Cincinnati in 1929 to partner with Glenn Rowell and form the popular children's team the Lullaby Boys. But soon after, Gene Carroll, another Chicago songster, lost his partner and joined Rush and Rowell at WLW. As it turned out, three was a crowd, and Gene and Glenn went off on their own as a successful duo while Ford Rush stayed on as WLW's "Old Man Sunshine." (MM.)

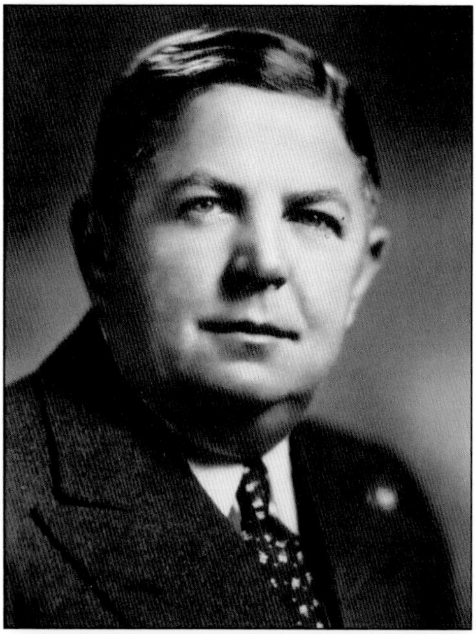

As a child, Covington's L.B. Wilson toured the country in a vaudeville tumbling act with his brother Hance. Back in Covington, L.B., who was named after his mother, Lida Beall, opened a small but successful cigar stand in an alley. In a matter of just a few years, Wilson's "empire" included two theaters, a bank, grocery stores, and several other businesses. In 1929, Wilson and some investor friends won the license for WCKY, which stood for Covington, Kentucky. WCKY went on the air on September 16, 1929, and the stock market collapsed a month later. Fortune smiled again as Wilson bought out his fellow investors for pennies on the dollar. (MH.)

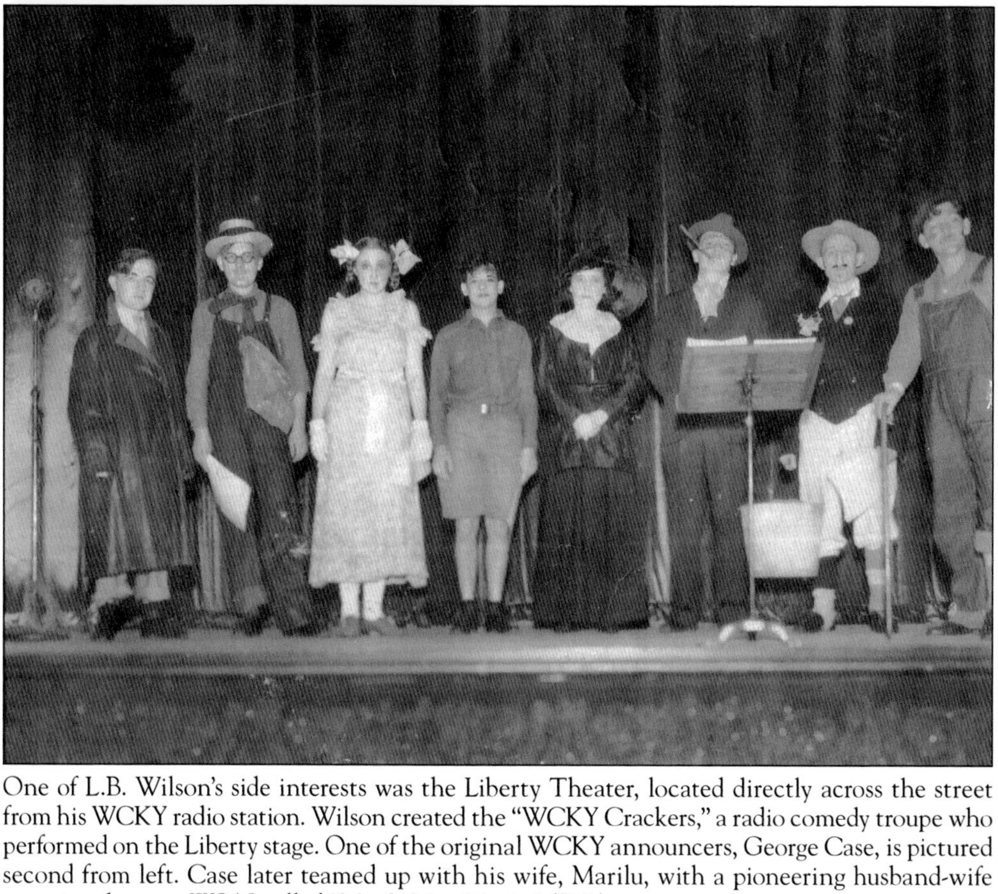

One of L.B. Wilson's side interests was the Liberty Theater, located directly across the street from his WCKY radio station. Wilson created the "WCKY Crackers," a radio comedy troupe who performed on the Liberty stage. One of the original WCKY announcers, George Case, is pictured second from left. Case later teamed up with his wife, Marilu, with a pioneering husband-wife morning show on WSAI called "Mr. & Mrs. Music." (RC.)

Work commenced in early 1930 on a new headquarters for Crosley's radio manufacturing and broadcasting business. An eight-story factory was built on Arlington Street in Camp Washington. Floors one through six were dedicated to manufacturing. There were offices on the seventh floor, and the studios for WLW and WSAI were located on the eighth floor. The facility was state-of-the-art with studio floors "floating" on sound-isolation chambers, air conditioning, and the latest in acoustics. The dozen studios provided ample space for rehearsals and broadcasts for both stations. (EDCH.)

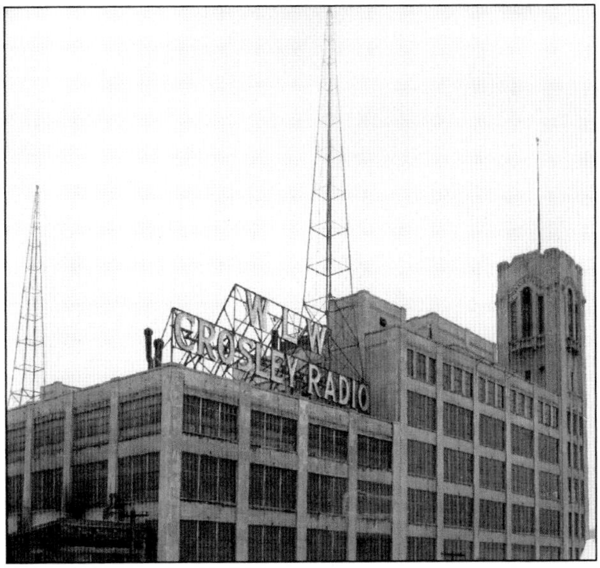

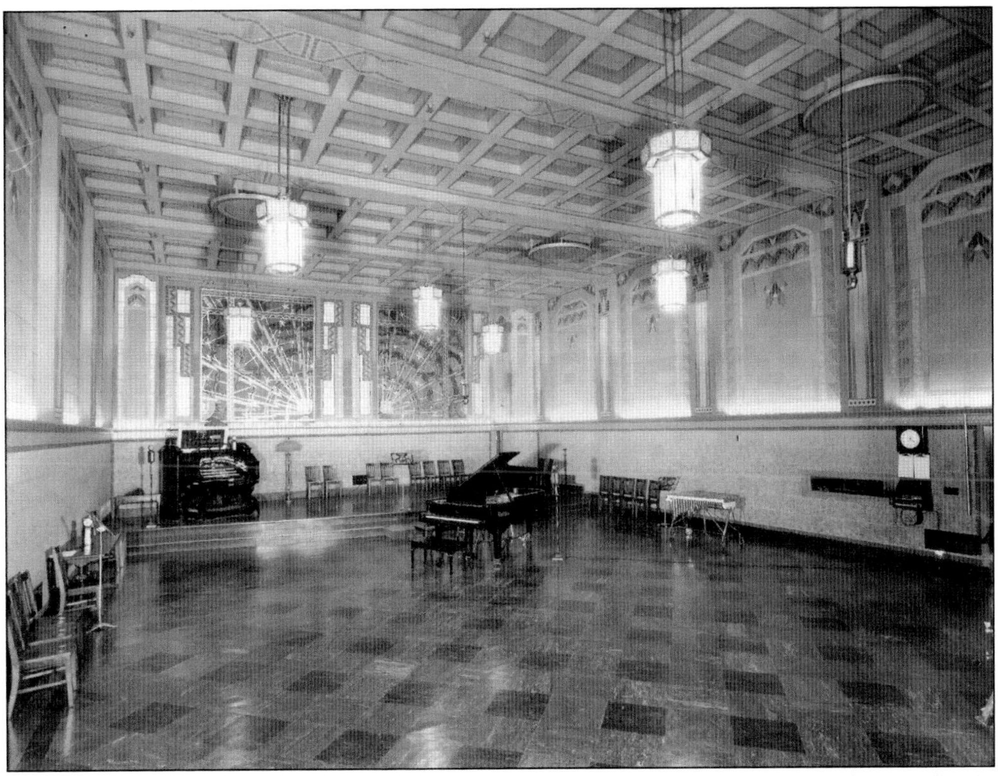

The showpiece of Crosley's Arlington Street facilities was the large main studio, Studio A. The elaborately decorated space could comfortably host the 60-piece WLW orchestra and still accommodate a large audience. Red Skelton's *Avalon Time* originated from here, as did many other live programs. The three-manual Wurlitzer Opus 1606 was installed in Studio A with its various ranks of pipes hidden behind the chromium Art Deco grillwork on the rear wall. After Crosley/Avco vacated the building in the 1950s, the room was stripped of its ornamentation and lost to the ages. (MA.)

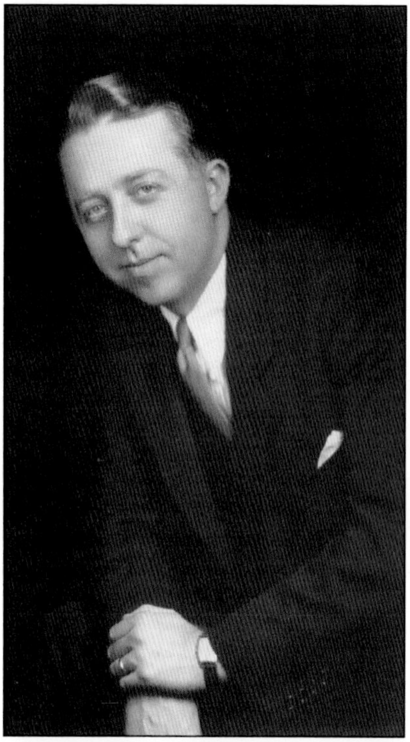

For all of his successes, Powel Crosley did have some dark sides, and one was a well-documented paranoia over Depression-era staff levels. Often, he would return from a vacation, look at the latest profit statement, and unceremoniously order across-the-board layoffs. In March 1930, John Clark was hired as station manager to carry out Crosley's orders. Beyond that, though, Clark aggressively pursued new talent by placing advertisements in newspapers in New York, Chicago, St. Louis, and other major cities, offering paid temporary positions to unemployed ex-vaudevillians and other talented performers. If they succeeded, they stayed, but if not, they were sent home. (MA.)

One of John Clark's first moves was to "steal" a popular entertainer who was one of WCKY's original program hosts—Sydney Ten Eyck. At WCKY, Ten Eyck had created a music and patter show called "The Doodlesockers of the Air." Based on fictional "Grandpappy Doodlesocker's" exploits, and featuring a small band, a vocal trio, and pianist "Ramona," the comedy program was very popular. After a stint in New York, Ten Eyck returned to WLW in 1946 where his Doodlesockers returned for a brief revival. (MM.)

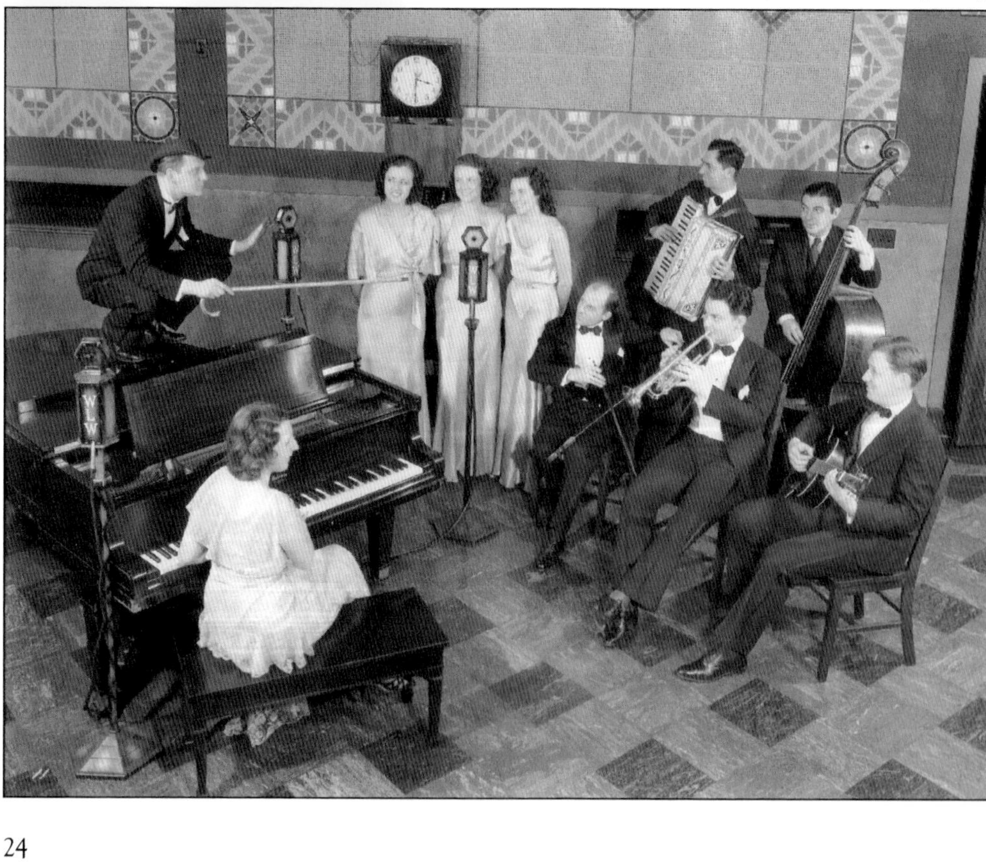

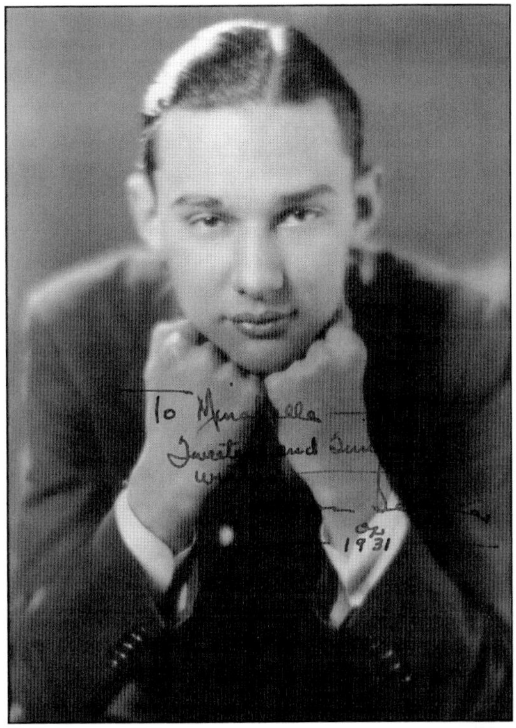

Covington-born Don Becker came to WLW as a ukulele player. However, the talented Becker quickly demonstrated skills as a program writer and producer. In just a few years, Becker focused exclusively on his typewriter, authoring scripts for a variety of shows. His legacy, however, was to be the radio soap opera *The Life of Mary Sothern*, which he helped create and write beginning in the fall of 1934. In 1936, Becker left WLW to write for a New York soap opera producer called Trans American. In 1937, the company acquired *Mary Sothern* for national distribution. (MA.)

Like the stylish studios of today, Crosley's Arlington Street studios had a greenroom where guests and performers could relax and unwind before and after broadcasts. While the Arlington Street "performers lounge" was not particularly plush, many performers and announcers camped out in chairs or couches for a nap during daylong schedules. (EDCH.)

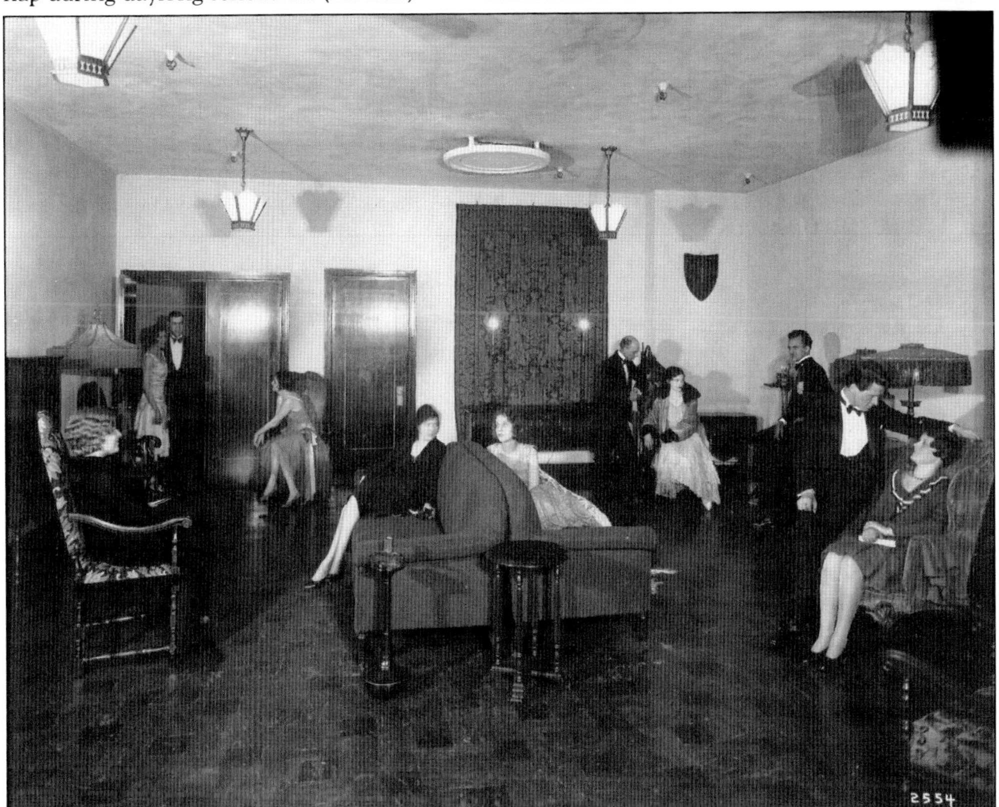

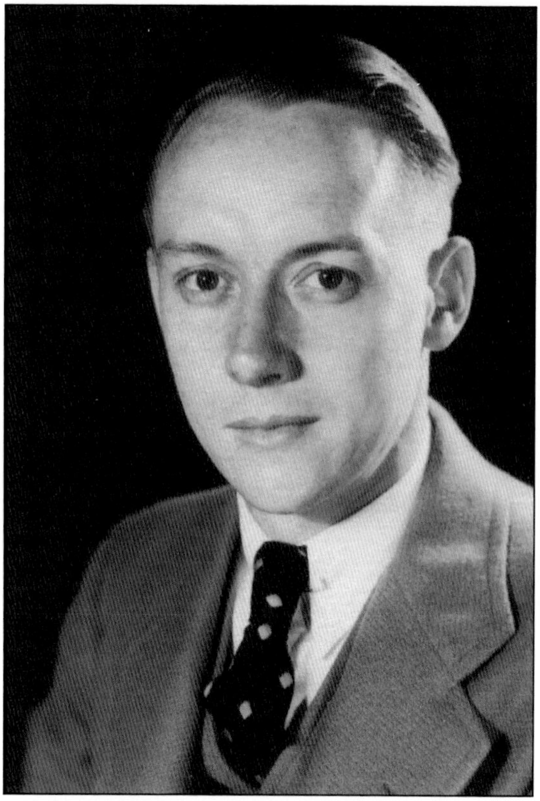

Joseph Chambers was the chief engineer charged with assembling and overseeing the operation of the 500-kilowatt transmitter. An engineering whiz, the baby-faced Chambers supervised radio's largest broadcast operation into the late 1930s. (EP.)

Almost immediately after being granted permission to broadcast at 50,000 watts in 1928, WLW quietly began planning for its next power increase application. By this time, they had moved the WLW transmitter to the Mason WSAI site and by 1933, had constructed an 851-foot, diamond-shaped Blaw-Knox tower in preparation for its superpower increase. To accommodate the new equipment, ground was broken by Powel Crosley Jr. on a new transmitter building that same year. (GHW.)

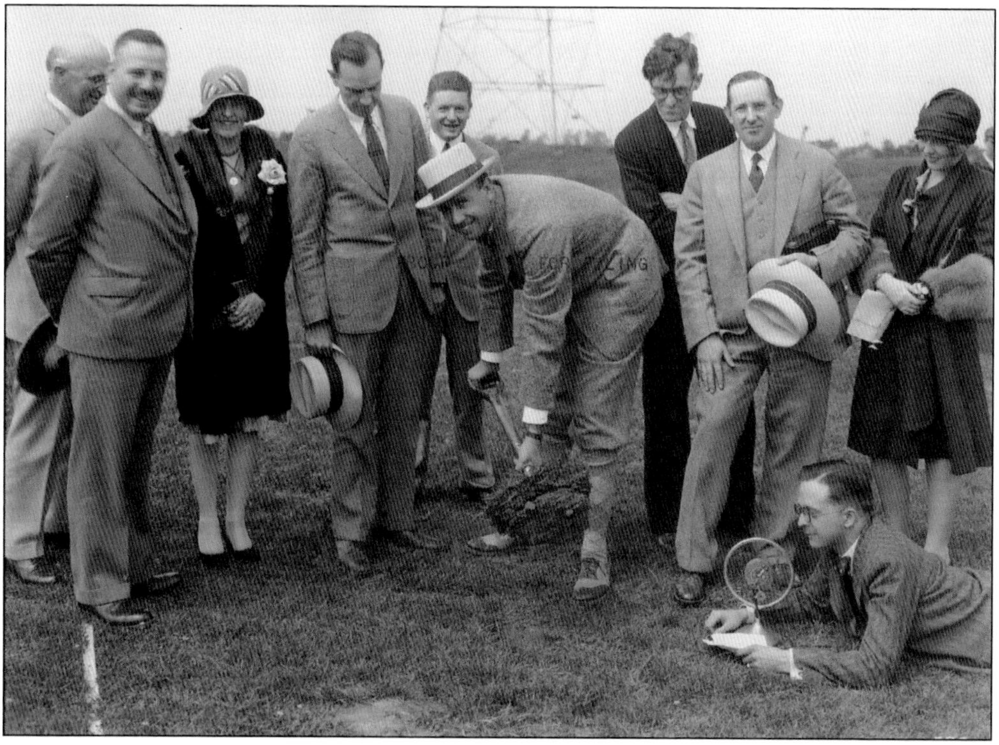

Powel Crosley's radio business model always had been to sell mass-produced, inexpensive radios, all the while offering to those radios the most powerful radio signal possible. Thus, WLW was among the first to be granted 10,000 watts (1926) and 50,000 watts (1928). But nothing gave Crosley more pride than the night of May 2, 1934, when the 500,000-watt transmitter went on the air. Operating as WLW until 1939 and later as the experimental W8XO, the "big-rig" transmitter was used into the 1940s. (MM.)

Logic suggests that a 500,000-watt signal will reach 10 times farther than a 50,000-watt transmitter, but that is not the case. While the daytime and nighttime coverage patterns did increase during the superpower operation, coverage only increases as the square root of the power increase. Rather, the quality of the signal within those areas improved markedly—particularly during the day. Many rural areas that could not receive a reliable radio signal of any kind could now be served by WLW with its farm reports, news, and entertainment. (DB.)

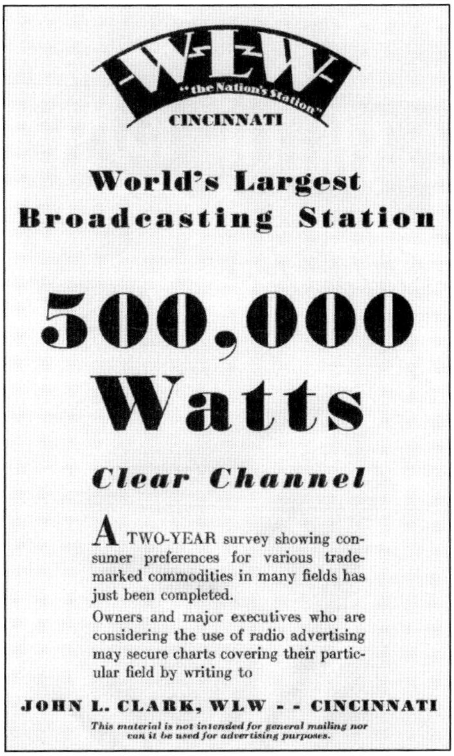

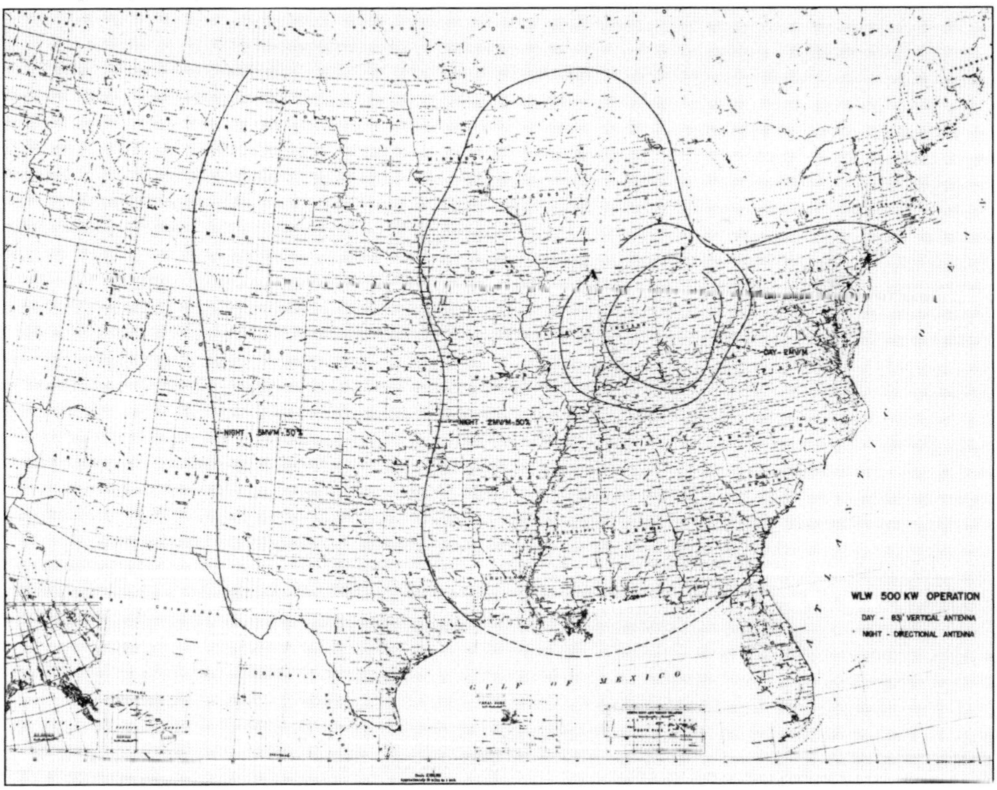

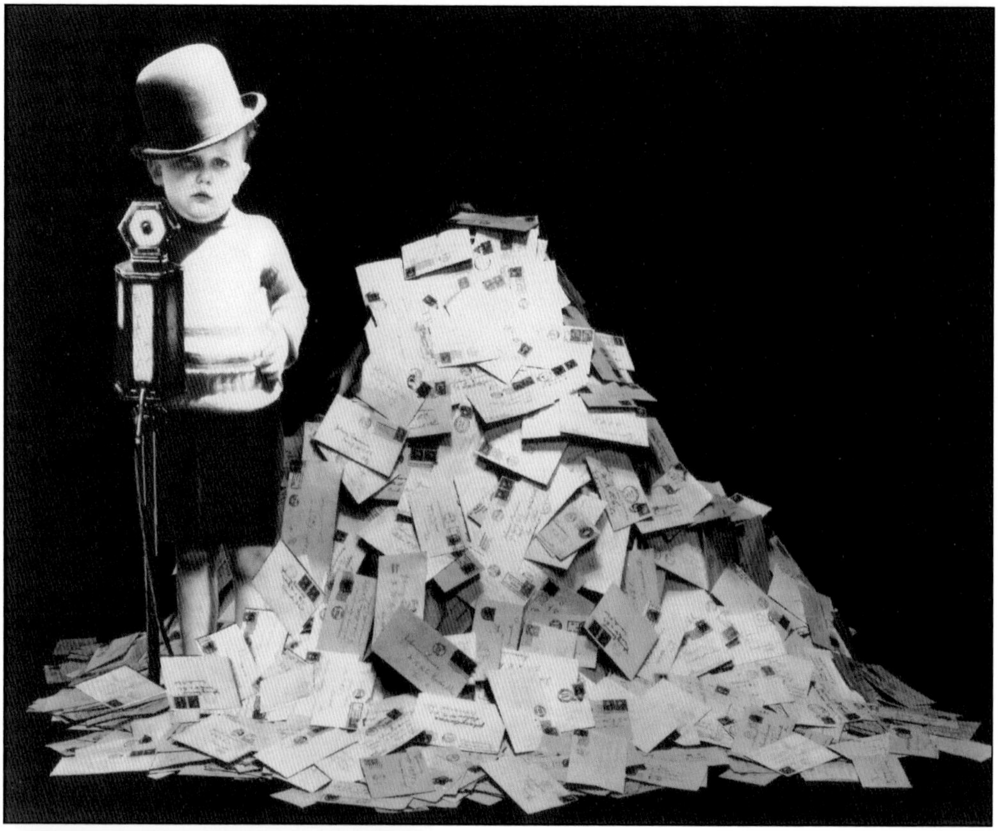

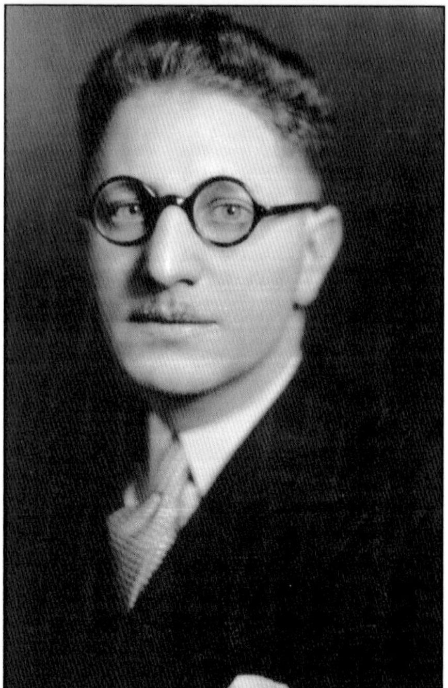

Frederic W. Ziv was trained in law in Michigan but returned to Cincinnati to work in advertising. In 1936, Ziv found a bread company willing to sponsor a children's show and created *The Freshest Thing in Town* about a tough kid in a bowler hat. Before long, other bread companies in other cities also wanted the show, and Ziv's syndication company was born. In just a few years, the creator of *Bold Venture*, *Cisco Kid*, *Sea Hunt*, and *Highway Patrol* was the largest radio and TV syndicator in the world. (FZ.)

Entrepreneur J. Ralph Corbett found his law degree unfulfilling and instead sought employment in radio broadcasting. Around 1932, he formed an independent production company that worked so closely with WLW that Corbett had an office next to the station manager. *Notes On Business*, a program examining new and successful business opportunities, was one of Corbett's creations. During one broadcast, a guest mentioned an idea that must have caught Corbett's imagination because in 1936, he gave up radio and invested in the innovation of electronic doorbells, and the world-famous NuTone Company was born. (MA.)

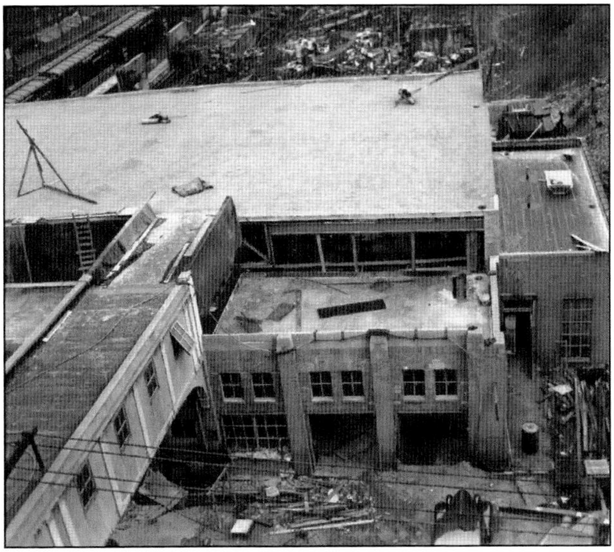

While the factories and businesses in the Mill Creek Valley experienced occasional flooding along Mill Creek, nothing in the past ever presaged the massive flooding that occurred in January 1937. But floodwaters aside, the real damage occurred on "Black Sunday," January 24, 1937, when a nearby fuel storage tank overturned, ignited, and caused a massive fire that destroyed several Crosley outbuildings and damaged the main building. The destruction prompted Crosley to shift manufacturing to other Crosley plants in Indiana. (EDCH.)

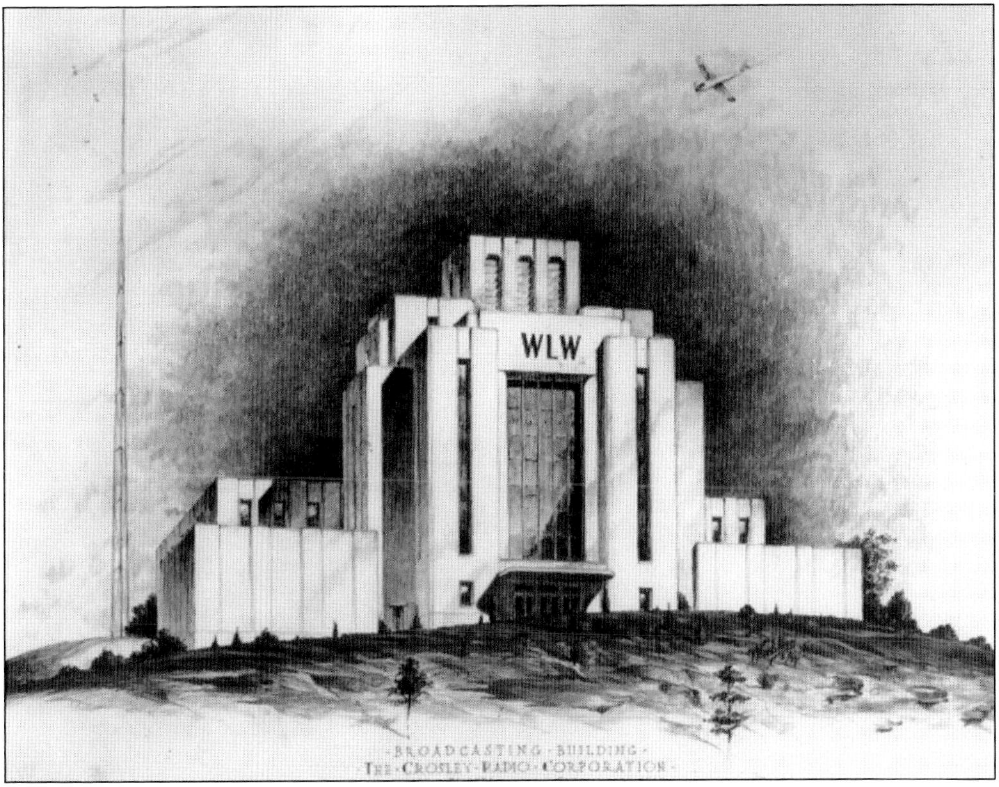

The Arlington Street Crosley facility was serviceable, but in 1937, Powel Crosley had even grander heights, literally, in mind. He acquired the knobby hilltop in Clifton Heights for FM experiments and proposed the construction of a one-million-dollar building to be called the Temple of Radio. The Hannaford-designed temple would have been an imposing sight overlooking the downtown area. But Powel's brother Lewis felt that the Depression-era project was ill timed and convinced Powel to cancel. The property later became the home of the WLWT Mt. Olympus television complex. (MM.)

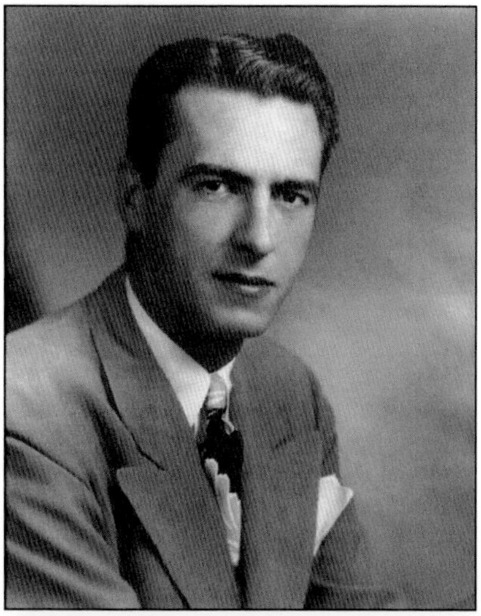

Newspaper owner Scripps-Howard acquired WFBE and a station in Tennessee in October 1935 and renamed their Cincinnati station WCPO to reflect their local daily newspaper—the *Cincinnati Post*. The studios were moved to the Hotel Sinton, and the new owners wanted to move away from the rather lackluster programming that had been the hallmark of the city's weakest power station. So in early 1938, the company brought in Mort Watters from a station it acquired in West Virginia. Watters quickly put his personal touch on the station by emphasizing the news-and-information advantages of being owned by a newspaper. With war in Europe brewing, Watters's decisions proved prophetic. (MH.)

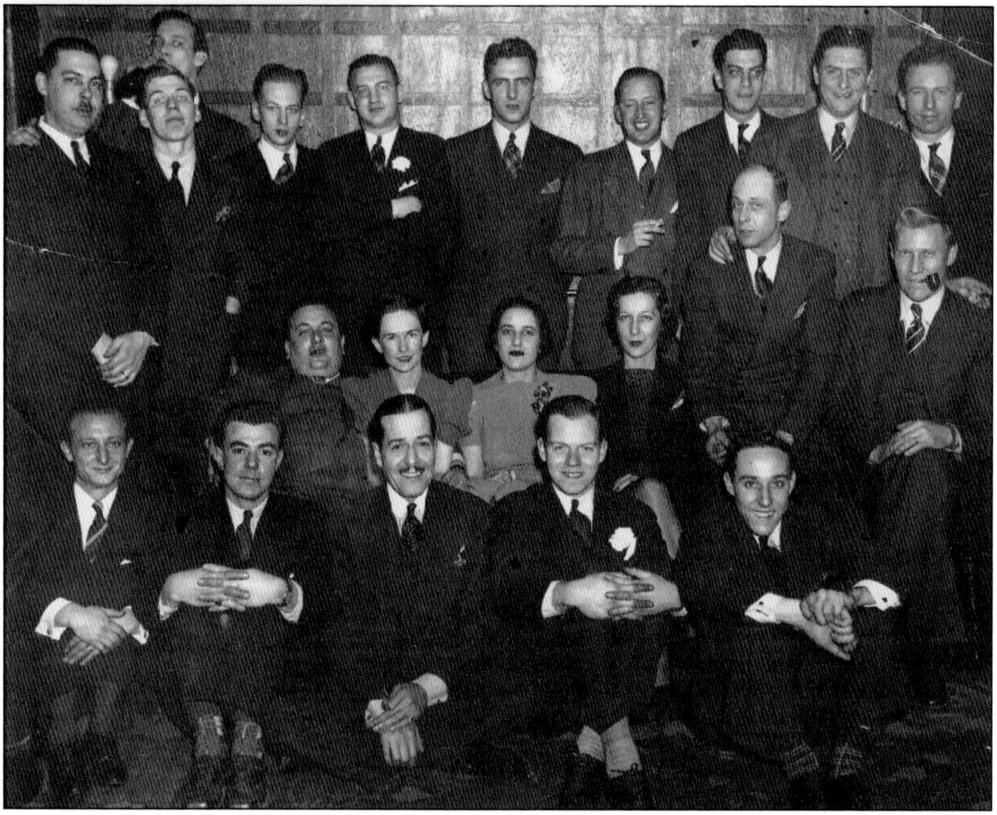

Christmas 1938 must have been different for the staff of WCPO when this photograph was taken. Mort Watters had just taken over as station manager, and the staff saw the format shift away from amateurish acts toward an emphasis on news and information. Harry Hartman is seated at left in the second row. Second from right in the second row (next to man with pipe) is announcer Andre Carlon, who soon after would leave WCPO and cofound the Cincinnati Local of the American Federation of Radio Artists (AFRA), which unionized radio actors, announcers, and performers for the next half century. (MH.)

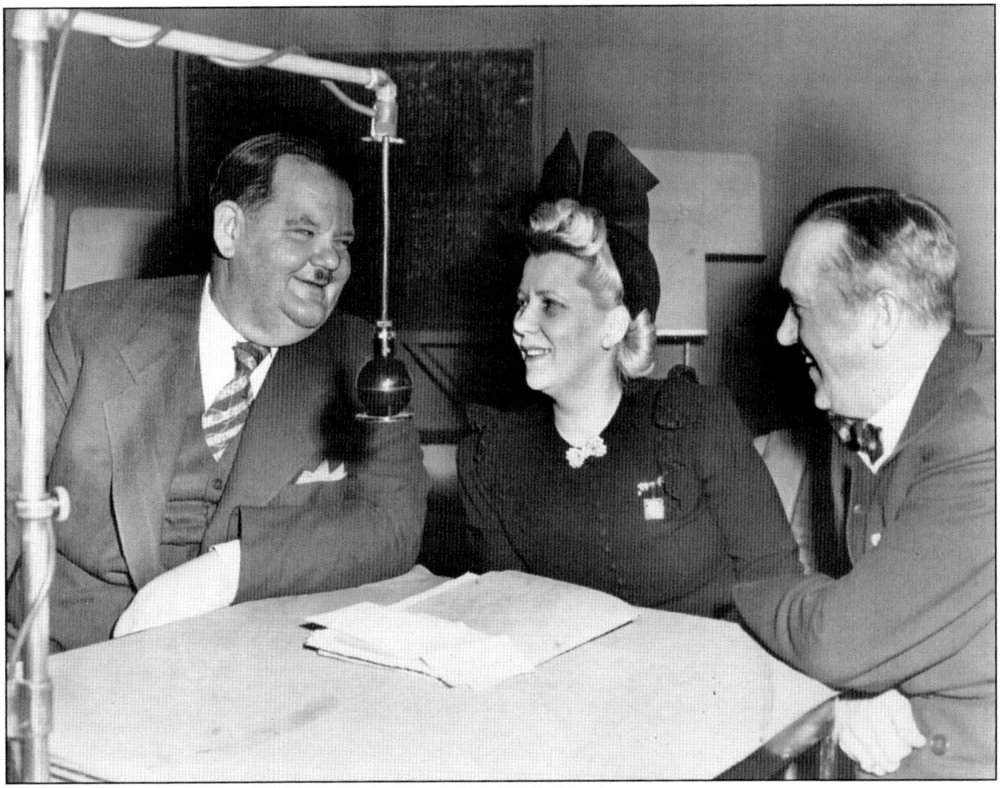

On November 1, 1931, WKRC was sold to the CBS radio network. Being an "owned and operated" or "O&O" CBS station was a source of great pride for the employees. For one, the network invested a great amount of money upgrading the facilities. Plus, it guaranteed WKRC's spot in the network "chain" of broadcasts. Ruth Lyons, pictured here with Laurel and Hardy, started at WKRC in 1928 as a piano accompanist. Lyons enjoyed the station's association with CBS and rose through the ranks to become one of the first female program directors in the country. (MM.)

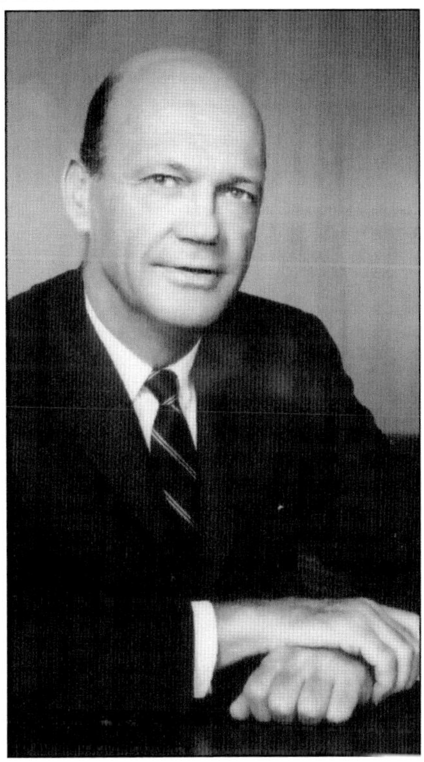

In the late 1930s, WCKY's L.B. Wilson wanted CBS affiliation for his station, and so he invited the prominent Cincinnati Taft family to a broadcast convention in Chicago to convince them to purchase WKRC from the CBS network. The family felt the radio station would be a perfect complement to its *Cincinnati Times-Star* newspaper and put in charge Hulbert "Hub" Taft Jr., the grandnephew of former president William Howard Taft. Although the transition was painful at first, the now Mutual-affiliated WKRC gradually demonstrated impressive growth into a ratings powerhouse in the 1950s and 1960s. (MM.)

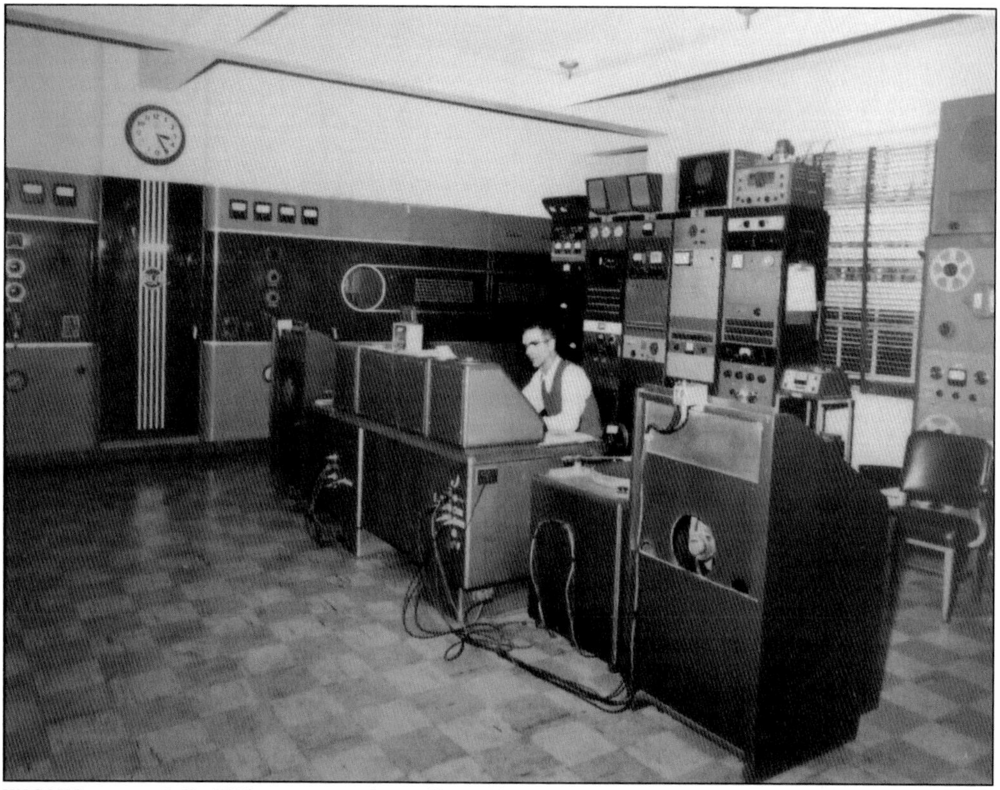

WCKY owner L.B. Wilson was politically well connected and was particularly good friends with Kentucky senator Alben Barkley. In July 1937, Wilson was granted permission to double the station's power to 10,000 watts. In 1939, the power was increased to 50,000 watts, and the studios moved to the Hotel Gibson in Cincinnati. Transmitter supervisor Jim Ranney is pictured with the new transmitter. Because WLW's superpower was revoked that same year, Wilson lost no time in placing the slogan, "As powerful as any radio station in the world," on all of WCKY's letterhead. (JR.)

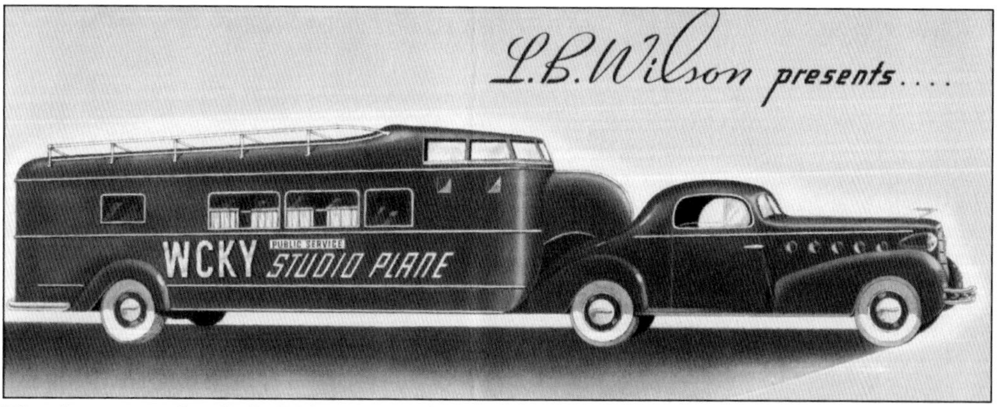

The showman side of L.B. Wilson came through in many forms over the years. In 1940, Wilson had constructed a unique vehicle called the WCKY Studio Plane. Basically an Art Deco trailer that inside had a custom-installed control room, broadcast studio, and lounge, the Studio Plane preceded by some 30 years the rock-and-roll remote vans of the 1980s and 1990s. Alas, the Studio Plane must not have been very durable; there is no mention of its existence by 1945. (MM.)

By the time superpower permission was rescinded by the FCC in 1939, Powel Crosley had lost some of his interest in the day-to-day operation of WLW and WSAI. At about the same time, Crosley hired two skilled managers from KMOX in St. Louis: James D. Shouse and Robert E. Dunville. Together, the talents of Shouse and Dunville so complemented each other that rarely was one name uttered without the other. Shouse, a skilled communicator and talent evaluator, eventually rose to chairman of the board of Crosley Broadcasting. (MM.)

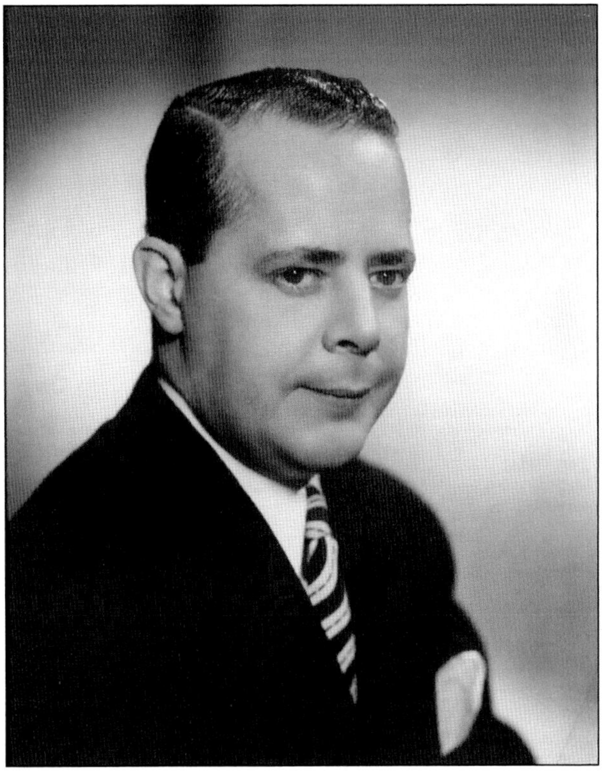

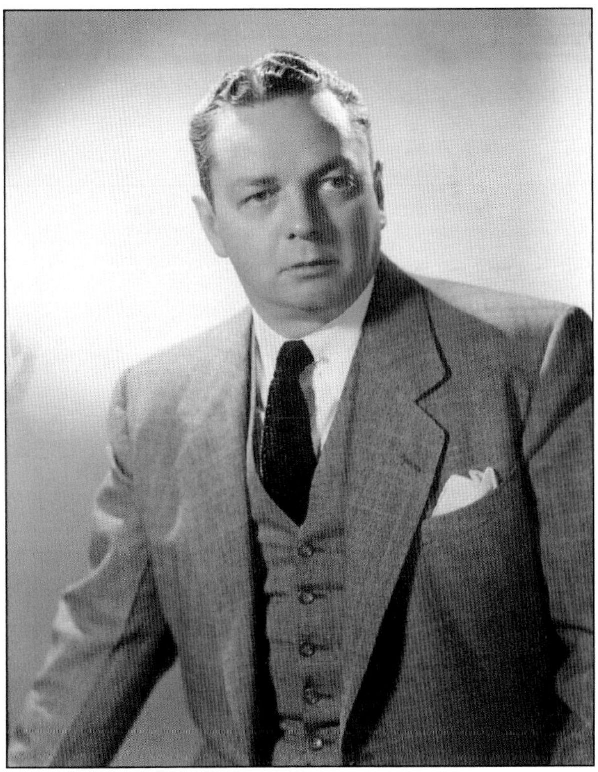

Robert Dunville, who eventually became president of Crosley Broadcasting, provided the strong business acumen needed to run a profitable company. Where the somewhat shy Shouse was focused on serving the community, Dunville used his organizational skills to put the programs and talent in place to carry out the vision and keep the company profitable. So tied together in life, Shouse and Dunville died young within three years of each other in the early 1960s. (MM.)

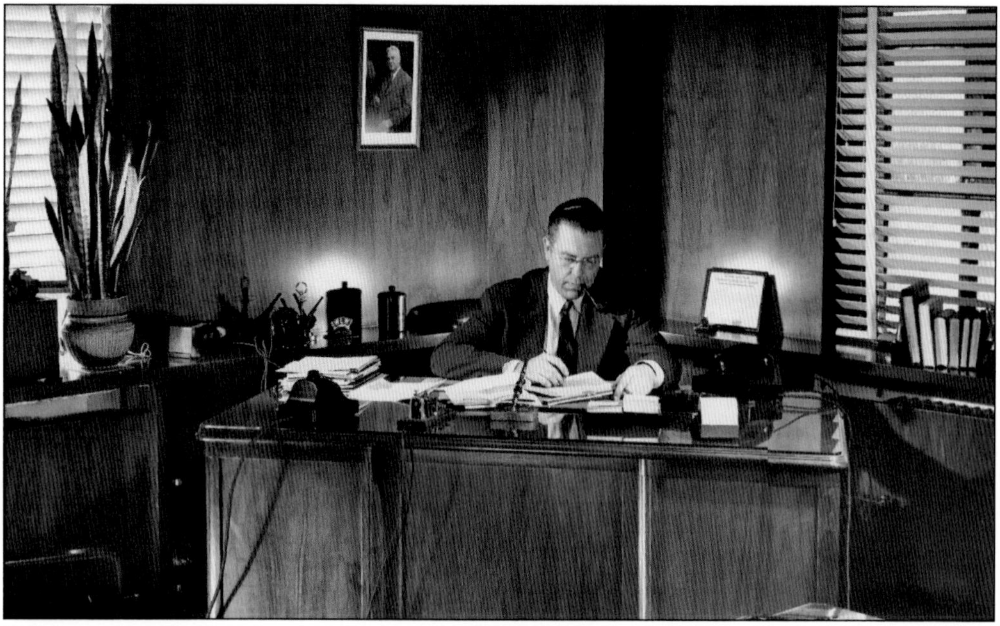

Following Joseph Chambers's departure as chief engineer at WLW in 1937, the station hired Ronald J. Rockwell to head the department. Rockwell was a brilliant engineer who oversaw the building of the Voice of America complex, the early experiments in television, and even designed and built from spare parts a 50,000-watt transmitter in 1959 called the Rockwell Cathanode System—the highest fidelity AM transmitter in the world. (GHW.)

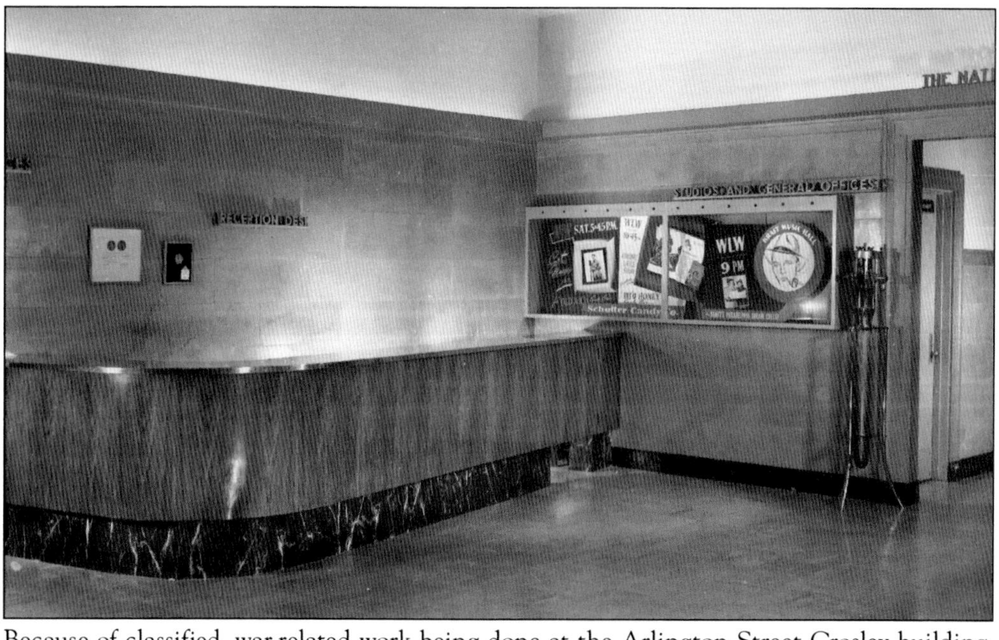

Because of classified, war-related work being done at the Arlington Street Crosley building, Crosley was forced to make plans to relocate WLW and WSAI in 1941. The company purchased the Elks Lodge No. 5 at Ninth and Elm Streets and renovated it into radio studios. The building was dubbed Crosley Square and became a showplace for radio broadcasts with large studios and an Art Deco lobby. Less than a decade later, it also housed WLWT television. (MM.)

Two

Behind the Microphone
The Announcers, Actors, and Newscasters of Cincinnati Radio

In the communication process, there needs to be a "sender" to impart the message. This sender could have a deep, rich voice or occasionally change his or her voice to sound like someone else. An entirely new character can be created, or perhaps an even stronger message is communicated through silence or a well-placed pause. In radio, the one truth is that no one can see the sender of the message. The announcer, the actor, the vocalist, the storyteller, the newsreader, and the voice in the middle of the night all are faceless ghosts dancing through space. In fact, radio listeners often are disappointed when they actually do meet their radio favorites. "Gee, you don't look the way I pictured you," is a common refrain.

The *theater of the mind* is a common term borrowed to describe this unique reality in radio broadcasting. The richness, color, and depth of the picture painted by an individual's imagination cannot be translated or completely described by words or description. Imagination is the greatest canvas, and the coloring paints and shadings of that mental image bests the finest that Vincent van Gogh or Leonardo da Vinci could have hoped to produce with their own hands. Brilliant as they may be, the pictures painted in our minds by radio are intensely personal and cannot be completely shared. Perhaps in this lies the strange intimacy and closeness that radio enjoys. A child's mental image of Jack Benny can be far different from that of his or her own sibling's, and there is no way to accurately compare the two individual perspectives.

Before television, there were limited opportunities to see radio idols in person. National stars might be featured in fan magazines or in film, but local stars were limited, in most cases, to public appearances or the occasional performance in front of an audience. Consequently, most local radio stars spent their time in the community in total anonymity and would walk down the street unrecognized. Occasionally, these performers would have publicity photographs made, and in radio, it was not uncommon to be posed in front of the station microphone. In addition, if the radio personality was lucky, there was the occasional photographic hobbyist at a radio station who would unknowingly capture a moment for eternity by snapping a candid image.

Cincinnati radio historians are fortunate that several dozen images, particularly from the early days, survive. The photographic hobbyist at WLW happened to be studio technician Eugene Patterson, who took hundreds of photographs of his peers between 1934 and 1940. Although local stations did not start recording their own audio until late 1934, and even then, with less than 10 percent of the sounds of the live-radio era ever recorded, the lack of surviving audio recording is at least tempered somewhat by visual remnants. In this chapter, the faceless voices of Cincinnati radio come to life, perhaps for the first time, to those who may or may not have painted their own individual portraits within their imaginations.

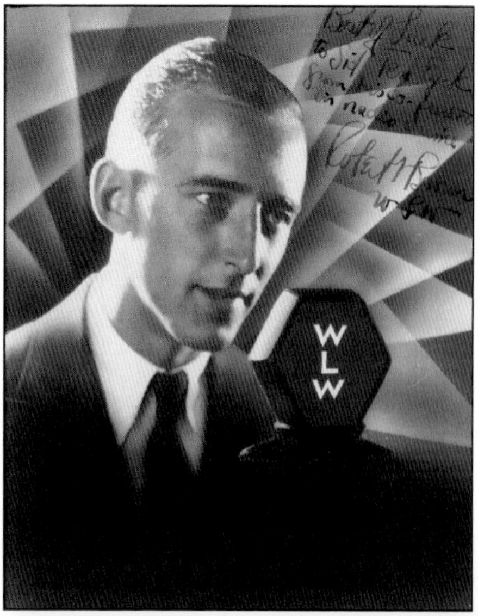

Without question, the first national star to emerge from the announcing staff of WLW was Bob Brown. Beginning in 1928, Brown was given the job of announcing WLW's most important programs. In early 1932, Brown joined the NBC network in Chicago as a staff announcer where he fulfilled the hosting duties for such shows as *Ma Perkins* and *Vic and Sade*. Coincidentally, the character Uncle Fletcher on *Vic and Sade* was played by Clarence Hartzell, the brother of longtime Cincinnati announcer Cecil Hale. (DB.)

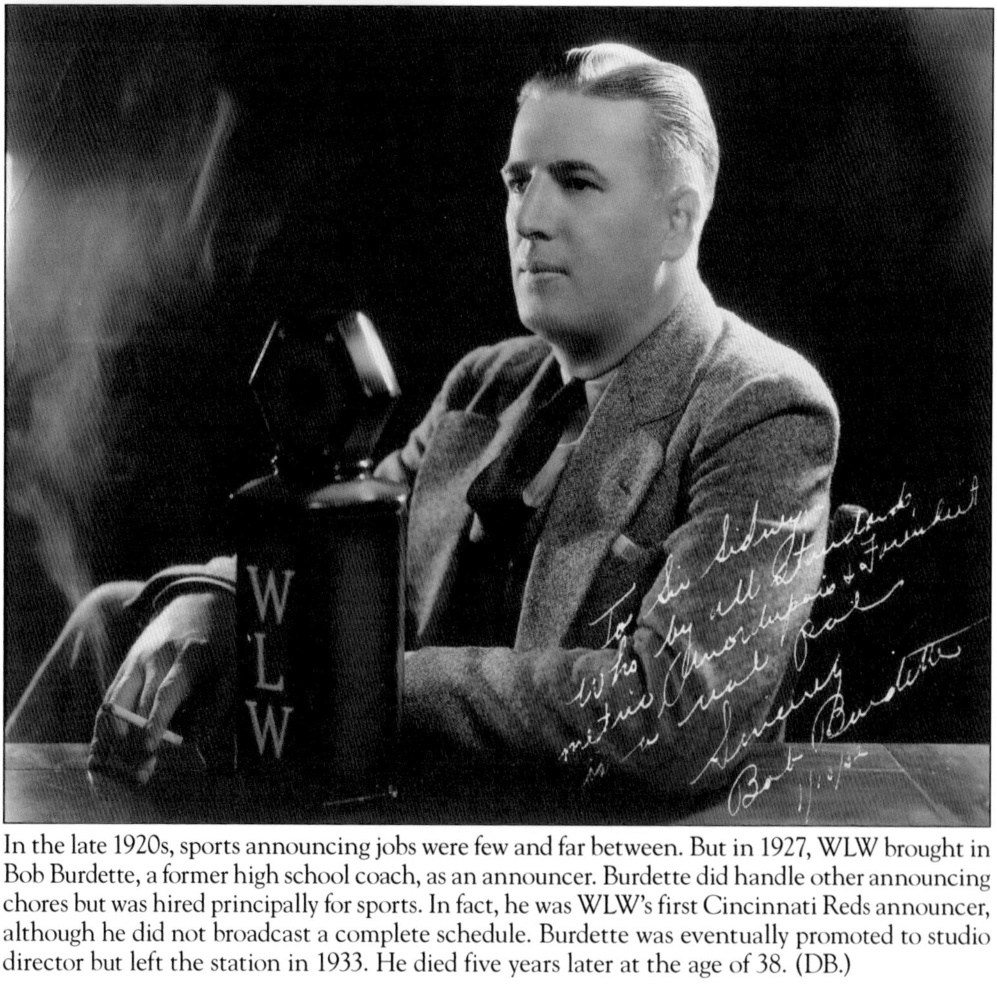

In the late 1920s, sports announcing jobs were few and far between. But in 1927, WLW brought in Bob Burdette, a former high school coach, as an announcer. Burdette did handle other announcing chores but was hired principally for sports. In fact, he was WLW's first Cincinnati Reds announcer, although he did not broadcast a complete schedule. Burdette was eventually promoted to studio director but left the station in 1933. He died five years later at the age of 38. (DB.)

Perhaps no broadcaster in Cincinnati history enjoyed the prestige and praise of his peers as did WLW's Peter Grant. Born Melvin Maginn, the former St. Louis law school graduate and radio actor came to WLW in 1931 and soon was promoted to chief announcer. Grant became the "go-to" announcer for any important audition or network broadcast, even announcing shows on WLW and WSAI simultaneously. Except for his service during World War II, Grant remained in Cincinnati, staying loyal to WLW into the television era. Grant retired in 1968. (MM.)

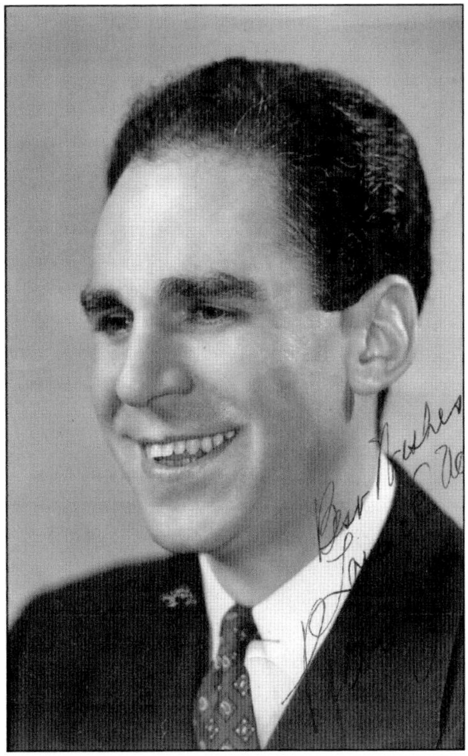

The job of radio announcer was difficult to land in the Depression era. Competition was fierce for a limited number of positions. Announcers had to have clear diction and the ability to pronounce a long list of difficult names and foreign-language terms and titles. The dreaded announcer's audition would strike fear into the heart of any able-tongued prospective speaker. Still, the announcers could have fun too, and many Cincinnati announcers went on to long local and national careers. (CG.)

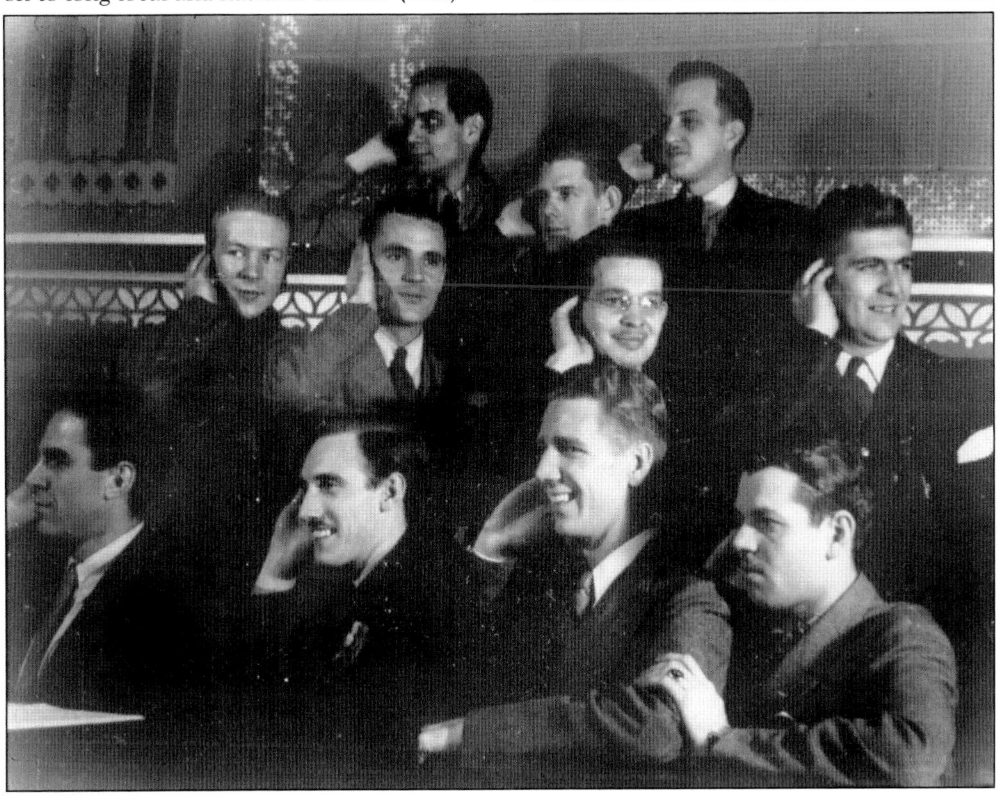

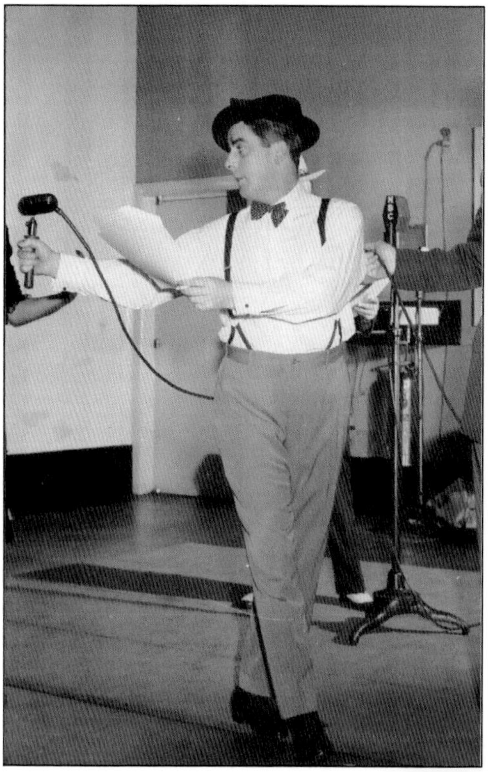

Producer-writer-director-announcer Ed Byron was a jack-of-all-trades at WLW in the early 1930s, but his greatest achievement perhaps was the creation of *Moon River.* He reportedly composed the poem that began, "Moon River, a lazy stream of dreams," on the back of a napkin at a local speakeasy because he was given less than a day to come up with a concept for the program. By 1939, Byron was in New York creating and producing the extremely popular *Mr. District Attorney*, starring former fellow WLW staffer Jay Jostyn. (MM.)

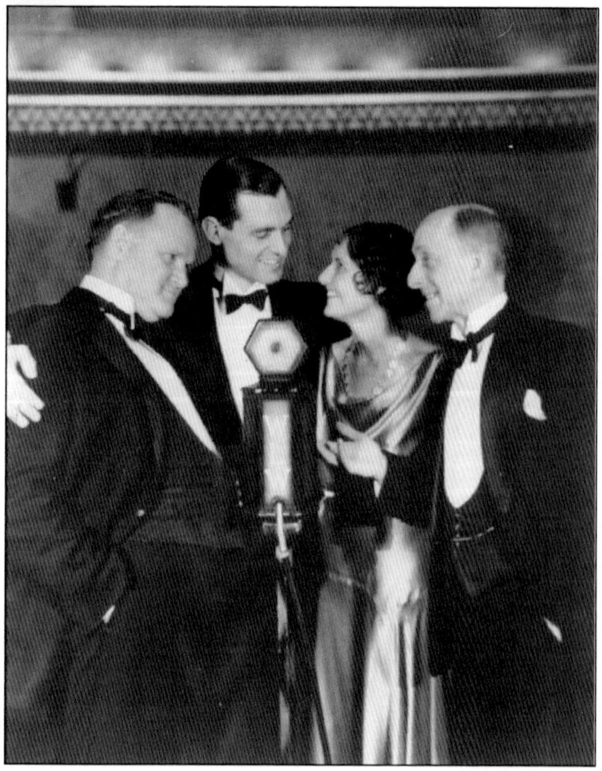

St. Louis cartoonist T.E. Tuttle brought his newspaper cartoon *The Bungles* to life as a WLW radio feature *The Puddle Family*. Produced by and featuring famed radio historian Erik Barnouw (second from left) and actor Charlie Egelston (right), the Puddles were good enough in 1931 to go national as a Procter & Gamble–sponsored serial. But Tuttle balked at the contract negotiations, and WLW and Procter & Gamble had to rework the entire concept of the show. The resulting revised concept became the classic soap opera *Ma Perkins*. (MM.)

Actress Virginia Payne grew up locally in Price Hill and was teaching drama and acting for radio when, at the tender age of 23, she was cast to play the matronly lead character on a new WLW drama called *Ma Perkins*. The show was an immediate success and Cincinnati-based Procter & Gamble, manufacturer of Oxydol, quickly took it national where it continued for an amazing 27 years. Payne, who never missed a performance in 7,065 episodes, was rarely permitted to be photographed without a gray wig and glasses, but this publicity shot was an exception. (MM.)

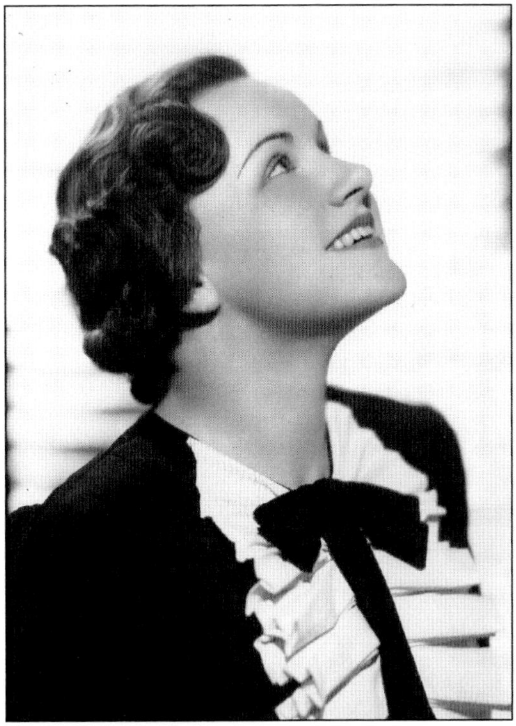

Former vaudevillians Hink and Dink portrayed blackface characters in a music-and-patter routine beginning in 1925. On WLW in the early 1930s, they had a popular minstrel act that they took on the road for live stage performances. Without makeup, Elmer Hinkle was an agriculture reporter at WLW, and George Ross was a popular barber in the Oxford, Ohio, area. (MM.)

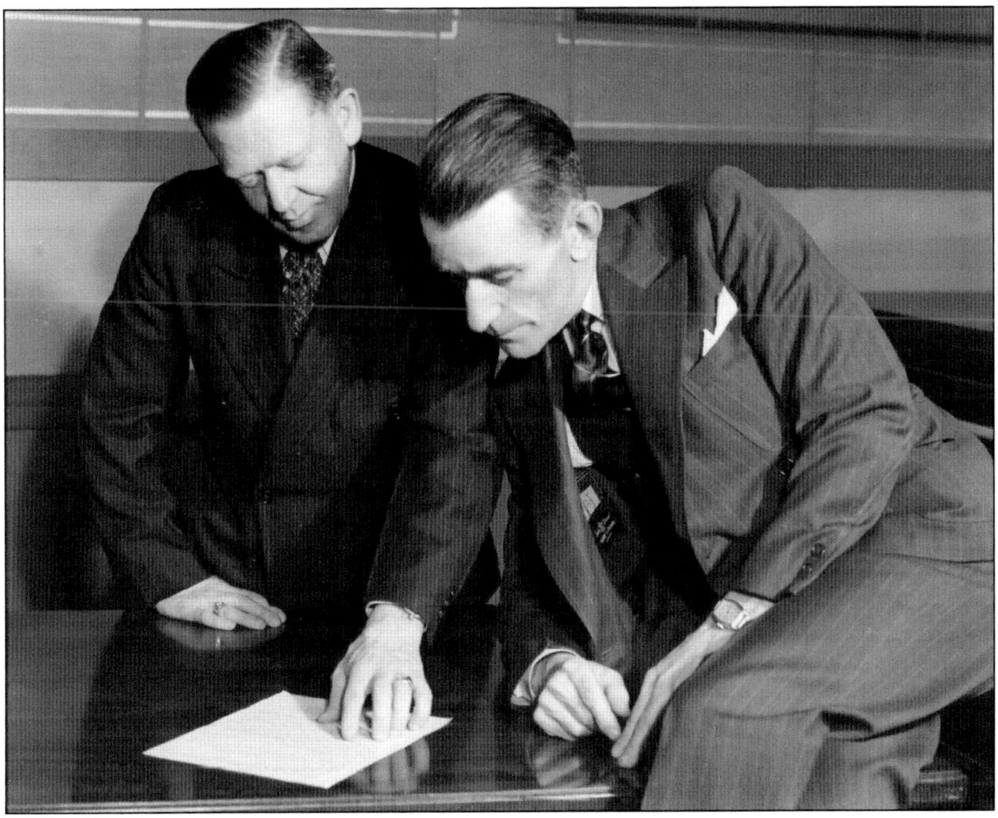

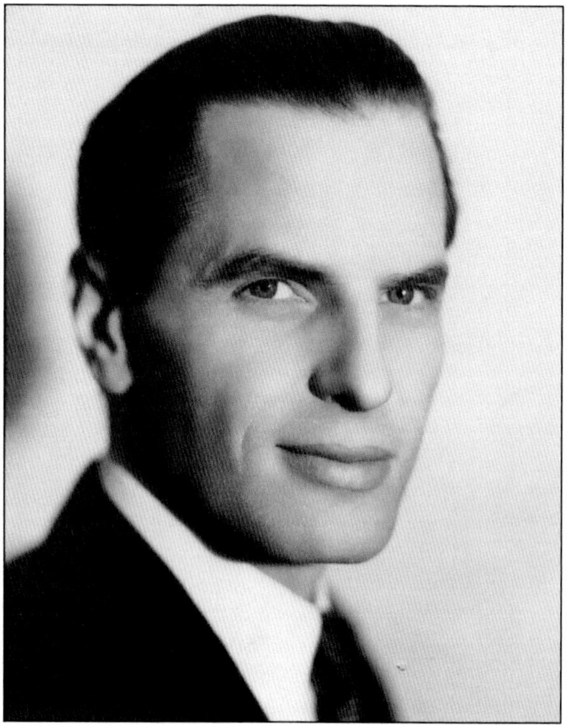

Anthony Snow was a sickly young man who collected poems and songs while recuperating in the 1920s. Regaining his strength, he changed his name by reversing it to become Tony Wons, a gentle-voiced host who read poetry and sang on the air. Wons was heard on WLW for most of 1930 and 1931 before moving to New York. To augment his radio income, Wons issued several volumes of *Tony Wons Scrapbook* booklets. (MM.)

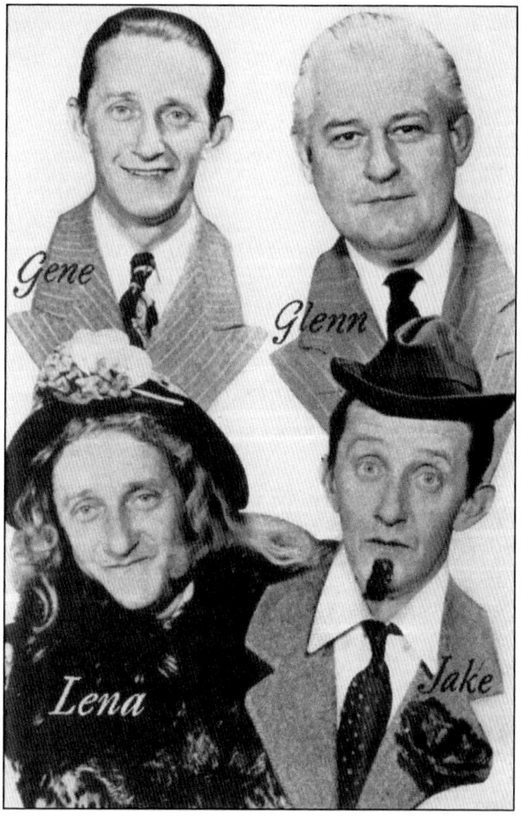

After teaming up at WLW as the Quaker Early Birds in September 1930, Gene Carroll and Glenn Rowell started appearing over NBC and on stations in Cleveland and Chicago. In addition to being Gene and Glenn, Carroll also invented two fictional country-bumpkin alter egos, Jake and Lena. After Gene and Glenn and Jake and Lena broke up in 1943, Gene brought Lena to *Fibber McGee and Molly* for one season. Glenn eventually ended up back in Cincinnati as "Captain Glenn," a WLWT kiddie show host. (MM.)

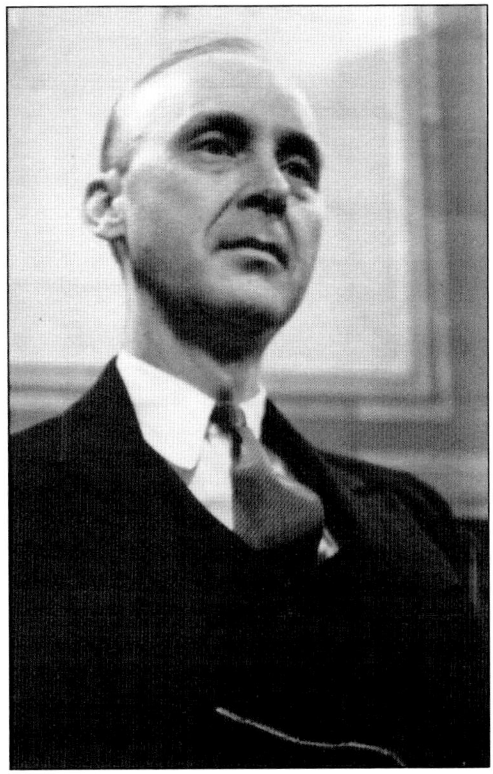

WLW drama director Rikel Kent studied under the famed 19th-century actress Minnie Maddern Fiske before appearing on stage in New York in the early 1900s. He was a popular WLW radio director because he challenged his performers into playing a variety of roles. He was also a stickler for the authenticity of sound effects. Kent directed most of WLW's dramatic programs of the 1930s into the 1950s with a brief stop in New York in the 1940s to direct the soap opera *Valiant Lady*. (CG.)

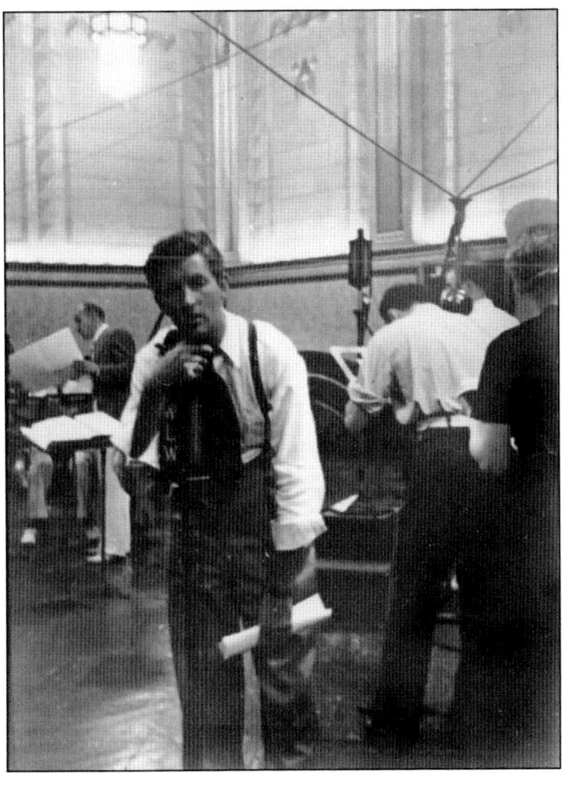

Actor Jay (or Jean) Jostyn came to WLW from Milwaukee in the mid-1930s and appeared on many programs, often playing gangsters and thugs. His character Max on *The Life of Mary Sothern* gradually transitioned from brute to Mary's love interest. When fellow WLW alum Ed Byron went to New York to create *Mr. District Attorney*, he recruited Jostyn to take over the lead role after the first season. Later, Jostyn enjoyed a long career in Hollywood as a versatile character actor. (CG.)

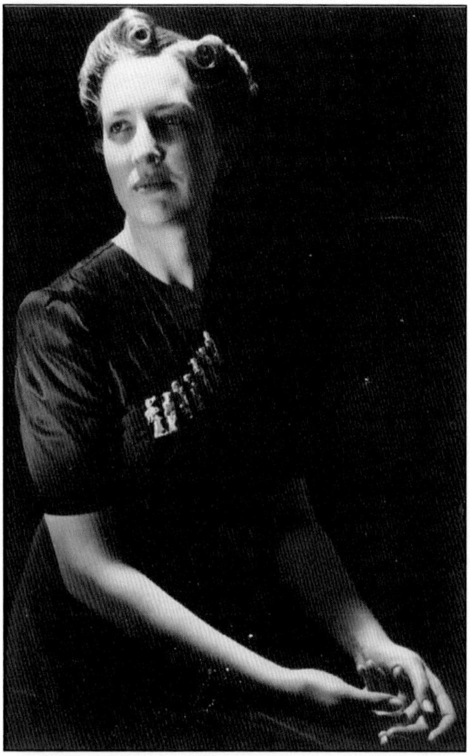

A native of Dearborn County, Indiana, Minabelle Abbott began her career at WLW as a secretary for general manager John Clark. In her spare time, Minabelle became a hillbilly character named Sara Wayne. This experience enabled her to win the role of the title character in the WLW-produced soap opera *The Life of Mary Sothern*, which ended up being carried nationally from New York. Minabelle returned to Cincinnati in 1938 to work on the *Mailbag Club* at WLW and in 1945, at WKRC as Suzanne Russell on the *Syd and Suzy* program. (EP.)

Mary Jane Croft came to Cincinnati in 1935 from her native Muncie, Indiana, to work on stage at the Guild Theater. Instead, she ventured into radio, joining the dramatic staff of WLW. Croft won the part of the cruel Letitia on *The Life of Mary Sothern*. Mary married WLW actor Jack Zoller and moved to Hollywood in 1939 where she enjoyed a lengthy career in film and television. Croft played Lucille Ball's sidekick after Vivian Vance on *The Lucy Show* and *Here's Lucy*. (MM.)

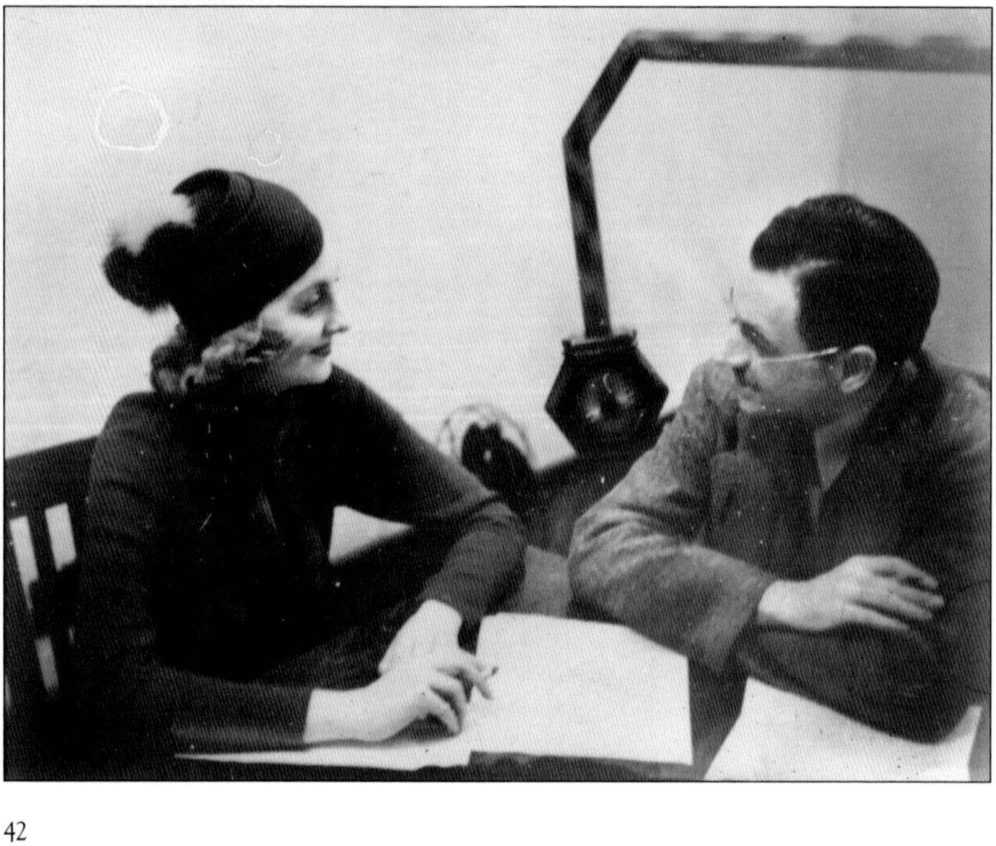

Stories of radio pranks are legendary at radio stations all around the country, and WLW was no exception. Studio technicians were known to place microphones at the tops of ladders or set fire to scripts as they were being read. Peter Grant, pictured here, had a great sense of humor but was the object of a prank that got several employees suspended. It seems one night some technicians were doing a slow striptease while Grant read poetry on *Moon River*, only to be surprised when Powel Crosley popped in while giving guests a tour. (CG.)

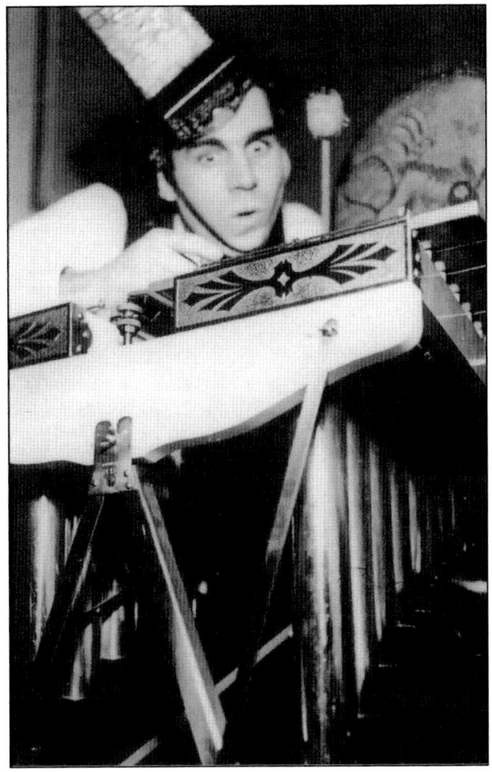

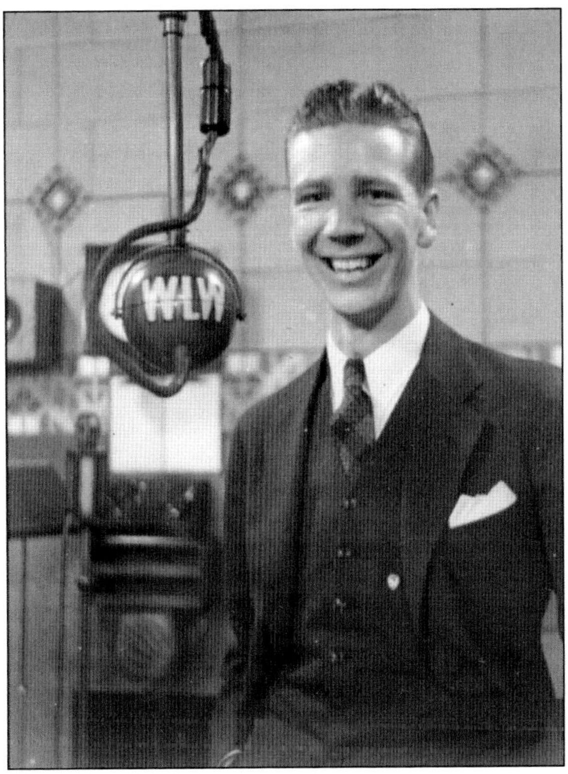

Durward Kirby was born in Covington, Kentucky, but came to WLW via Indianapolis in 1936. As a staff announcer, Kirby hosted a variety of programs, including the comedy quiz show *Stumpus*. The tall, lanky Kirby left the station in 1939, along with vocalist-wife Mary Paxton, and went on to fame on television with *Candid Camera* and the *Garry Moore Show*. (CG.)

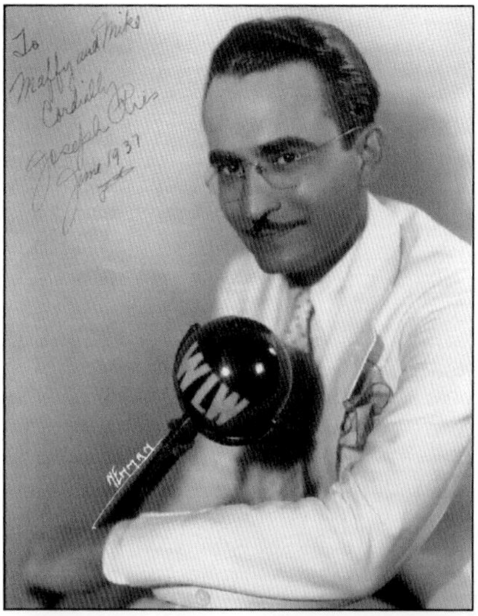

Distinguished and nattily dressed, Joseph Ries filled many roles at WLW in the 1930s: announcer, program producer, and director of educational and public affairs programming. Ries hired and fired famed radio writer Norman Corwin during a two-week stint at WLW in 1936. A former professor at Butler University, as one of his duties, Ries hosted the *Ohio School of the Air*, which was carried nationally on NBC-Blue. During World War II, Ries, who reportedly could speak 15 languages, left the station to work for the Department of State in Venezuela. (MM.)

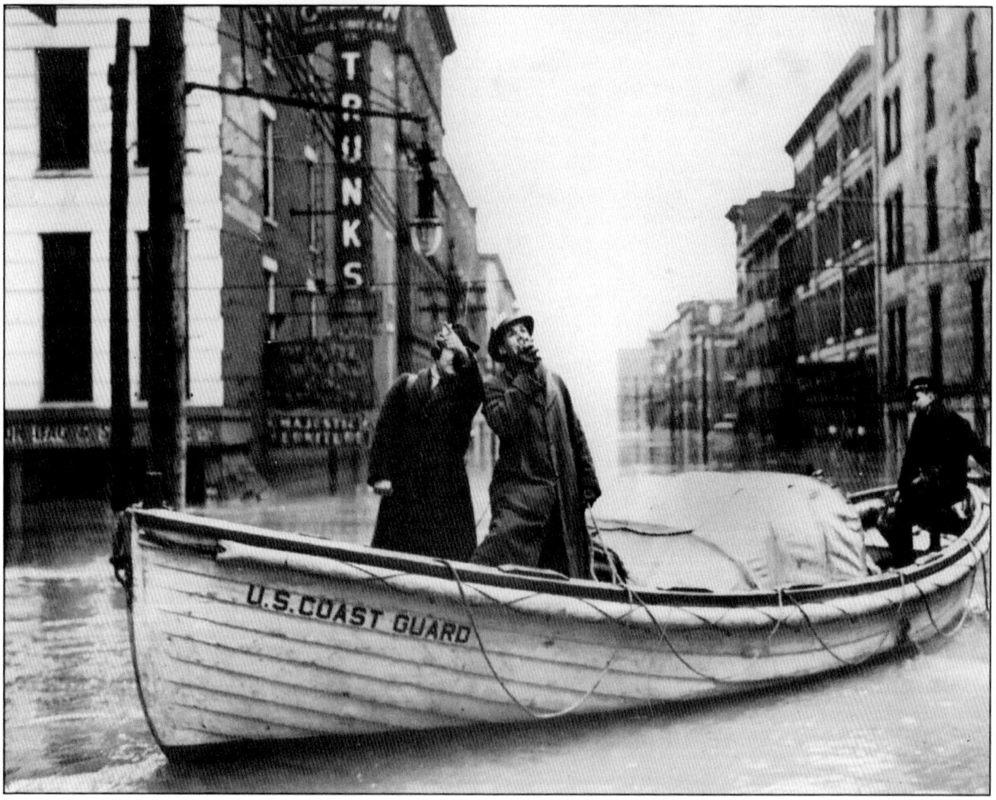

The January 1937 flood affected the lives of millions of people up and down the Ohio River. One positive, albeit unintended, consequence was the impact the month-long disaster had on the development of radio news. Prior to this, newspapers and syndicates distrusted radio as a competitor in delivering news and public service information. After the flood and other national events, radio proved it could ably handle the immediacy of emergency situations, and newsmen, like Peter Grant (in the boat, center), shared with the nation and the world the latest reports live from the scene. Broadcast news in Cincinnati would never be the same. (MM.)

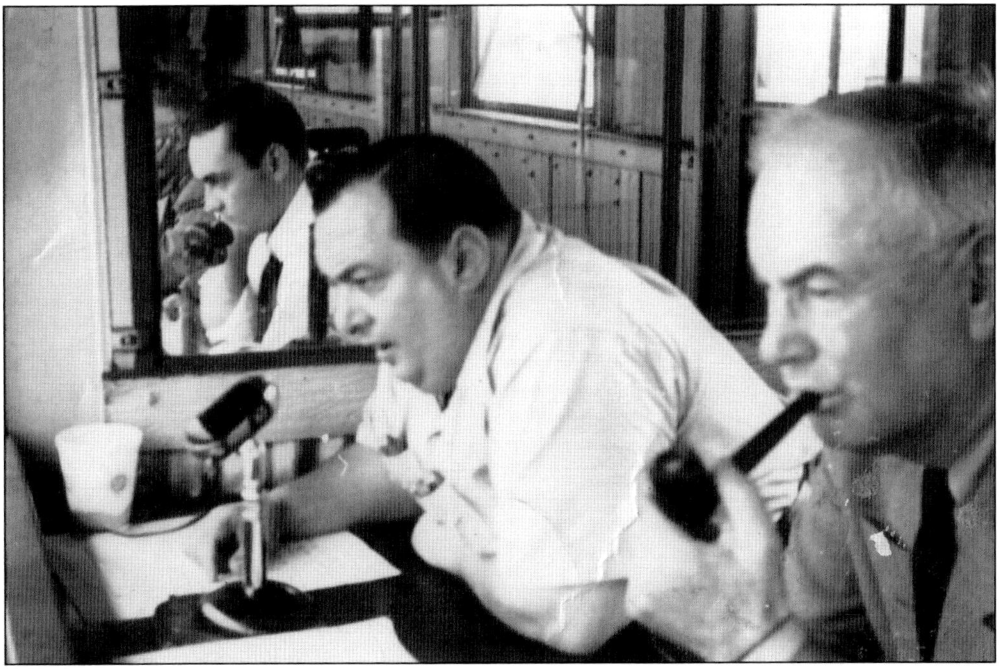

Although nearly forgotten today, WFBE-WCPO announcer Harry Hartman (at microphone) was one of the most powerful sports announcers of his time. Hartman won the 1932 and 1936 *Sporting News* awards for the nation's best sportscaster. He coined the phrase, "Going, going gone!" and even had it turned into a song. Hartman was friends with many national celebrities, but his fame diminished after 1940 when WCPO dropped its baseball broadcasts. (MM.)

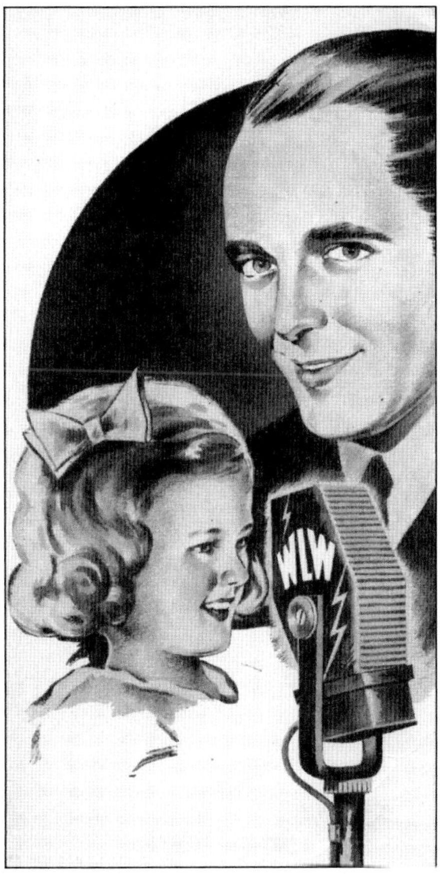

Tommy Riggs was a baritone songster on a radio station in Pittsburgh when, fooling around, he invented a falsetto voiced little-girl character named Betty Lou. The new act was very popular, and the *Tommy Riggs and Betty Lou Program* ended up at WLW in 1937 where it added vocalist Anita Ellis. Betty Lou even did public service announcements during the 1937 flood. A year later, songster Harry Frankel contacted an agent in New York, and Riggs ended up airing his show nationally, off and on until 1946. (MM.)

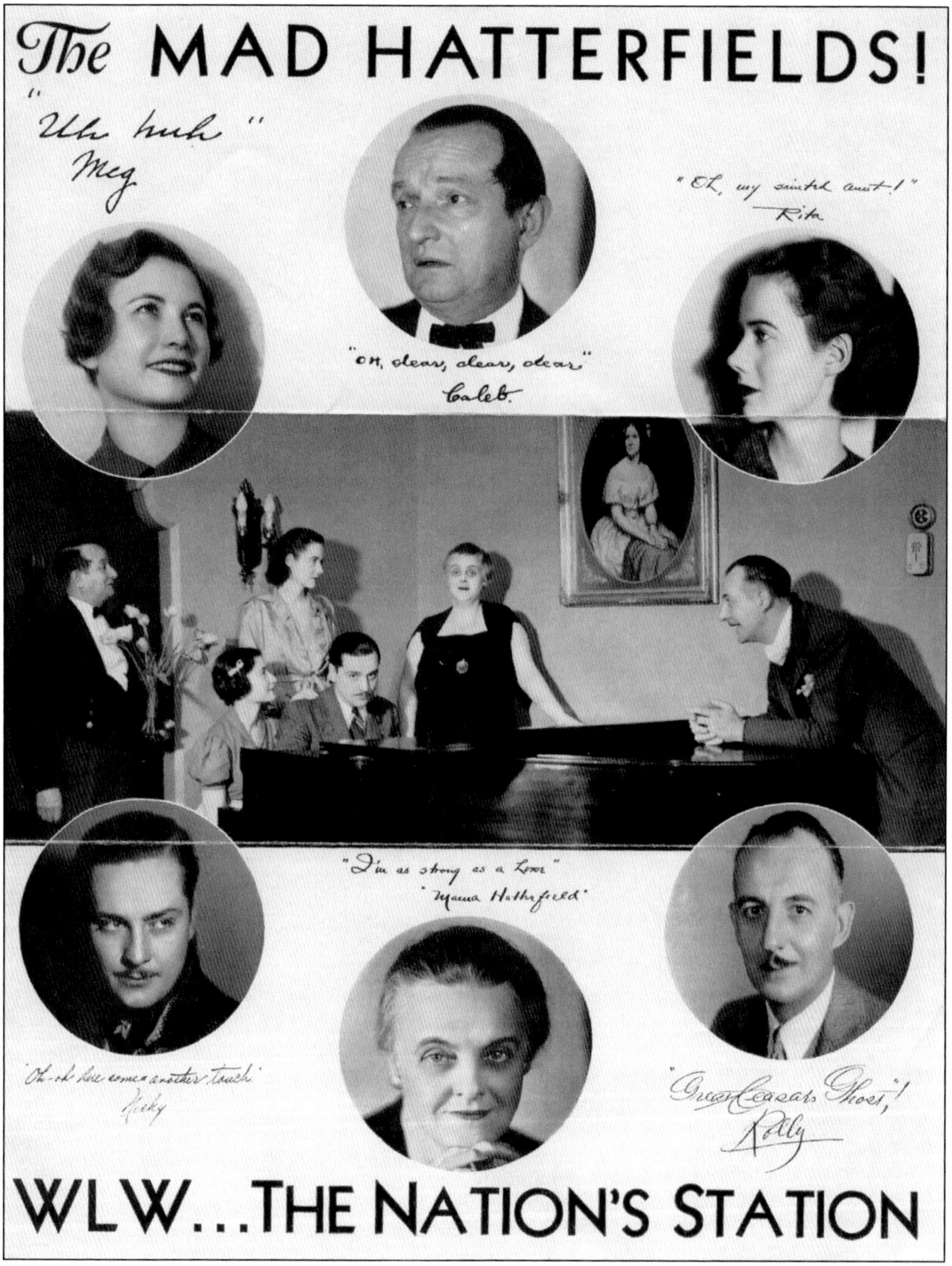

There are many long forgotten but once popular dramas and comedies that were featured on WLW during the 1930s. *Dr. Kenrad's Unsolved Mysteries*, *My Lucky Break*, *Famous Jury Trials*, and *Theater of Romance* were among them. Perhaps none was as popular as *The Mad Hatterfields*. A dramatic comedy much like television's *Soap* in the 1980s, the *Hatterfields* poked fun at a stodgy, wealthy family led by matriarch Mama (bottom center), played by popular, longtime WLW actress Bess McCammon. McCammon soon after left for Chicago and was later heard on *The Romance of Helen Trent* with Nanette Sargent, fellow Cincinnati radio actress on WKRC. (MM.)

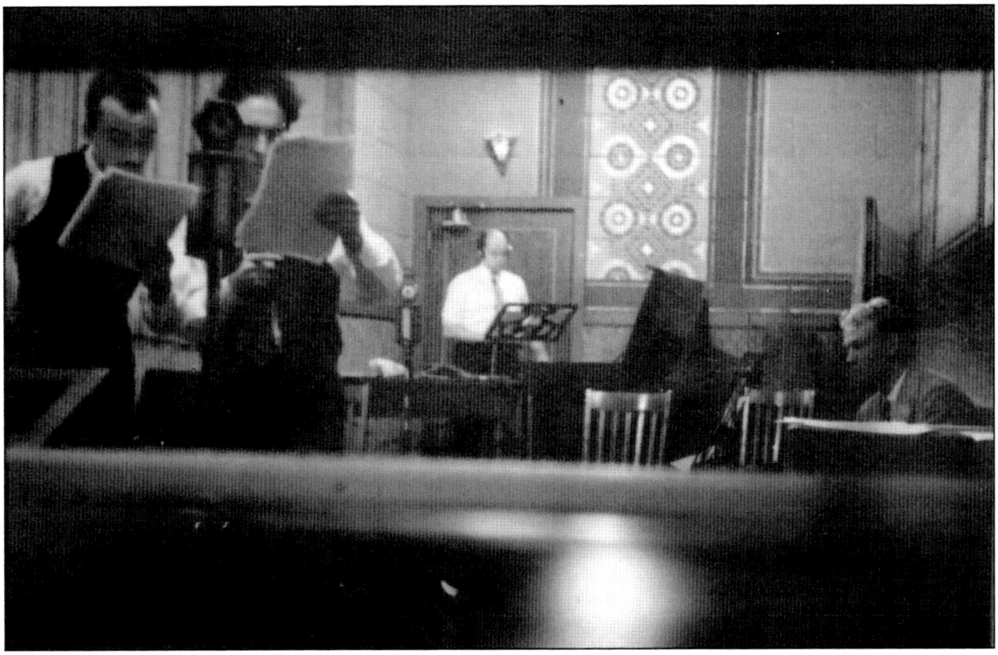

During the mid-1930s, the WLW-WSAI Arlington Street studios were busy with a constant din of activity. Hallways were filled with pacing announcers and impromptu rehearsing, and the studios were alive with productions in the various stages of broadcasting. This rare image shot through the control room window shows a broadcast in progress from Studio B, with announcer Red Barber seated at far right. (CG.)

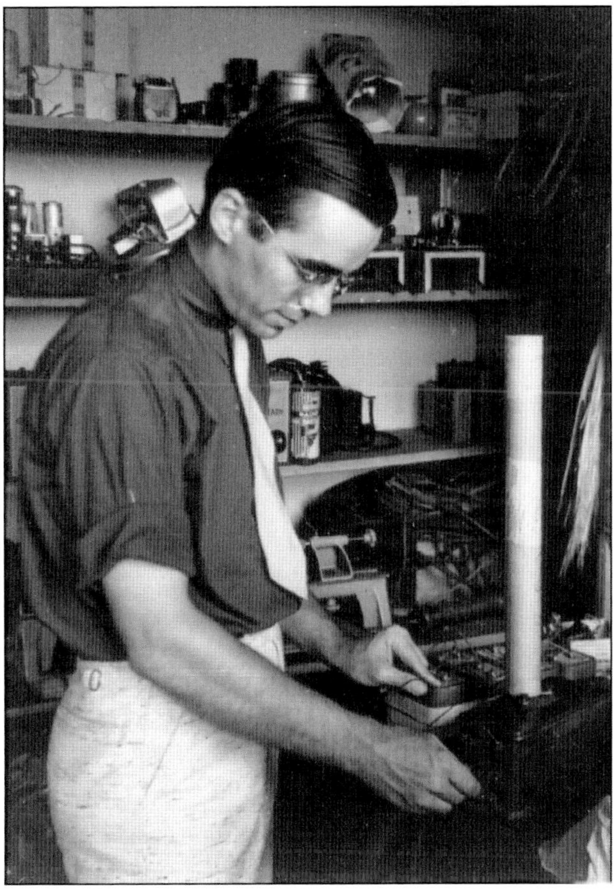

Although not an actor or a vocalist, WLW's Don Winget's talent was heard on many broadcasts. The studio technician was head of the station's sound effects department and, along with his brother Byron, supplied the *clanks*, *buzzes*, and door slams needed to bring WLW's radio dramas to life. (CG.)

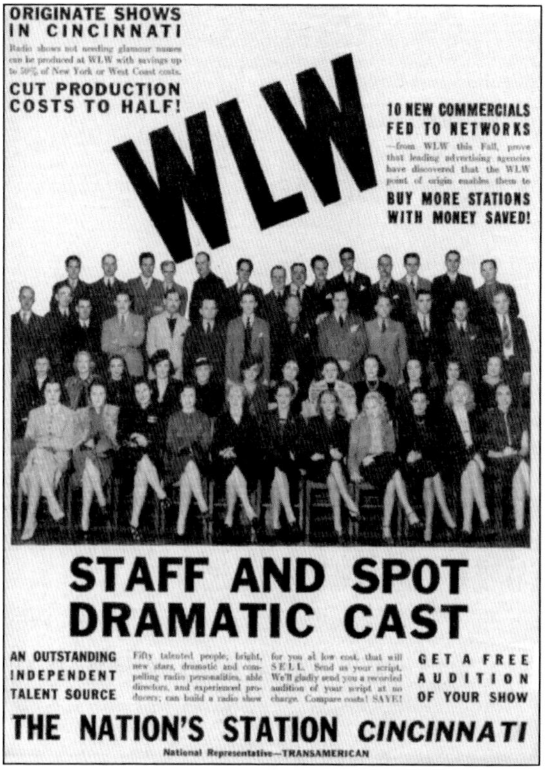

There is power, and then there is *power*—and at 500,000 watts, WLW certainly had the attention of the NBC and Mutual networks. In some cases, WLW rejected the networks' offerings, instead asking for the script so the station could produce it with its own actors. NBC in particular was often frustrated with stubborn WLW. In the end, though, the "world's most powerful station" usually won out. (MM.)

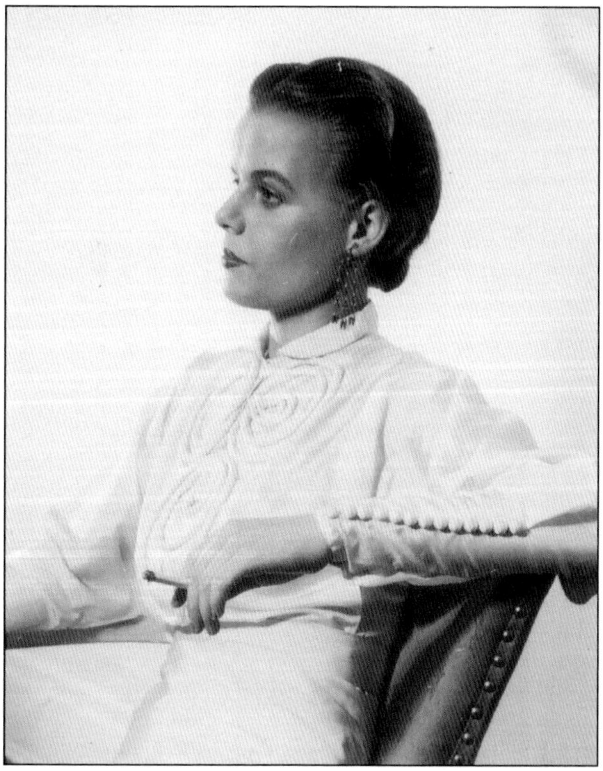

The attractive actress Eileen Palmer came to WLW in 1935 from Portland, Maine, and played the role of Mrs. Benson on the soap opera *The Life of Mary Sothern*. Palmer moved to Chicago where she was married, briefly, to actor Les Tremayne. Eventually, Palmer ended up in New York where she appeared on radio's *Perry Mason* and coached other actors. (EP.)

Despite living in Gainesville, Florida, Walter Lanier "Red" Barber auditioned several times to work at WLW to no avail. But when Powel Crosley purchased the Cincinnati Reds during the 1934 off-season, he found no one among the WLW announcing staff who had any experience broadcasting baseball games. Although he had never seen a professional game before opening day in April 1934, Barber did broadcast University of Florida games and was hired. When not at Crosley Field, Barber would host other programs on both WSAI and WLW and was a very popular member of the staff, leaving reluctantly in 1939 to work for the Brooklyn Dodgers. (MM.)

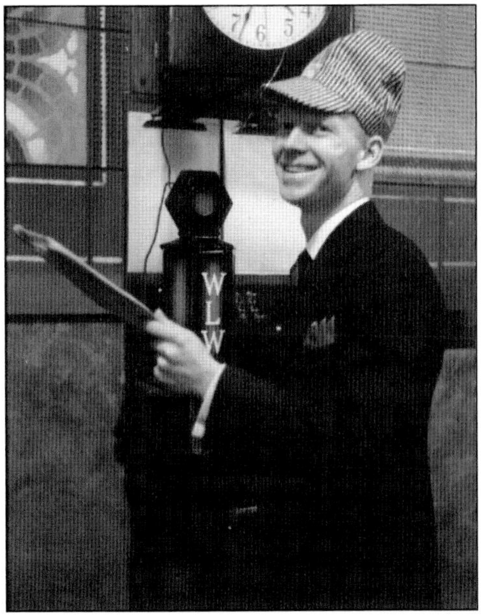

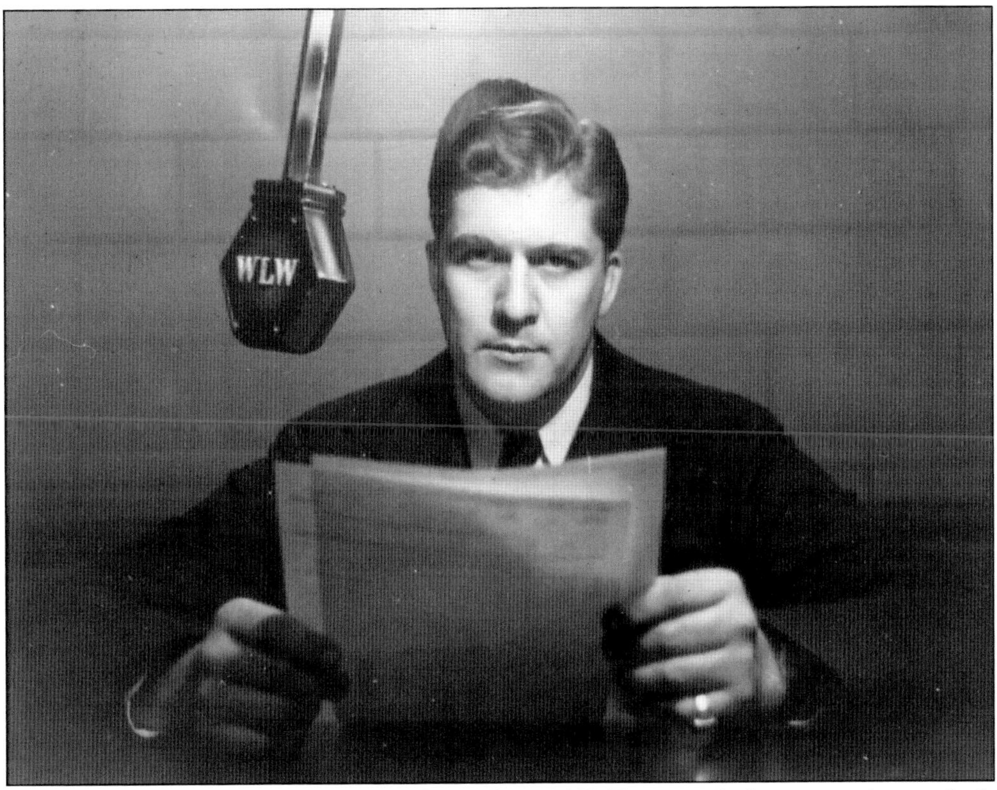

Nicknamed "Mr. Radio Baseball," Pennsylvania-born Al Helfer enjoyed a long career during which he worked six World Series and ten All-Star games. Beginning in 1935, he assisted Red Barber on the WLW Cincinnati Reds broadcasts. Helfer left for a job at CBS in 1937, and in 1944, he married Lockland-born vocalist and pianist "Ramona" Myers, who coincidentally got her start at WLW back in the early 1930s. (CG.)

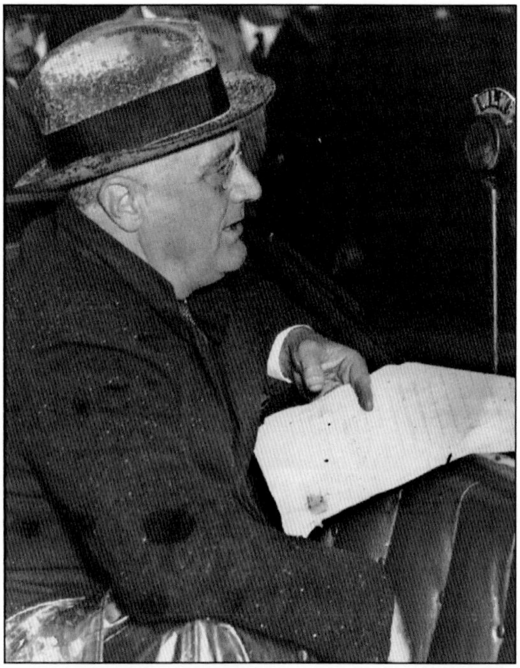

Although politicians recognized the power of radio dating to its early days, it was no surprise that Franklin D. Roosevelt and his rivals sought out the local microphones on their visits to Cincinnati. On October 16, 1936, FDR did not let a little rain prevent him from addressing the WLW microphone from the back seat of his open touring car during the final days of the presidential campaign against Alf Landon. (MM.)

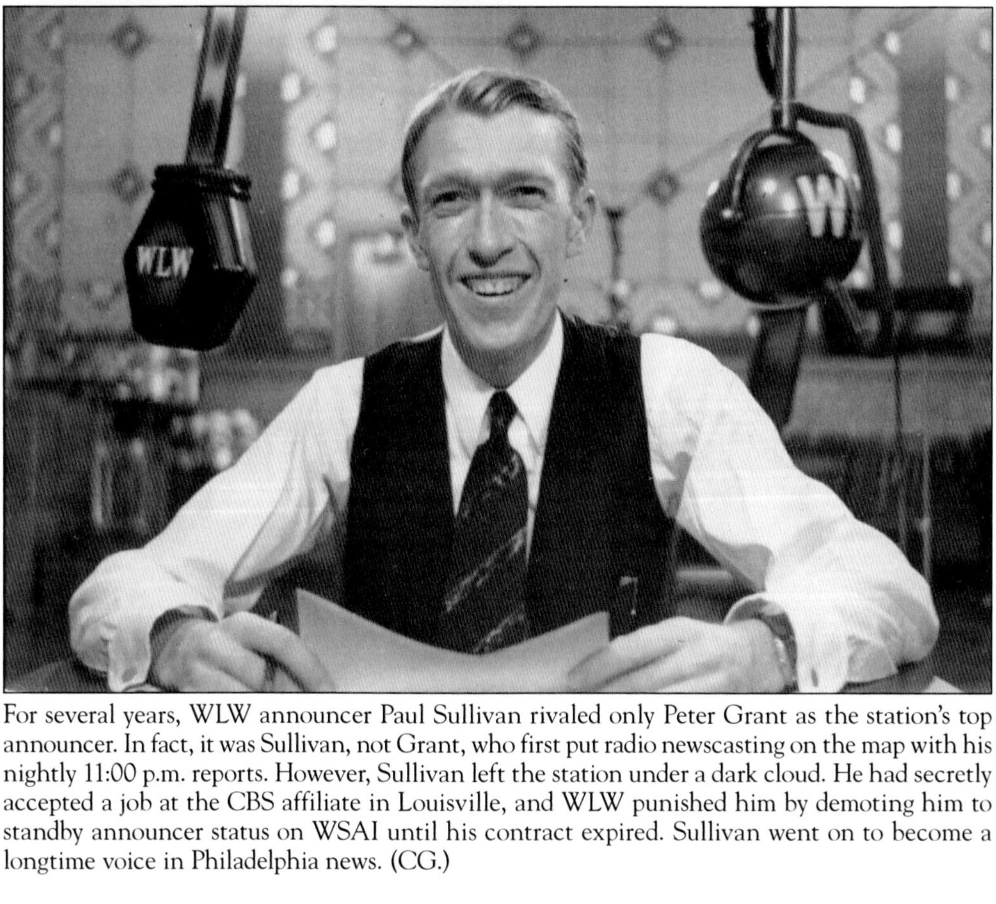

For several years, WLW announcer Paul Sullivan rivaled only Peter Grant as the station's top announcer. In fact, it was Sullivan, not Grant, who first put radio newscasting on the map with his nightly 11:00 p.m. reports. However, Sullivan left the station under a dark cloud. He had secretly accepted a job at the CBS affiliate in Louisville, and WLW punished him by demoting him to standby announcer status on WSAI until his contract expired. Sullivan went on to become a longtime voice in Philadelphia news. (CG.)

Huntington, Indiana, native Howard Chamberlain enjoyed an announcing career at WLW that rivaled only Peter Grant in terms of longevity and popularity. Arriving in 1937, Chamberlain happened to be on duty December 7, 1941, when the first Pearl Harbor bulletins came across the wire. He hastily arranged an impromptu panel discussion, which garnered such praise the station turned it into a weekly news analysis program called *World Front*. In the 1950s and 1960s, he assisted the Farm Department programs on radio and television. (EP.)

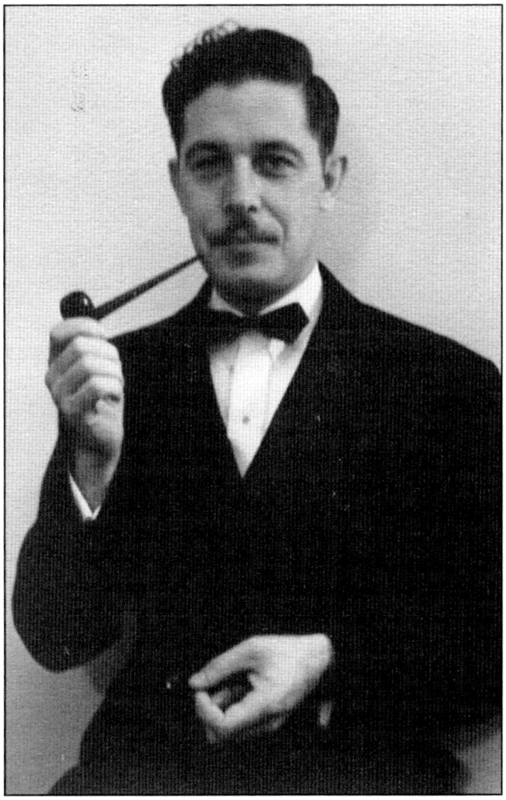

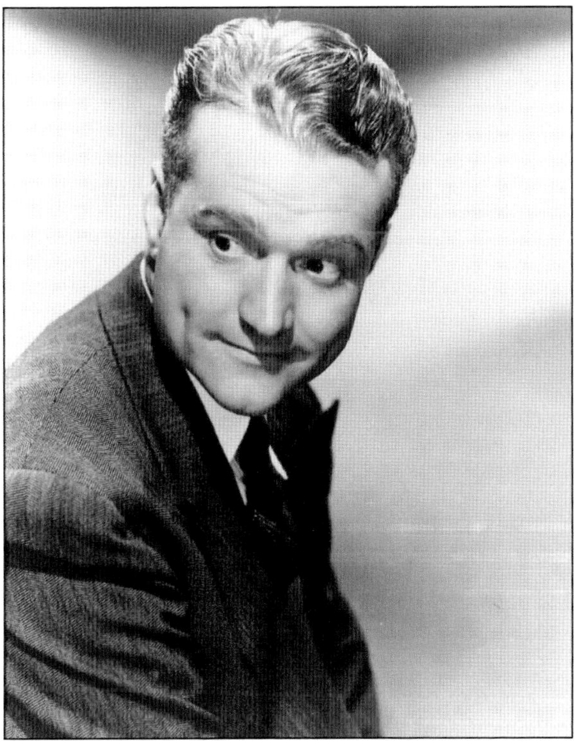

Red Skelton was still developing his physical comedy style when he was added to the cast of Red Foley's *Avalon Time* country music program in early 1939, which was broadcast out of WLW's studios for the NBC network. But as Skelton gained in popularity, Foley's role and the country theme quietly disappeared. By the time it left Cincinnati for Chicago in April of that year, the show belonged entirely to Skelton and gave a national push to the careers of bandleader Phil Davis, vocalist Jeanette Davis, and announcer Del King. (MM.)

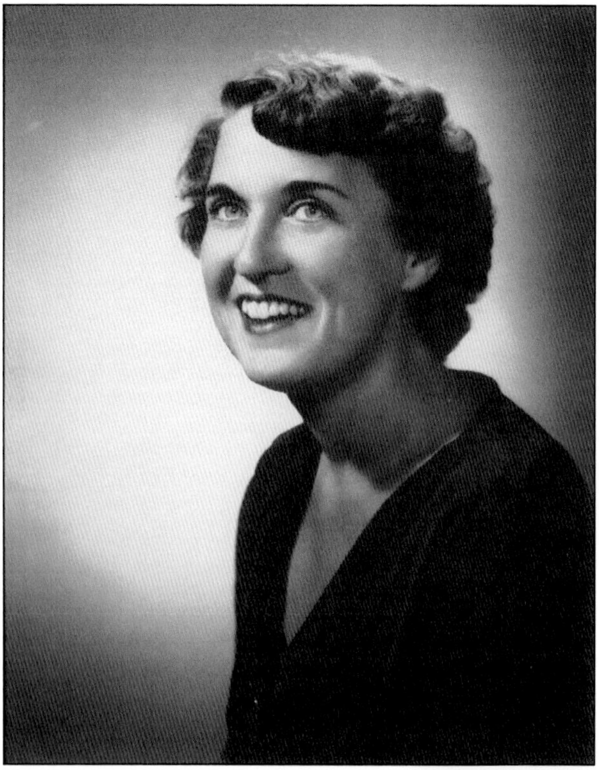

Although best remembered for her many years as media critic for the *Cincinnati Post*, Mary Wood began her career in the late 1930s as a continuity writer for WLW. Wood spent a couple of years churning out scripts for WLW before a request for a pay raise ended in unemployment. She quickly found work at the *Post* writing obituaries and because of her experiences in radio, was eventually given the radio-and-television beat. (MH.)

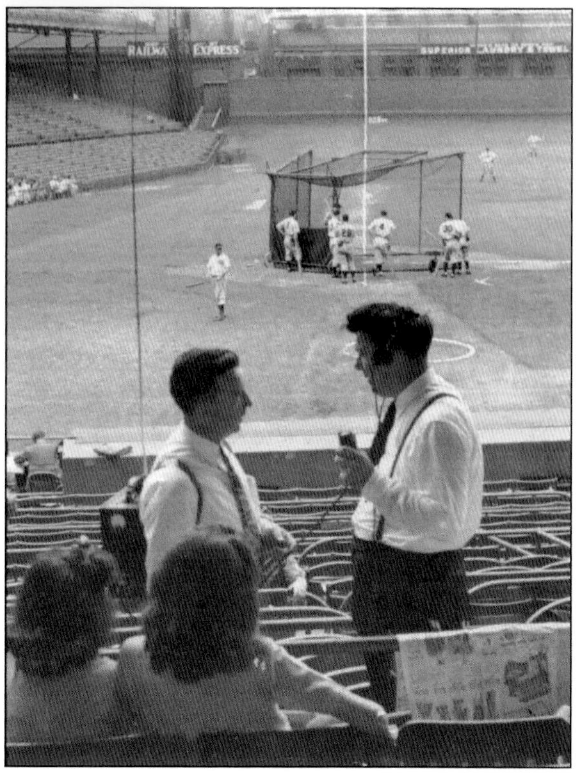

As a two-sport, college and high school referee, Dick Bray had plenty of experience to bring to WSAI and WLW in 1936. Bray assisted on Cincinnati Reds broadcasts and hosted an evening sports show. But Bray gained even more attention when he hosted the *Fans in the Stands* program on WLW, WCPO, and WKRC for Ruebel's Rye Bread. Before home games, he would wander the ballpark with a transmitter backpack interviewing patrons and handing out bread coupons. For away games, he would stand in front of the Albee Theater downtown. Bray is pictured here (left) at Crosley Field interviewing a fan before a June 1943 game. (WR.)

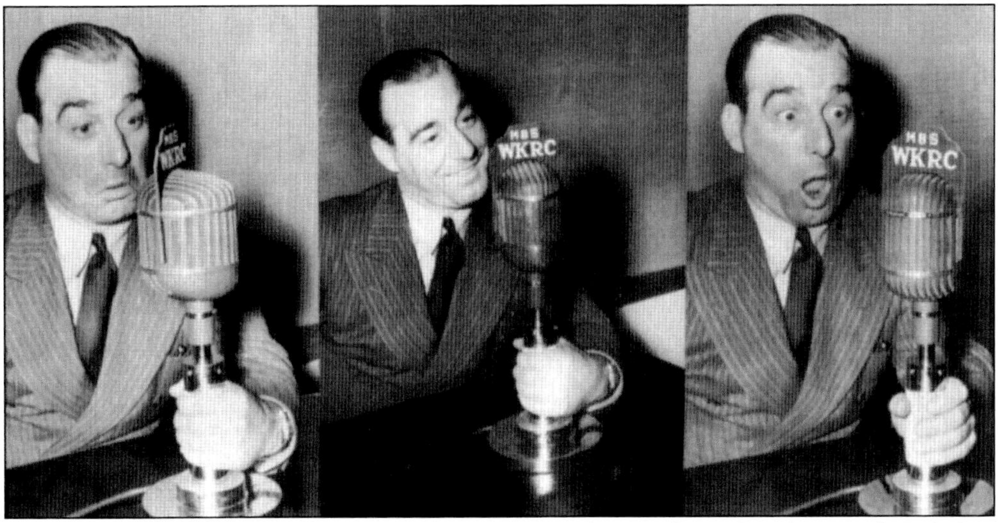

Described as a "poor man's Amos and Andy," Jimmy Scribner's *Johnson Family* was a daily dialect comedy that was heard on WLW and WKRC for several years in the 1930s. Scribner voiced all 22 characters himself, and WKRC actually built a special swivel microphone to accommodate his vocal variations. In fact, Scribner had a lucrative side business selling items related to his characters Pee Wee, Papa, Lawyer Philpotts, and Lucy, which he continued nationally into the 1950s. (MM.)

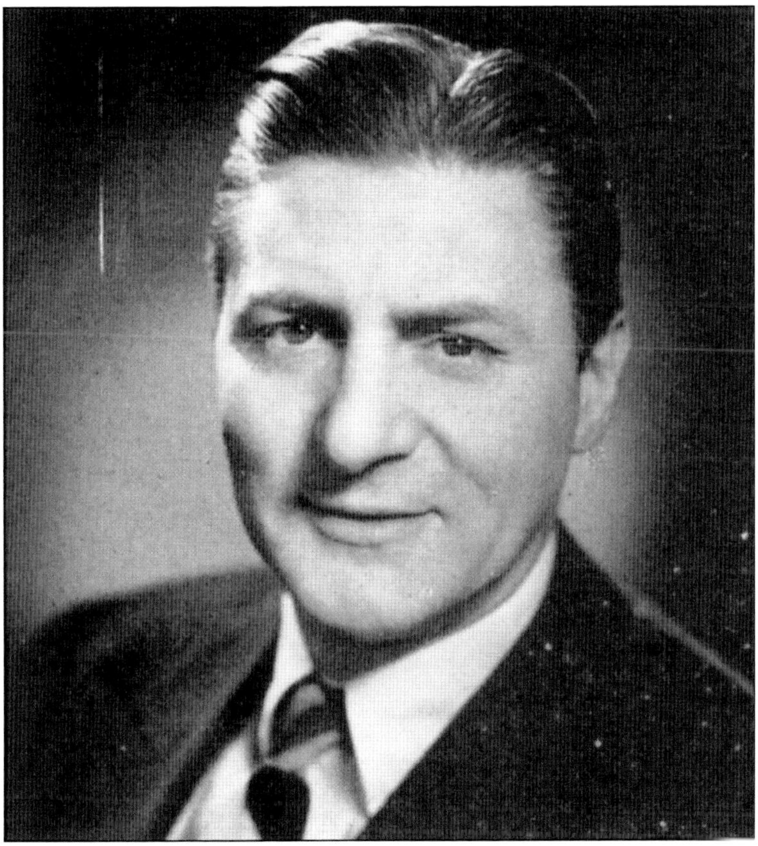

Between trains at Cincinnati's Union Terminal, it was possible that travelers would be accosted by a man with a Southern drawl and a microphone. Tennessee native Paul Hodges came to Cincinnati in 1935 after Scripps-Howard purchased both his Knoxville station and WCPO. Hodges's specialty was man-on-the-street interviews, and he did *Train Time*, *Travel Time*, *Bus Time*, and even *Skating Time* from a local rink for WCPO, WLW, and WCKY. (MM.)

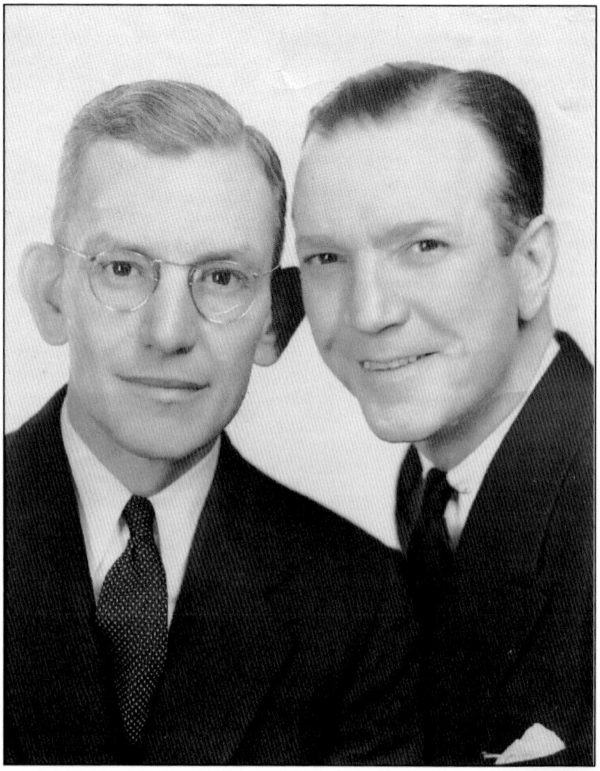

As co-creator of the popular man-on-the-street national program *Vox Pop* in the early 1930s, Jerry Belcher was already well known when he was hired to announce and to head-up the public affairs department at WCKY in 1942. Pictured with fellow *Vox Pop* host Parks Johnson (left), Belcher helped give average Cincinnatians a chance to voice their opinions about politics, government, sports, and the other issues of the day. (MM.)

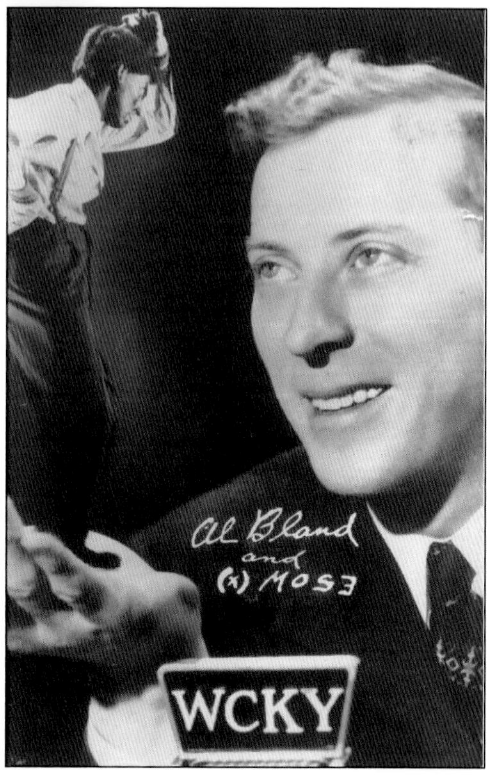

Brothers Lee and Thomas "Al" Bland came to WCKY in the mid-1930s but took different career paths. Lee became a recording technician with CBS and worked with Norman Corwin's *One World Flight*. Al became the morning host and created a blackface character named Mose, who commented on the Cincinnati Reds during the 1940 championship season. Later, after rising in the management ranks at KMOX in St. Louis, Al Bland returned to Cincinnati in 1954 as program director at WLW. (MM.)

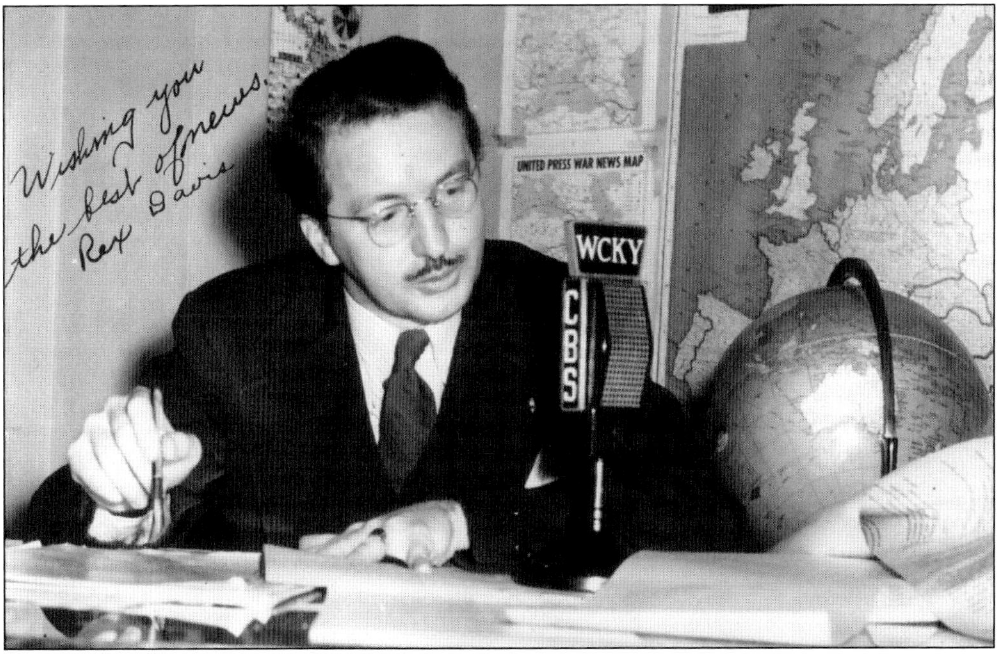

He started on Cincinnati radio using his real name, Frank Zwygart, in the late 1930s, but WCKY management realized that other than having a winning Scrabble name, their young newsman would be better served with the nom de plume "Rex Davis." Davis rose quickly in stature and in 1946, was hired away by KMOX in St. Louis where he remained as a news icon until 1981. (MM.)

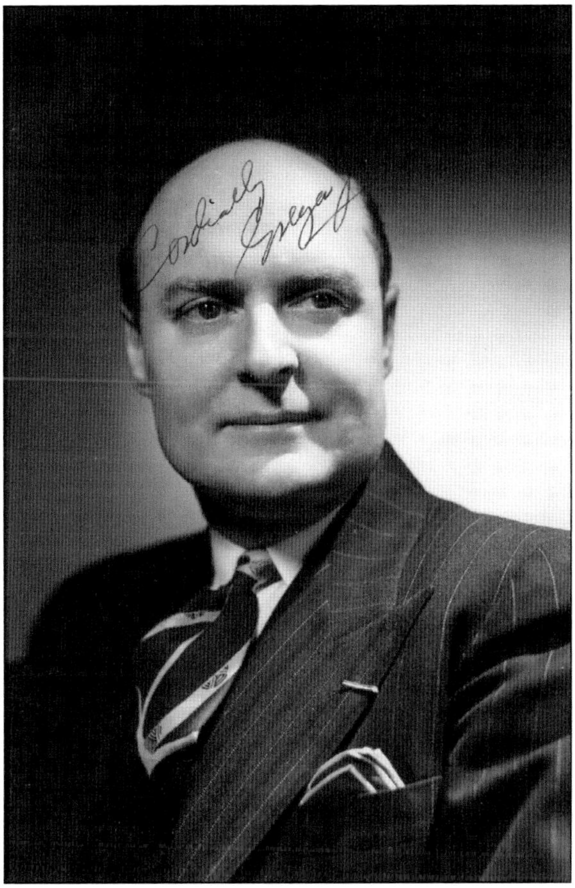

With the advent of World War II, WLW assembled a set of news commentators to discuss world events, including Carroll Alcott, who wrote *My War With Japan*, and Gregor Ziemer, who was well known for *Education of a Nazi*, the 1941 book on which the film *Hitler's Children* was based. However, Alcott and Ziemer disliked each other and actually got into a well-publicized fistfight following a May 1943 broadcast. There is no word on who won, but Alcott left WLW for WCKY two weeks later. Ziemer stayed long enough to send this photograph to a fan. (MM.)

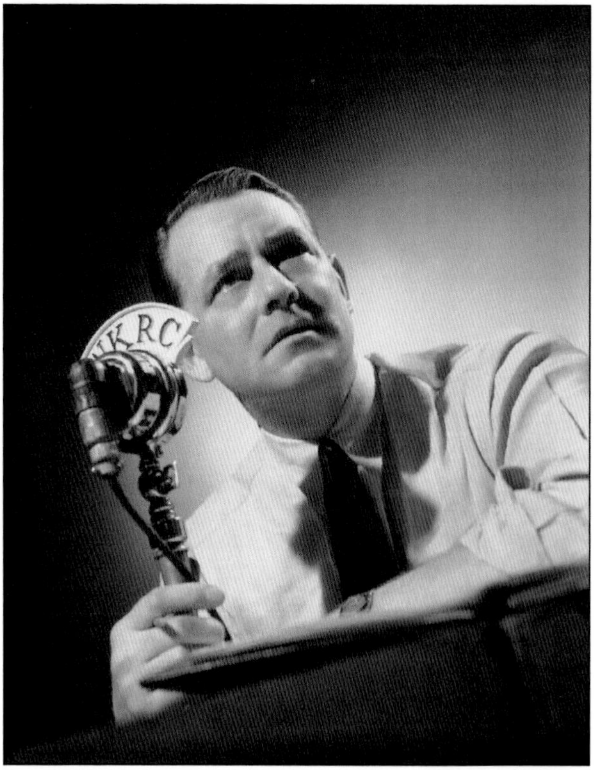

By 1941, famed New York Yankees pitcher Waite Hoyt had struggled in retirement for three years trying to land a broadcasting job in New York. Thinking he would come to Cincinnati for a year or two to hone his announcing skills, Hoyt auditioned for and won a job at WKRC for the 1942 season. After a rocky start, Hoyt ended up embracing the city and calling Reds games until 1965, celebrated as one of Cincinnati's favorite rain-delay storytellers. (MM.)

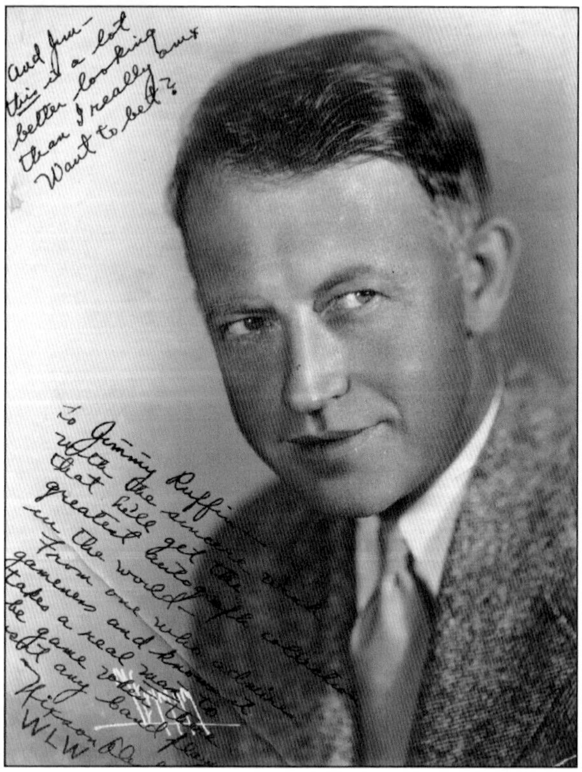

In the late 1930s, as tensions between print and broadcast thawed, newspapermen and women gradually found themselves moonlighting on radio as commentators. Popular *Cincinnati Times-Star* sportswriter Nixson Denton was one who was invited by WLW to share his views. Unlike other cut-and-dry scribes, Denton had a flair for words, often quoting the classics of literature. Denton's writings later were celebrated in a book by WKRC's Bob Jones. (MM.)

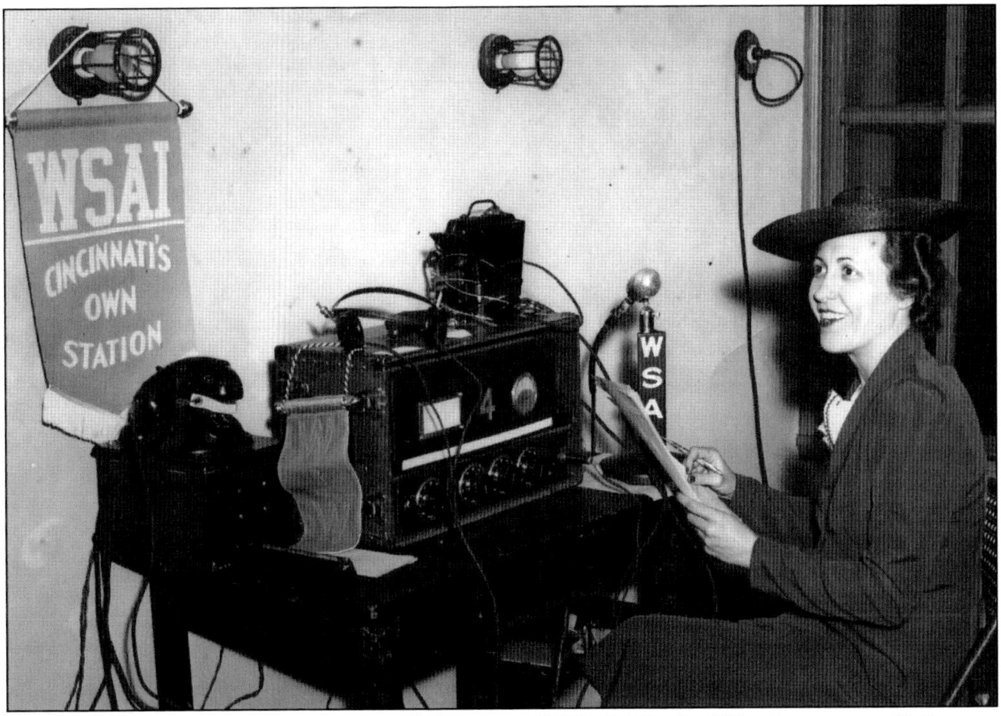

While Ruth Lyons was creating quite a following at WKRC, Marsha Wheeler was equally busy at WLW. Like Lyons, Wheeler entered broadcasting in 1928 and was featured on her own *Woman's Hour* program. On Thursdays, Wheeler read listener letters over the air, and this became known as the WLW Mailbag Club. By the 1940s, the Mailbag Club was a full-fledged club, complete with a monthly newsletter, regular picnics, and wartime service projects. Wheeler became a news analyst and later retired to open a coffee shop in Milford, and Hilda Weaver helped run the club. (MM.)

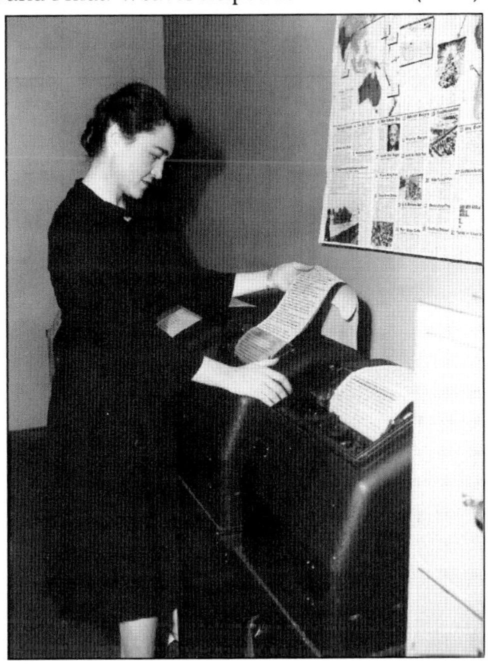

Elizabeth Bemis studied medicine at the University of Paris but returned to her home in Denver in 1938 to work as a journalist after war clouds enveloped Europe. With experience in both newspapers and radio, Bemis came to WLW in early 1940 to work as a news analyst on a program called *A Woman's View*. After two years at WLW, Bemis was hired by CBS in New York where she worked as the network's first female commentator until 1944. After the war, she joined her soldier-husband Louis DeBus in California where she remained active in radio and environmental causes. (MD.)

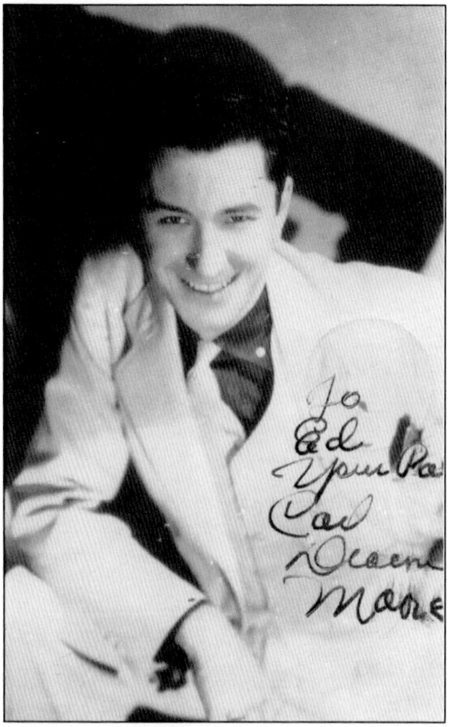

Carl Moore was a drummer and bandleader of regional renown who came to Cincinnati from Chicago in 1942. Surely, he fooled some people when he would broadcast on WSAI and WLW as his fictional alter ego the "Squeakin' Deacon." Full of cornpone humor, the Deacon would launch into countrified commentary reminiscent of television's later *Hee Haw* programs. Moore left the station in 1945 to try his luck as a disc jockey in California. (MM.)

In the autumn of 1930, WLW owner Powel Crosley wanted a midnight program of soft music and poetry to showcase the newly purchased Wurlitzer studio pipe organ. Program director Eddie Byron composed the legendary poem that opened the *Moon River* program while violinist Virginio Marucci, who suggested the theme song, played "Caprice Viennois" in the background. *Moon River* changed subtly over the next 37 years but was always popular, especially for late-night romance. On October 27, 1945, WLW invited back many of the vocalists, announcers, and organists for a 15th anniversary reunion broadcast. (MH.)

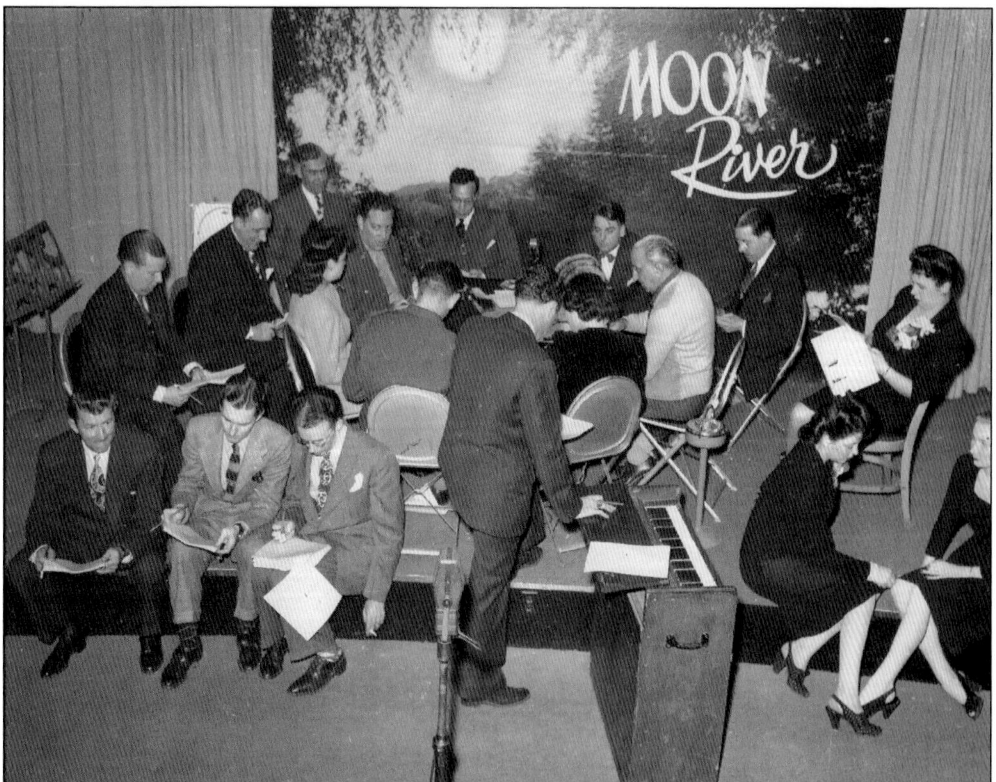

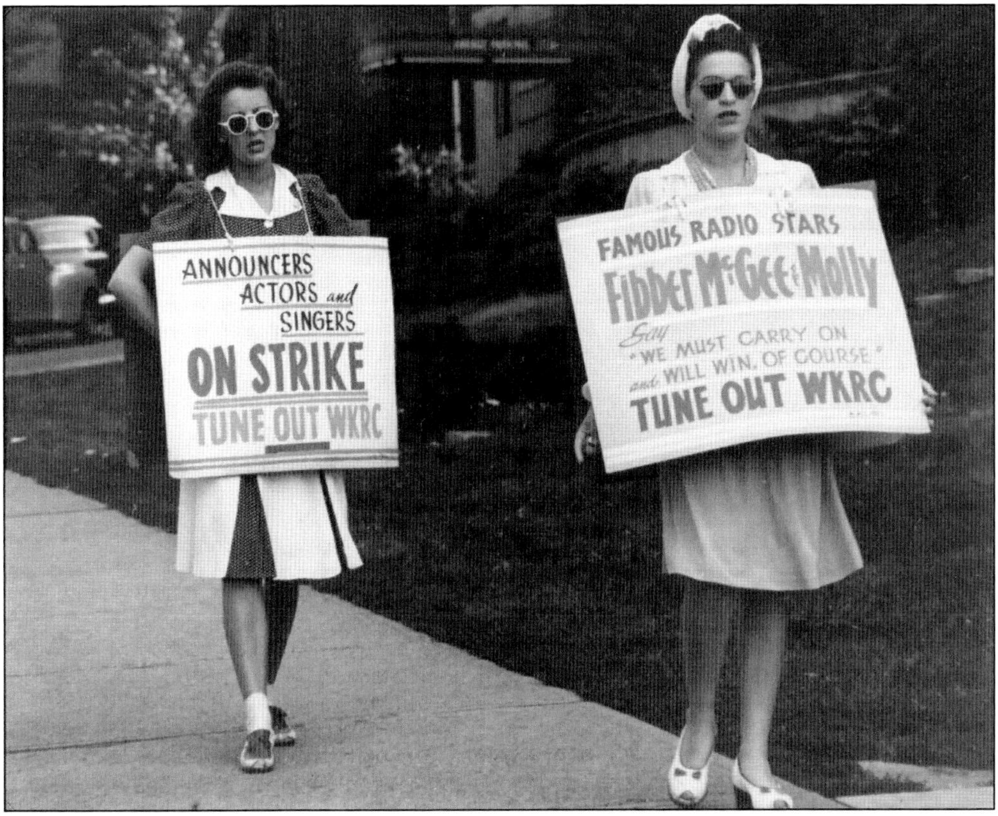

While Cincinnati radio technicians and musicians had their unions from nearly the beginning of the broadcast era, actors and announcers were not represented until the American Federation of Radio Artists (AFRA) organized locally in 1938. At WKRC, a new show produced by the government's WPA project called *Edith Adams' Future* premiered in early 1941. Months later, after prolonged negotiations with WKRC broke down, AFRA went on strike. Instead of capitulating, WKRC cancelled all dramatics programs, and *Edith Adams* vanished forever. (MH.)

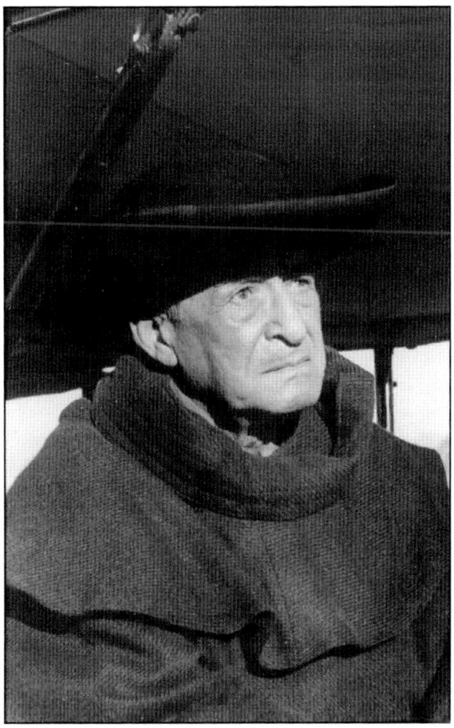

Ralph Moody was already one of the older members of the WLW-WSAI dramatic staff in the early 1940s. He had a great talent for dialects and portrayed the character of Old Rhinelander as host of the German-themed *Canal Days* program, which celebrated Cincinnati's Over-the-Rhine neighborhood. In spite of his age, Moody left for Hollywood in 1945 where he enjoyed a long career playing prospectors and Native Americans in films and on such television shows as *F-Troop* and *Circus Boy*. (MM.)

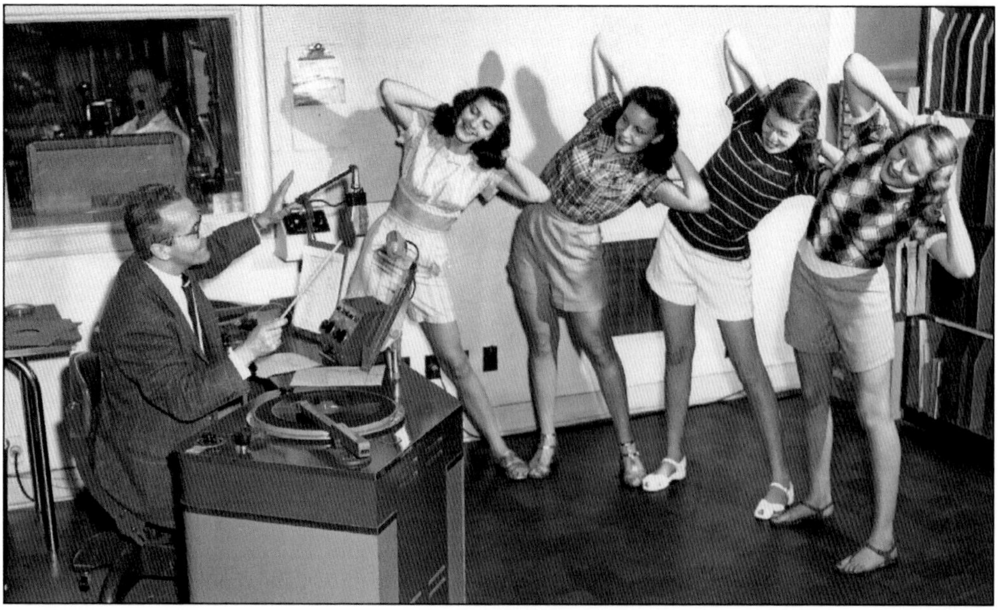

Brooklyn native Bill Dawes appeared in several Broadway plays in the early 1930s and arrived in Cincinnati in 1936 to teach dramatics at the Schuster-Martin School of Drama. He found radio to his liking in 1940 when he began hosting the *Make Believe Ballroom* on WCKY. In 1949, he moved over to WCPO radio and in 1952, was named program director there. Dawes remained in various management capacities until his death in 1968. Dawes is pictured here at WCKY conducting a radio physical fitness exercise. (BS.)

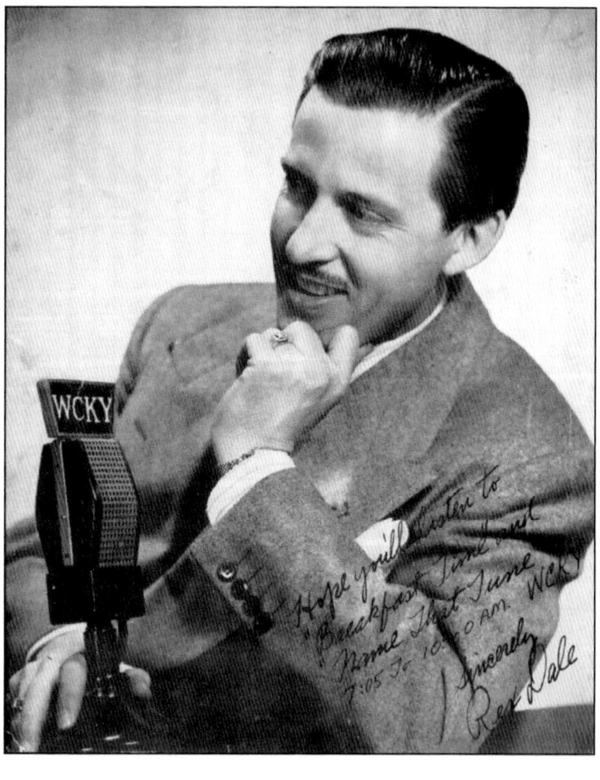

In 1949, six years after one Rex—Rex Davis—departed WCKY for St. Louis, Rex Dale arrived at the station as a disc jockey. Dale was quickly voted one of the top DJs in the region, and thousands enjoyed his "platter time." But when Rex decided to leave the station in 1958, WCKY claimed to own his name. The matter ended up in court with Dale keeping the moniker. (MM.)

Announcer Paul Jones arrived at WLW from West Virginia in 1939. Except for a two-year stint away during the war, Jones spent over 30 years on Cincinnati radio and television. In the mid-1940s, Jones was the announcer for Ruth Lyons on her early WLW radio programs. After working as a disc jockey at WSAI in the early 1950s, Jones ended up spending the next 16 years at WKRC radio and television. (MM.)

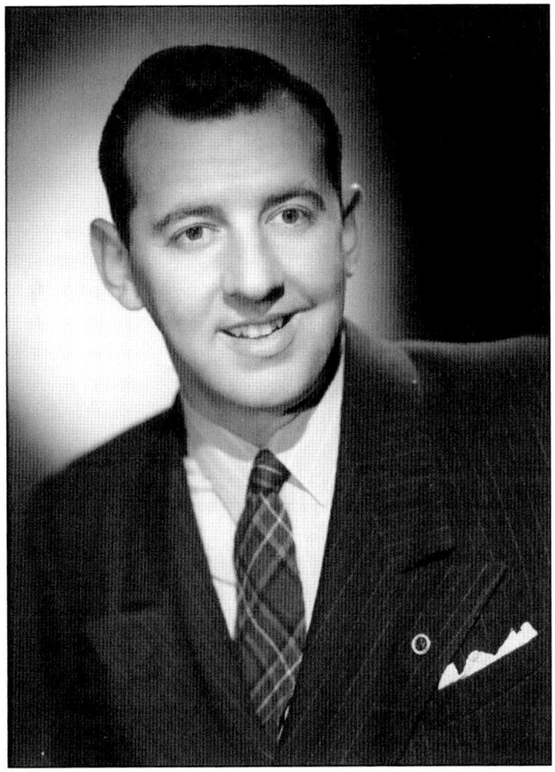

Radio drama did not die completely in the 1950s, but it certainly tailed off. In 1950, before creating *The Twilight Zone*, WLW writer Rod Serling spent most of his time working on television scripts for shows like *Melody Showcase*. But he did sneak in an occasional radio drama, such as *It Could Happen To You*. Meanwhile, pictured here (standing) is Verne Jay, another popular WLW writer working with longtime producer-director Charlie Lammers (left) and technician Robert Kleiber. (MM.)

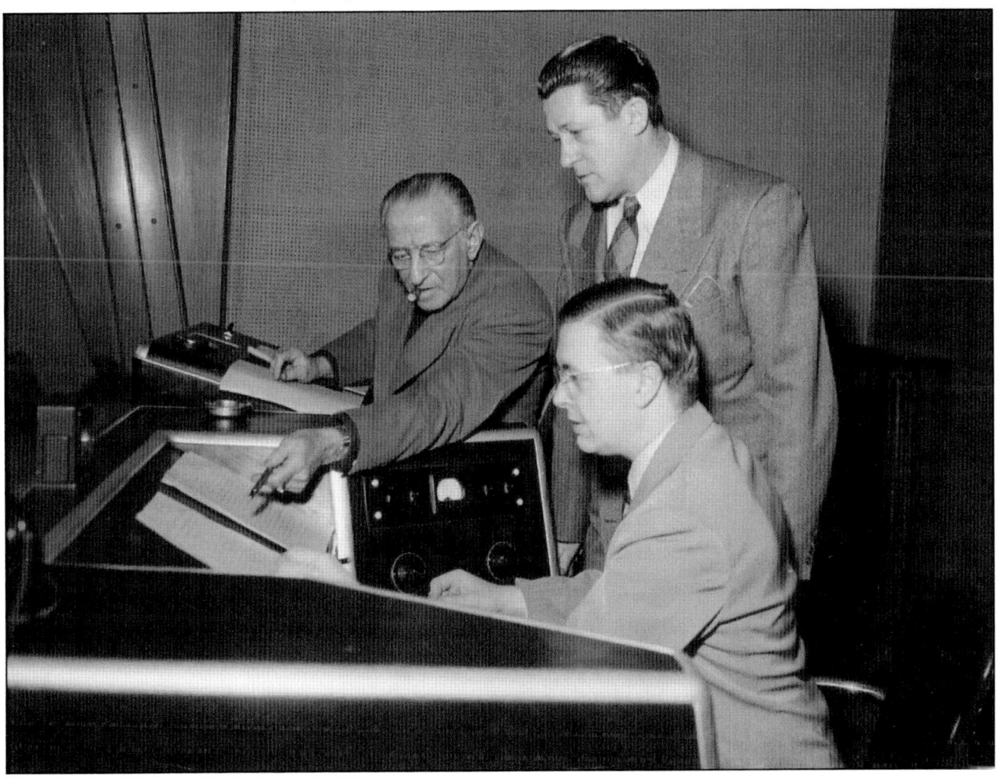

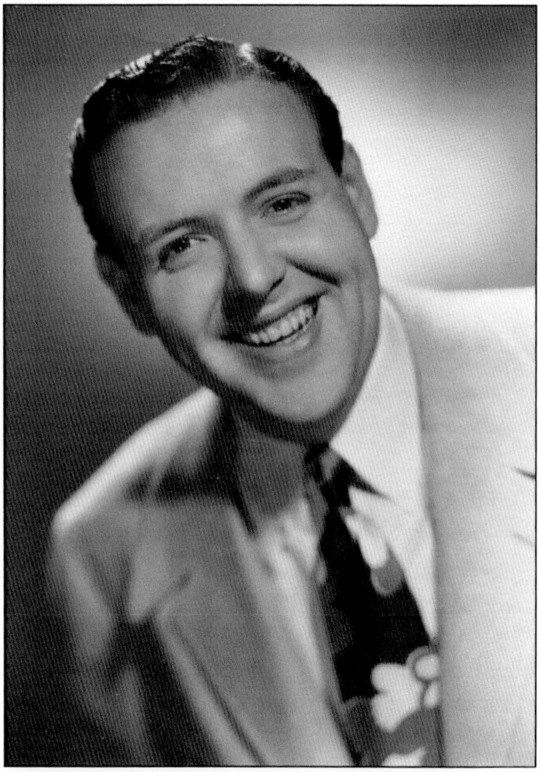

Another radio sidekick for Ruth Lyons on WSAI and WLW was Frazier Thomas, who came to Cincinnati in 1936 as a summer replacement announcer. Thomas hosted *I Cover the Movies* and *Inside Radio* for Crosley, but his true legacy began in 1950 during a one-year stint at WKRC television. Thomas and his wife invented the character Garfield Goose and then moved to Chicago where both Frazier and Garfield became kiddie-show icons for decades. (MM.)

As original radio drama became a lost presence on radio in the 1950s, so did opportunities for actors and actresses. Rather than maintaining a fulltime dramatics department, stations like WLW would hire freelance actors for productions. Mary Lou Lantz (right) started at WLW in the late 1930s and was heard on Red Skelton's *Avalon Time*. She later married WLW newsman Bob Merriman. (MM.)

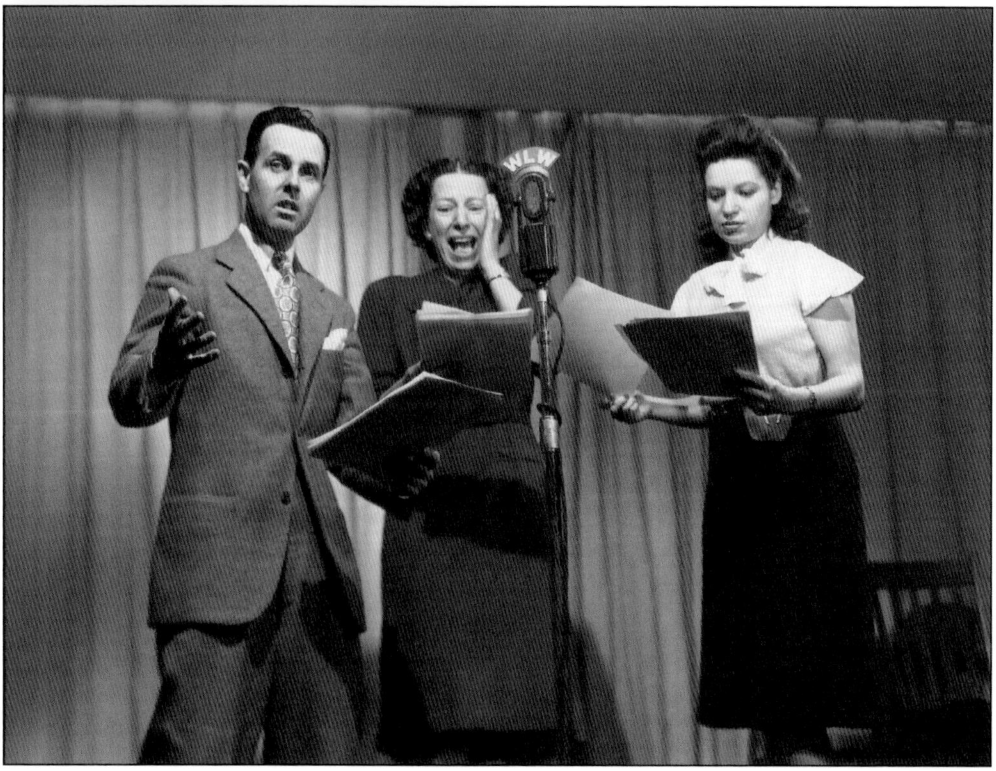

Three

Music to the Ears
The Bands, Vocalists, and Musical Acts of Cincinnati Radio

While it might not date back to "day one" of radio, certainly by "day two," radio invited musical programming to the microphone. Music and radio are very well suited for each other despite the fact that early vocalists had to literally insert their heads into rustic "morning glory horn" microphones to be heard. Music entertains and enlivens a broadcast, bringing energy and escape to the listener. To this very day, providing music is one of radio's most profitable and popular programming options.

Despite the popularity of music in general on radio, there have been, on occasion, the internal wrestling and struggles over exactly what type of music to provide. Clearly, fine arts music, operatic arias, and the classics were the favorites among programmers in the early 1920s. This emphasis on the arts, however, was not always shared by the listeners, who often clamored more for the base of popular culture—that is, jazz. Fred Smith, the program director of Cincinnati's WLW, for example, had to constantly resolve the conflict between his preferred desire to present the sweet soprano-performing Tosca and the restless listener groundswell that called for the latest licks from Jelly Roll Morton. Smith understood the show business adage, "Give 'em what they want," and reluctantly included jazz on his station, but numerous programmers in many other cities did not. The eternal struggle continues today in an era of fragmented audiences and formats so specific that one can turn the dial and receive not only "country," but also "young country," "classic country," "country rock," and "classic, young country rock."

Radio vocalists and musicians were often a transient lot. To many of them, radio was an avenue toward better things and larger audiences in bigger cities. Radio performance was an adjunct to their live, stage work. Often, a vocalist would come to a station for only one or two years and then move on. Rare was the vocalist who spent more than five years at a particular radio station. Instrumentalists might have stayed a little longer, but even they seemed to have had happy feet.

During the superpower era in the teeth of the Depression, talented musicians were attracted to WLW like moths to a porch light. With two full-sized orchestras of over 60 performers each, with dozens of composers, arrangers, soundmen, and technicians on staff, and with a 500,000-watt powerhouse that blanketed most of the country, if not all, musical acts and vocalists fought to be a part of the "Nation's Station." As one WLW performer stated, "you never knew who was listening. WLW, in those days, could be a springboard to anywhere."

This chapter celebrates the men and women who launched music into the radio winds, providing comfort to the infirm, causing the toes of the young to tap, and creating an atmosphere of romance for the late-night couples seeking quiet togetherness.

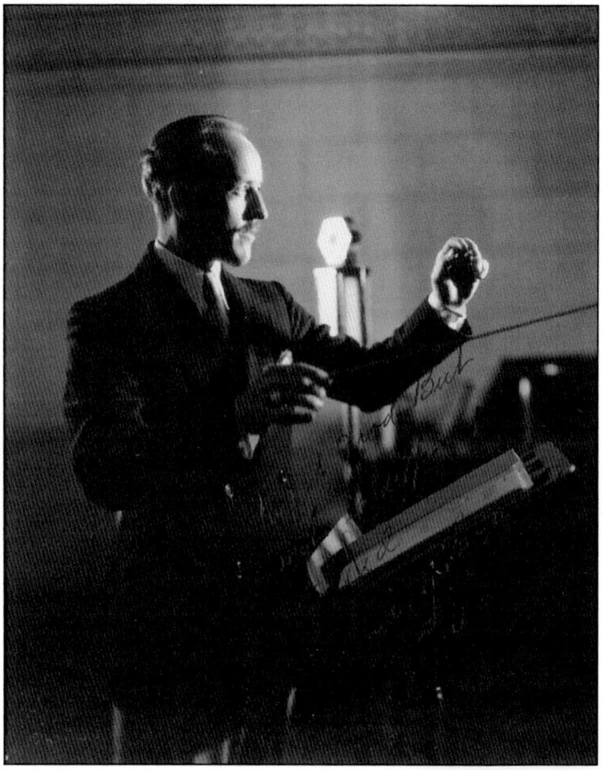

William Stoess was a violinist who also had conducted a small ensemble on Cincinnati radio as early as 1921. He was hired by WLW in 1926 and was the musical director for the better part of the next decade. In time, Bill Stoess gained the reputation as the most respected director on the WLW musical staff, whether leading a small ensemble or the entire, 60-piece WLW orchestra. In 1944, Stoess left Cincinnati for New York to become musical director for the ABC religious drama *The Greatest Story Ever Told.* (DB.)

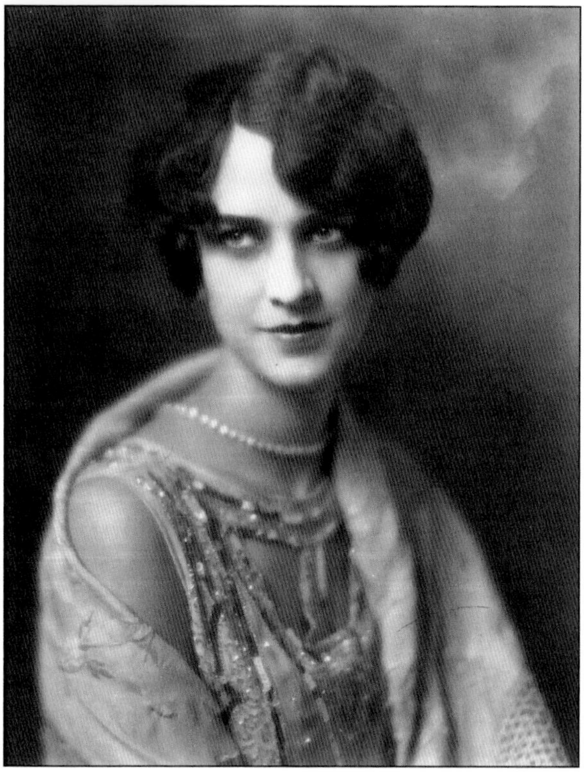

WLW owner Powel Crosley is credited, by some, with discovering Jane Froman. The Cincinnati Conservatory of Music student was singing at a dinner party when Crosley heard her. In 1930, Froman recorded with WLW's Henry Thies and his orchestra, but it was singer Don Ross, her agent, who convinced her to go to NBC in Chicago in 1932 and then on to New York in 1933. Hollywood fame was not far behind. (MM.)

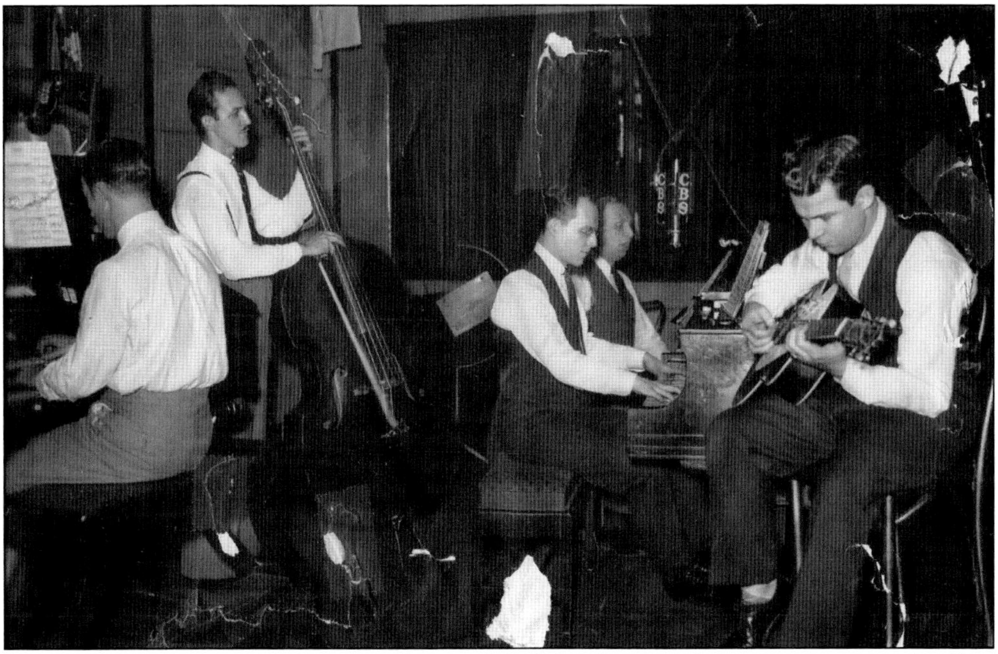

Harry Frankel (seated at the piano in background) had already enjoyed a long career as a vaudevillian and minstrel showman when radio came along. Not wishing to stray far from his farm in Richmond, he performed on Cincinnati radio station WLW beginning in 1930 and on WKRC in 1934. On the network, he was known as Singin' Sam the "Barbasol Man," but on WLW, sponsored by Great States Lawnmowers, he was known as the "Lawnmowin' Man." The guitarist in this image is longtime WLW strummer Chick Gatwood. (EP.)

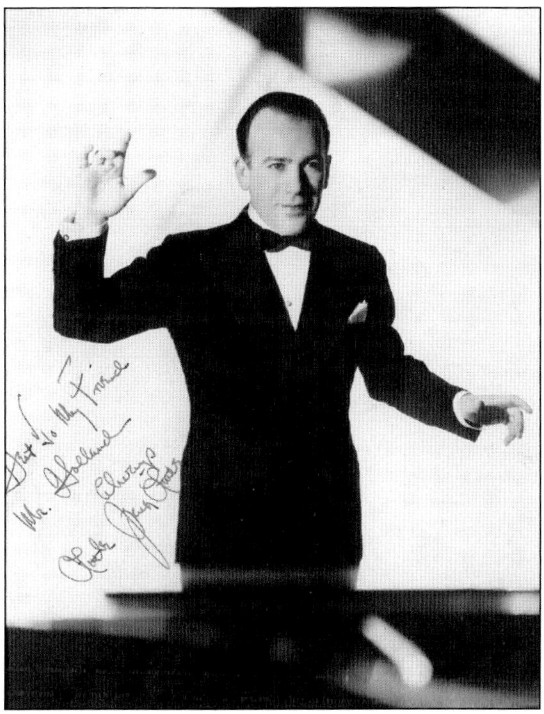

Little Jack Little was born in London, England, as John Leonard and grew up in Iowa before embarking on a vaudeville career as a pianist and vocalist. He brought his song-and-patter style to WSAI and WLW in the late 1920s. By 1932, he was in New York leading an orchestra and broadcasting over the NBC network. He later ended up in Hollywood where he appeared in some films before taking his life while chronically ill in 1956. (MM.)

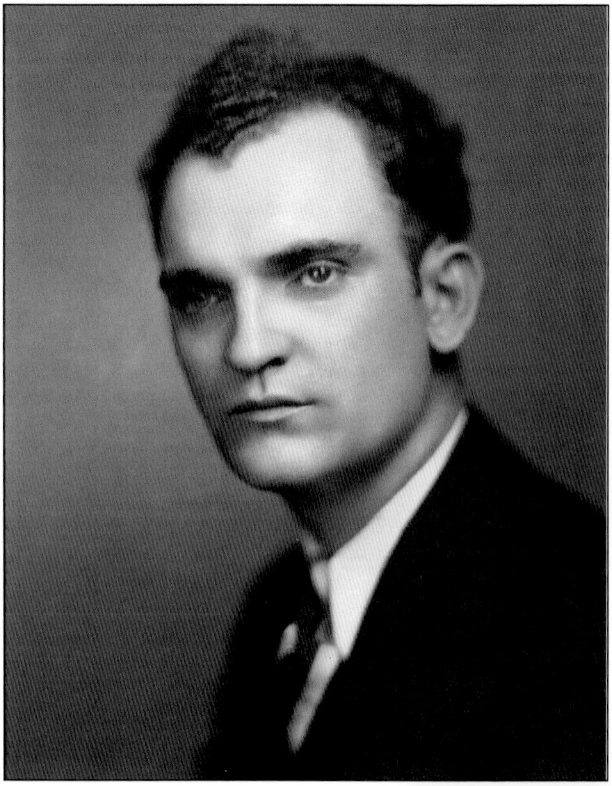

The Sunshine Boys were brothers Joe and Dan Mooney. Very popular for their peppy songs and flawless harmonies, the Mooney brothers came to WLW around 1932. They were also totally blind, having lost their sight from a childhood disease. Dan (left) left the act and radio station around 1936, and very little is known about him. Joe (below), however, enjoyed a long career as a jazz accordionist and was featured on recordings into the 1960s. (EP.)

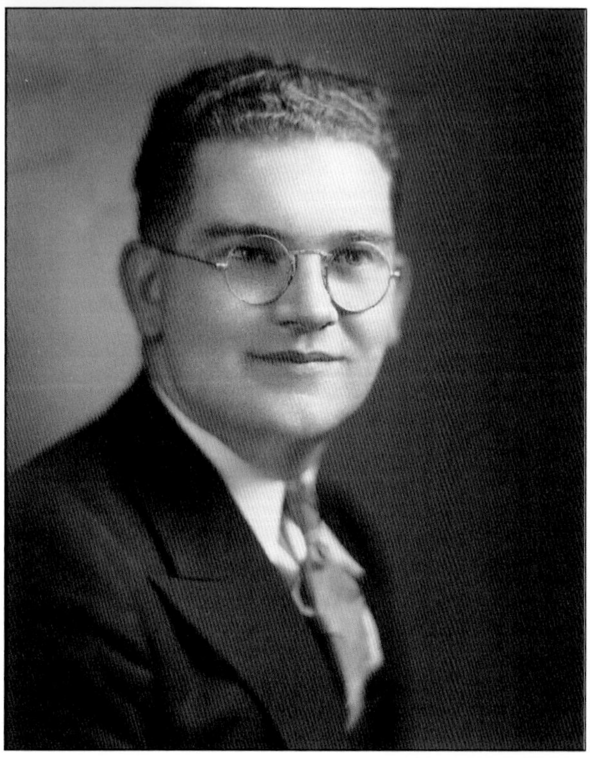

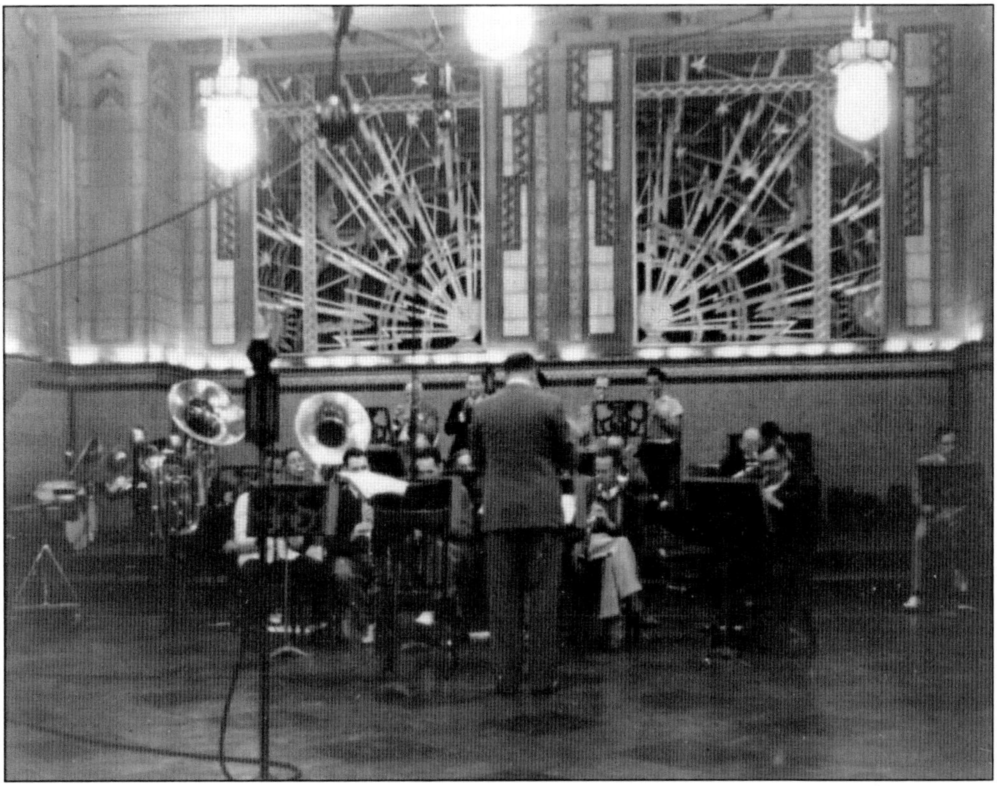

Frank Simon, the former cornetist and assistant conductor under John Philip Sousa, returned to his native Cincinnati in 1921 and was convinced by Middletown's Armco Steel Company to direct their company band. It was not long before Simon had a professional march band that was broadcasting nationally every Sunday afternoon for nearly 10 years from WLW over the NBC network. (FSB.)

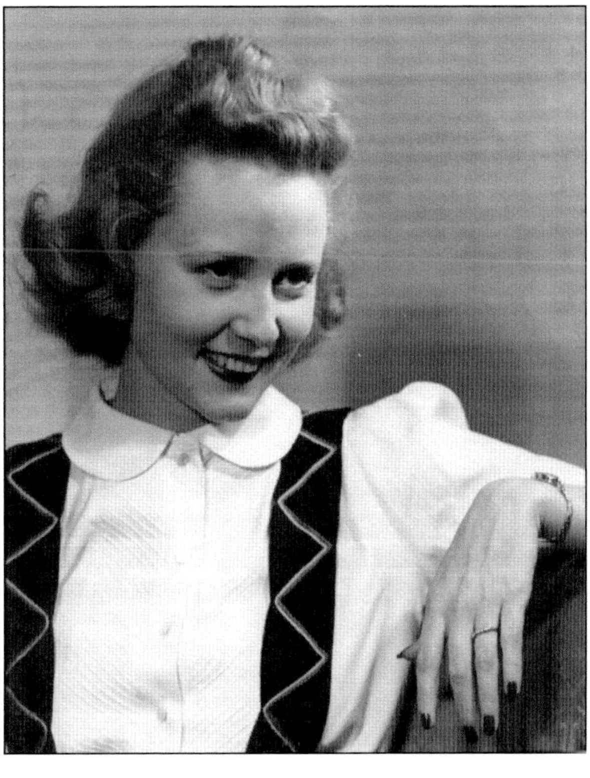

As daughter of the family behind Cincinnati's Tresler-Comet Oil company, WLW vocalist Jane Tresler was reluctant to use her real name on the radio in 1936, so she used the pseudonym Jane Gerrard. But as vocalist for Burt Farber's orchestra at the Netherland Plaza, she was still Jane Tresler. By 1940, Jane married WLW staff musician Bud Ruskin and retired from radio. (EP.)

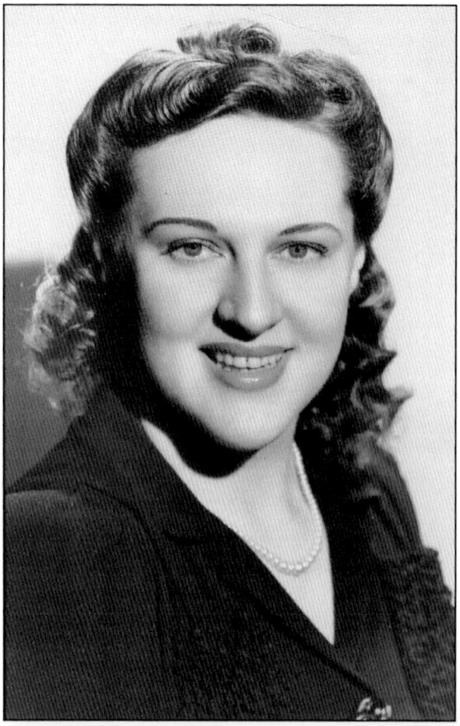

She was a terrific pianist and had a pleasing voice; Lockland-born Estrild Raymona Myers was known simply as "Ramona" when she joined WLW in 1931 to perform on a variety of programs, including Sid Ten Eyck's *Doodlesockers*. In 1932, Paul Whiteman happened to be in town and hired her for his band. Later, she replaced Mildred Bailey on her own CBS network show. Ramona married sports announcer Al Helfer in 1941 and returned to Cincinnati in the late 1940s for another WLW stint. (MM.)

The theater organ was a mainstay in radio in the 1920s and 1930s. Always on standby in case a program ran short, the staff organist was an important part of all five local stations. Broadcast legend Ruth Lyons was an organist at WKRC early in her career, and Fats Waller preferred the organ to the piano at WLW. Pictured here is longtime WLW organist Eugene Perazzo at the console of the station's three-manual Wurlitzer Opus 1606. His guest this day is none other than legendary network organist Rosa Rio. (EP.)

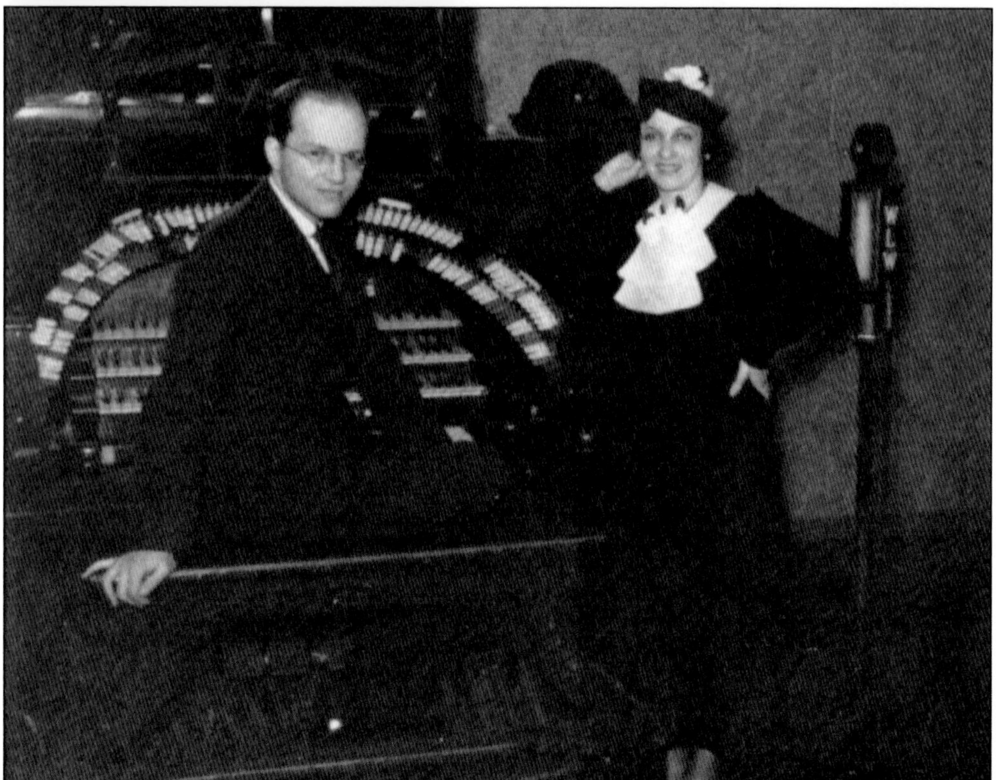

WLW staff violinist Virginio Marucci had an ensemble called the South Americans on the air but is perhaps best remembered for suggesting to program creator Ed Byron the theme song for the long-running *Moon River* program. Marucci felt the gentle strains of Fritz Kreisler's "Caprice Viennois" matched beautifully the poem Byron had written to open and close the program—and he was correct. (DB.)

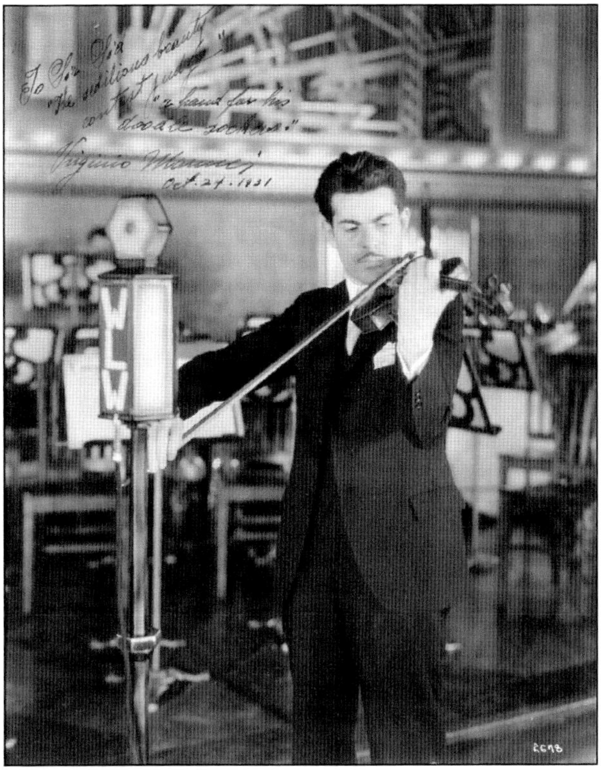

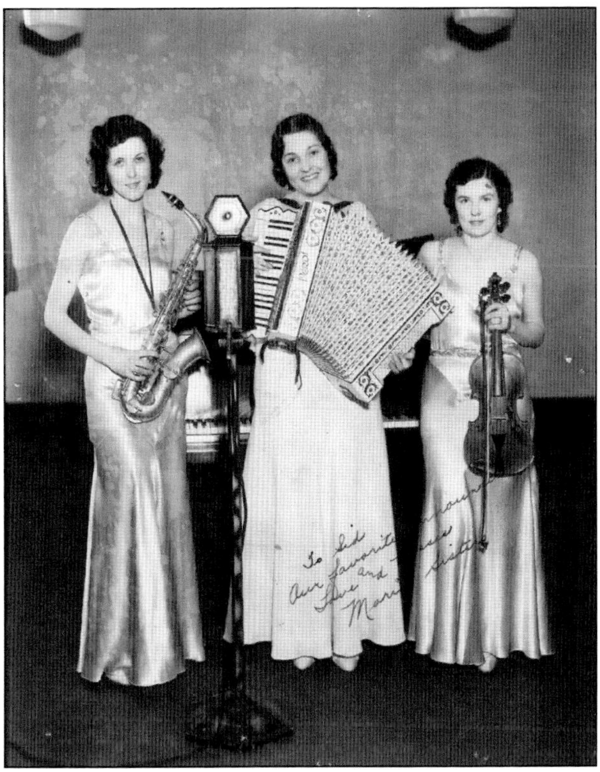

Now a ghost town, the former Dunn, Indiana, produced a talented set of sisters who performed as the Morin Sisters. Evelyn, Pauline, and Lucille Morin could sing and play instruments and were heard on WLW beginning in 1931 until they were discovered by Paul Whiteman two years later. Eventually, they ended up in Chicago on Don McNeill's *Breakfast Club*, but in 1939, Evelyn married, and the act disbanded. (DB.)

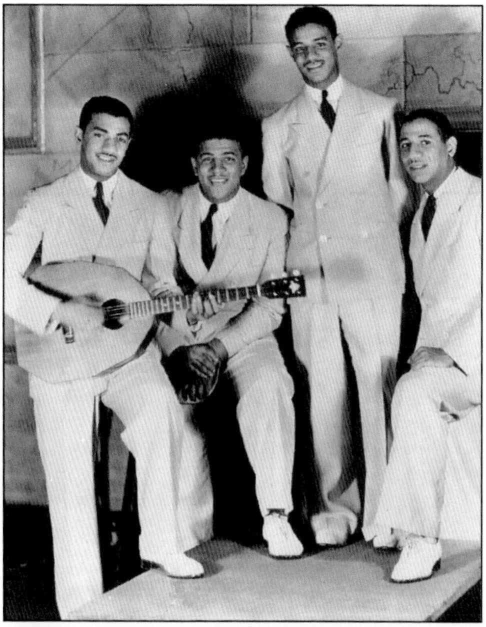

Touring Ohio with the Michael Hauer Orchestra, Piqua's Mills Brothers found a radio home at WLW in 1928 where their unique sound—one guitar and four voices imitating instruments—was immediately popular among jazz listeners. WLW pianist Seger Ellis, friends with high-powered New York agent Tommy Rockwell, had a hand in bringing the Mills Brothers to the attention of CBS in New York in 1930. Ellis's efforts may have benefitted the careers of, from left to right, John, Harry, Don, and Herbert, but ended up costing him his job at WLW. (MM.)

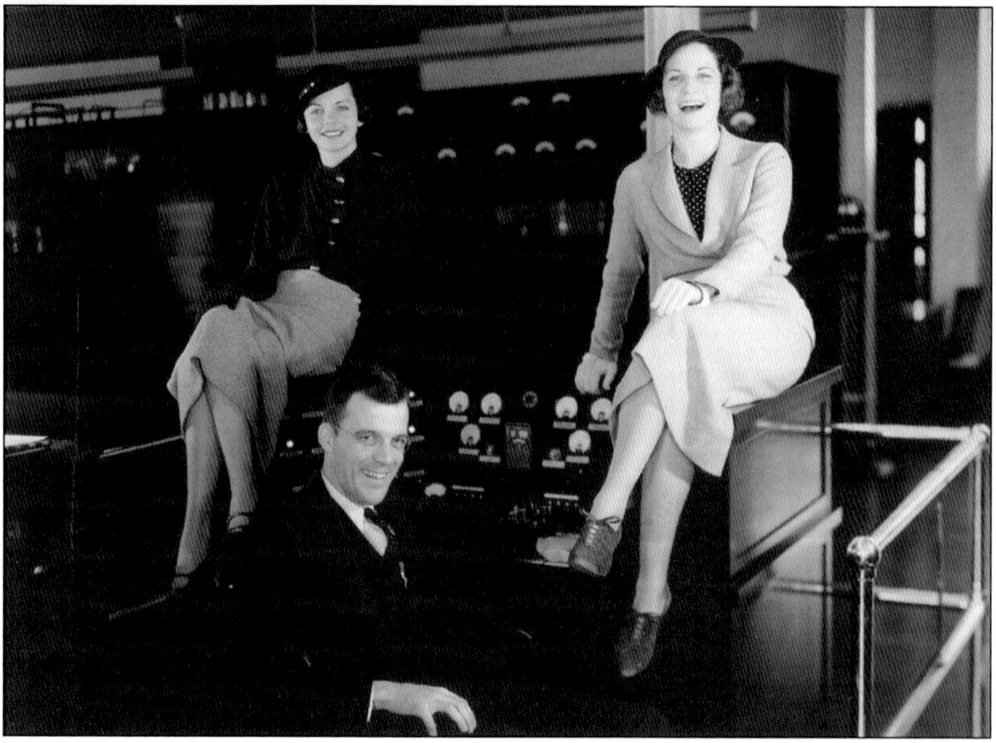

Singing sisters Dorothea "Dobbie" (left) and Ethel Ponce enjoyed great success in New York City as the teenage Ponce Sisters. They headlined at the Palace, recorded two dozen sides on Edison and Columbia, and were even featured in some MGM short films. But by 1932, as they entered their 20s, the Ponces' popularity began to wane, and so their manager and father, Phil Ponce, felt their career would benefit from a move to WLW along with Phil's other client Fats Waller. Dobbie Ponce was active at the station until 1937. (EDCH.)

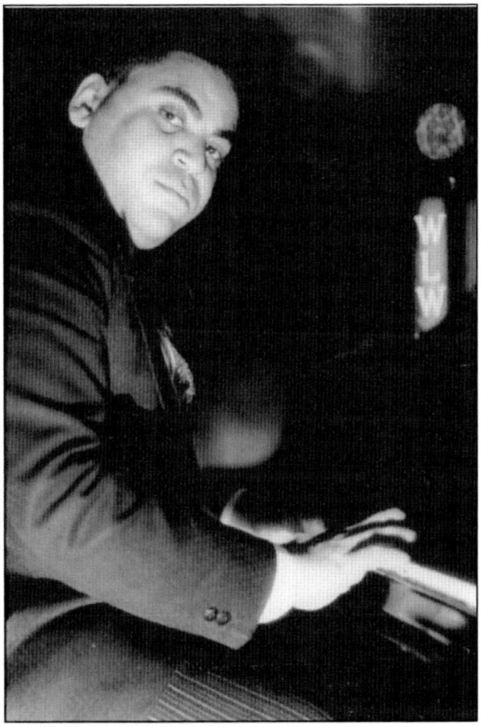

Thomas "Fats" Waller was building an excellent reputation in Harlem and around New York but wanted to boost his reputation outside of the city. His manager Phil Ponce found out about an opportunity in Cincinnati where Waller could hone his broadcast skills. From October 1932 until January 1934, Waller was heard on WLW on his own *Rhythm Club* jazz program and as an organist on the dreamy *Moon River*. He also performed in clubs around the region until he missed the excitement of New York enough to return. (MM.)

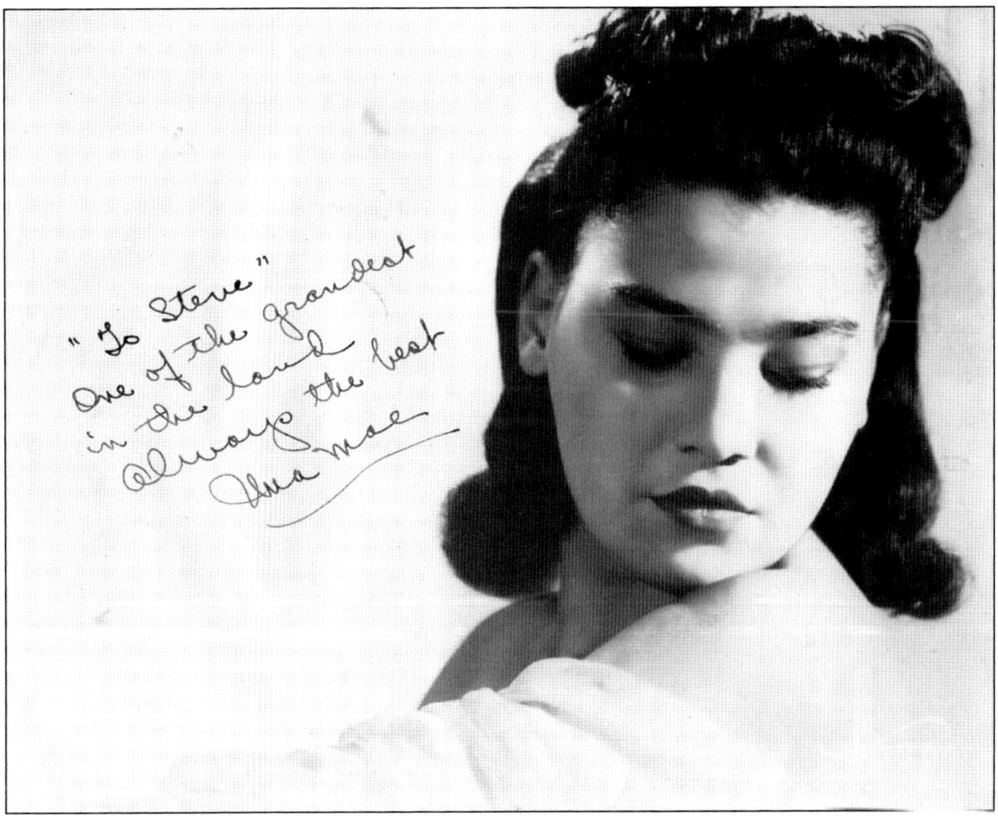

The 17-year-old vocalist-pianist Una Mae Carlisle was on Christmas break from school in Xenia when she was invited to perform on Fats Waller's WLW radio program in December 1932. Carlisle impressed Fats and the station enough to be added to the staff, although she had to leave behind her family and school. When Waller left to return to New York a year later, Carlisle went out on her own, touring Europe and recording hundreds of sides—many her own original compositions. (MM.)

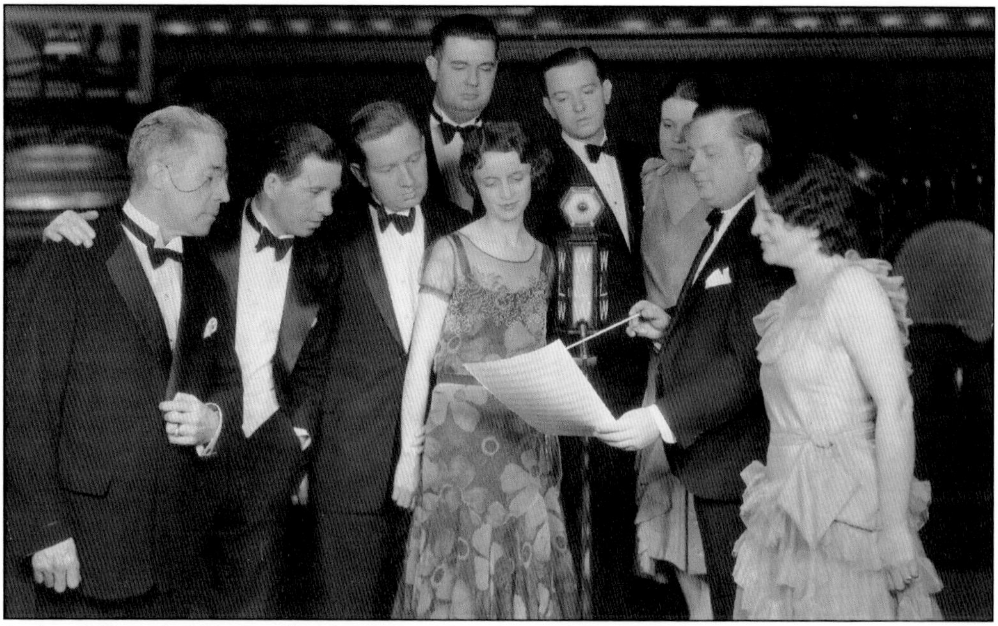

In the 1920s and 1930s, bandleader Henry Thies (second from right) had several orchestras touring the Midwest and appearing in Chicago, Detroit, and Cincinnati. But life on the road gave way to a job as a conductor at WLW in 1930, and Thies supplied the music for several prominent WLW shows, including the *Pure Oil* program. Still, in 1935, pressures and personal matters caught up with him, and Thies was found dead in the bathroom of his suite, the victim of a self-inflicted gunshot. (TF.)

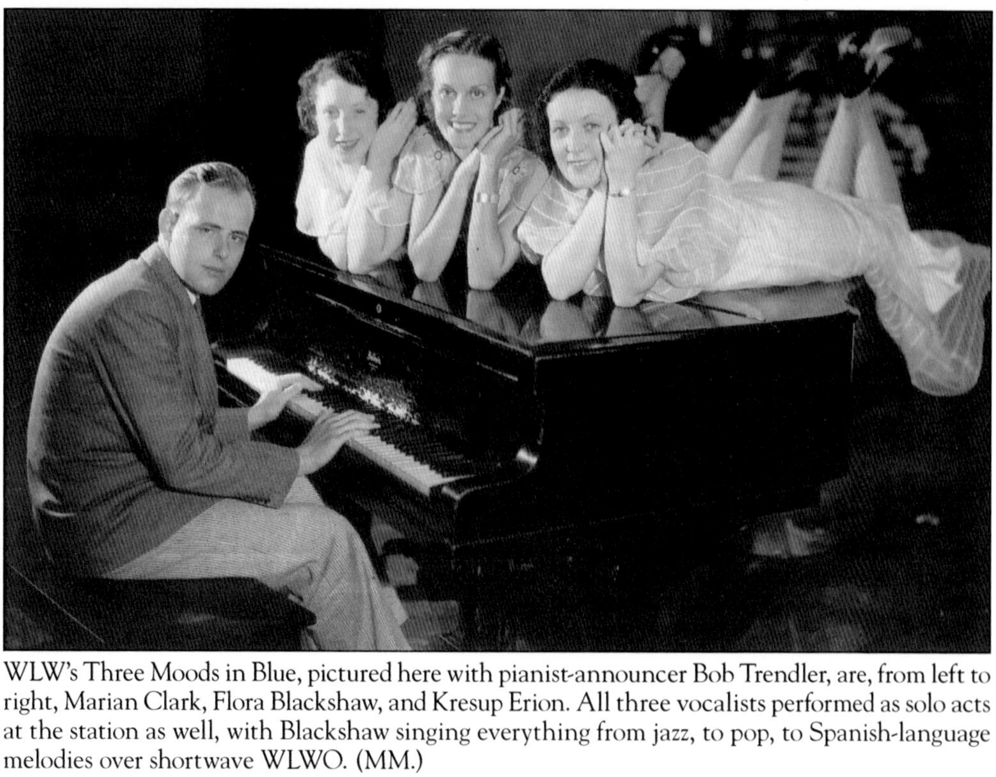

WLW's Three Moods in Blue, pictured here with pianist-announcer Bob Trendler, are, from left to right, Marian Clark, Flora Blackshaw, and Kresup Erion. All three vocalists performed as solo acts at the station as well, with Blackshaw singing everything from jazz, to pop, to Spanish-language melodies over shortwave WLWO. (MM.)

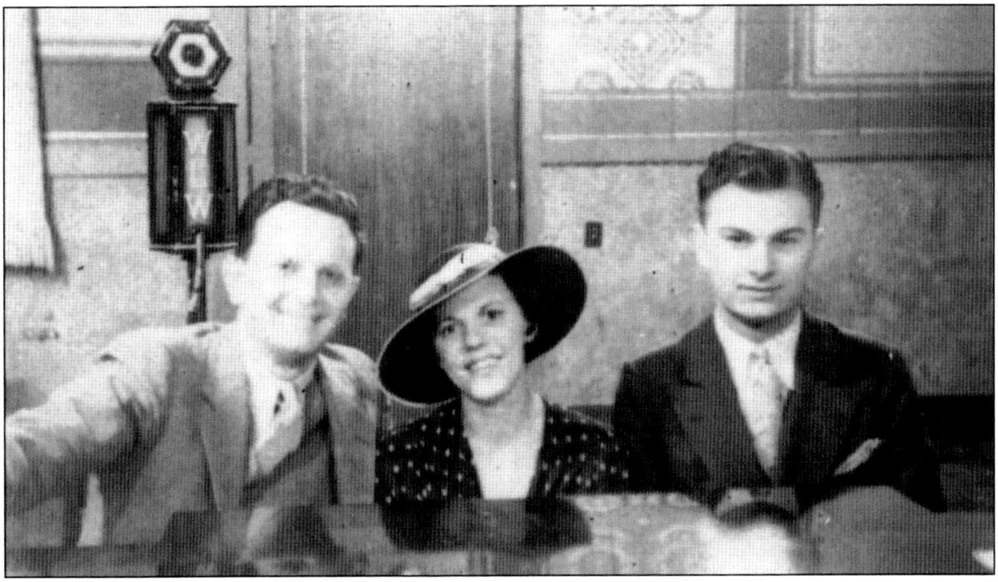

The vocal trio The Threesome, consisting of, from left to right, Herb Nelson, Grace Brandt, and a young Eddie Albert, arrived at WLW around 1932. Albert was a tenor who also was a soloist on other programs, including *Moon River.* As was the policy at the time, even vocalists were encouraged to try acting, and to his dying day, Eddie Albert credited WLW for developing him into the actor seen for years in movies and on television's *Green Acres.* (EP.)

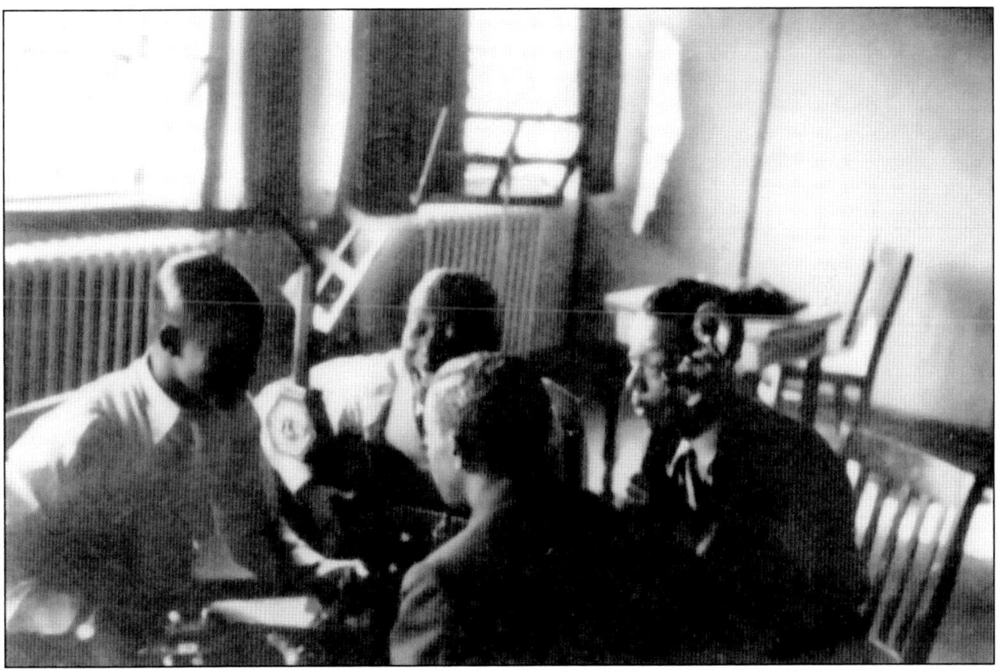

In the summer of 1933, just months after the Mills Brothers left, WLW turned to another African American vocal quartet who had been busy working on radio in Indianapolis and who appeared on Fats Waller's *Rhythm Club.* Called the Four Riff Brothers and later, King, Jack, and Jester, the group eventually became the Ink Spots. This is the only known photograph of the quartet practicing in the rehearsal room at WLW sometime in 1934. (EP.)

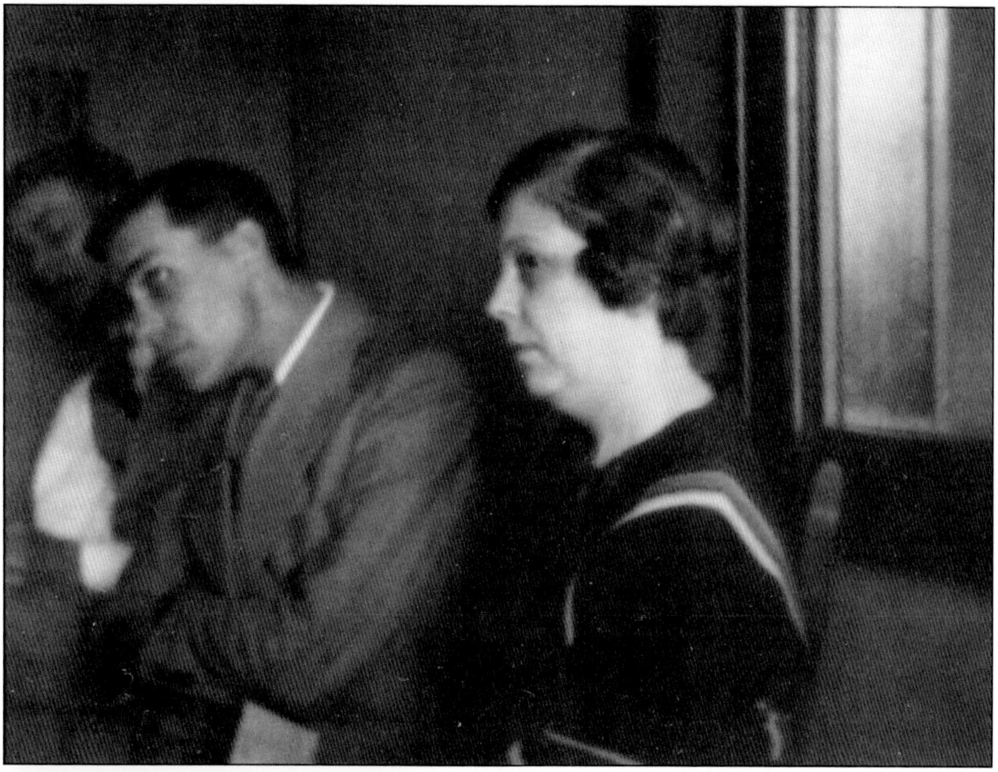

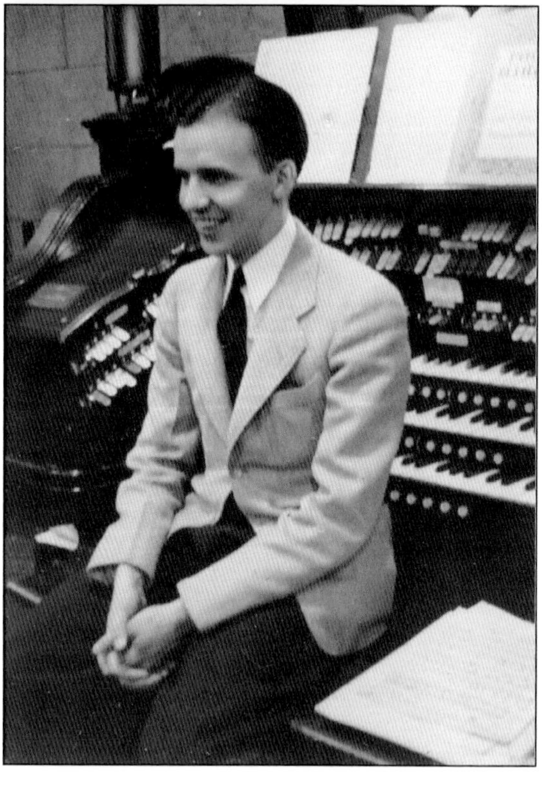

In terms of behind-the-scenes contributions, perhaps no individual had more of an influence on WLW singers in the 1930s and 1940s than vocal coach Grace Raine. In her autobiography, Doris Day gave high praise for Raine, who came to WLW in 1928 after working at WSAI. In addition to her work at WLW, Raine operated a private studio in Clifton and taught breathing, phrasing, and diction to hundreds of vocalists, including Day, the Clooney Sisters, and Anita Ellis. (CG.)

Organist Lee Erwin was WLW's primary *Moon River* organist from his arrival at the station in 1933 until he left in 1943, working closely with the DeVore Sisters, among others. A native of Alabama, Erwin worked extensively during the silent film era and was also a composer. Beginning in 1944 in New York, Erwin was a popular organist for Arthur Godfrey and others. Other WLW organists at this time include Gladys "Hap" Lee, Arthur Chandler Jr., Pat Gillick, and Herschel Luecke. (CG.)

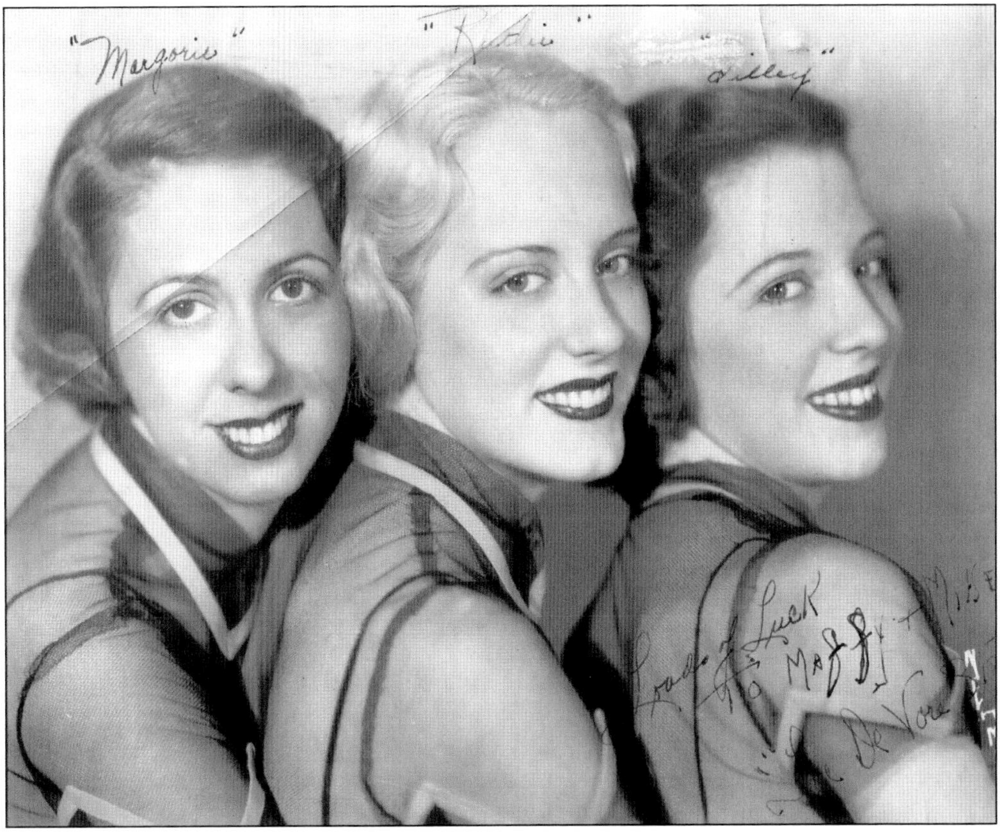

Another sister act, the DeVore Sisters, enjoyed a longer stay on Cincinnati radio. Beginning on radio in their native Indianapolis in 1932, Marjorie (left), Ruth (center), and Billie DeVore came to Cincinnati in 1934 to be heard across the country on the 500,000-watt WLW, where their gentle harmonies enlivened *Moon River*, *Vocal Varieties*, and several other programs. Ruth temporarily left the act in 1941 and was replaced in 1946 by honorary sister Barbara Cameron, but Ruth rejoined her sisters in 1947. (MM.)

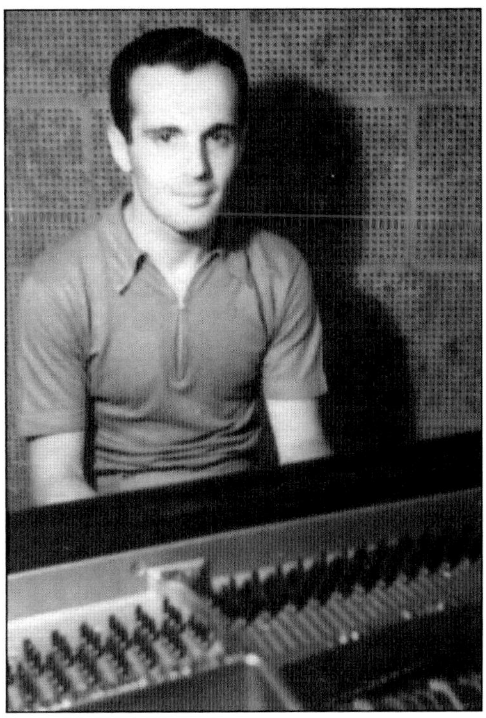

Popular longtime Cincinnati pianist Burt Farber was discovered by bandleader Henry Thies in 1933 when the orchestra was performing at a fraternity party at Farber's college Washington and Lee. Soon after, the Farber Fingers could be heard on WLW and WSAI as well as at the Netherland Plaza Hotel for nearly two decades. The Brooklyn-born Farber did work in New York City in the late 1950s into the early 1970s but always called Cincinnati his home. (EP.)

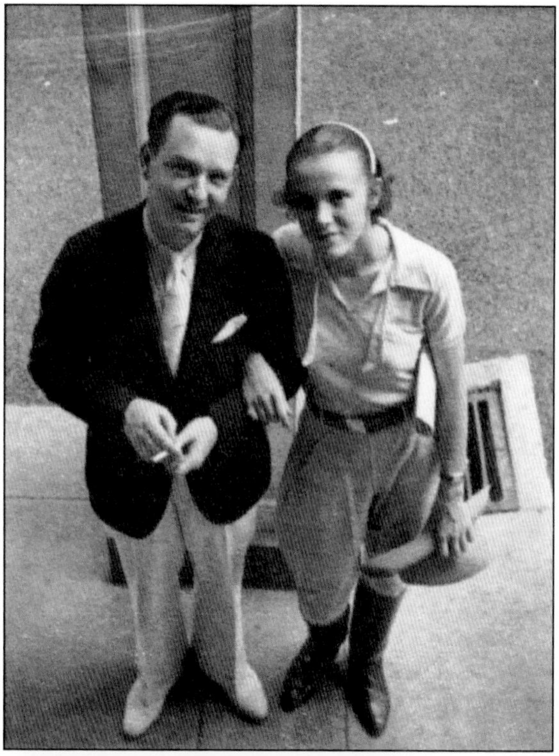

Among the WLW vocal staff of the mid-1930s, Mary Alcott was one of the most admired singers, having worked for several years in Chicago before coming to WLW. Alcott sang blues and popular music and is pictured with Charlie Dameron, one of the "workhorse" male vocalists at WLW through the 1930s. The Kentucky-born Dameron could be found singing country music, an operatic aria, and even recording a popular tune with the Henry Thies Orchestra. (EP.)

The vocal trio the Smoothies came to WLW in 1936 and stayed for about three years. Singing brothers Charlie (left) and Little Ryan, along with Arlene "Babs" Johnson, already had a national following—thanks in part to their time working with Fred Waring—and were paid accordingly. The trio was featured on WLW's *Vocal Varieties* program, which was broadcast nationally over NBC. (MM.)

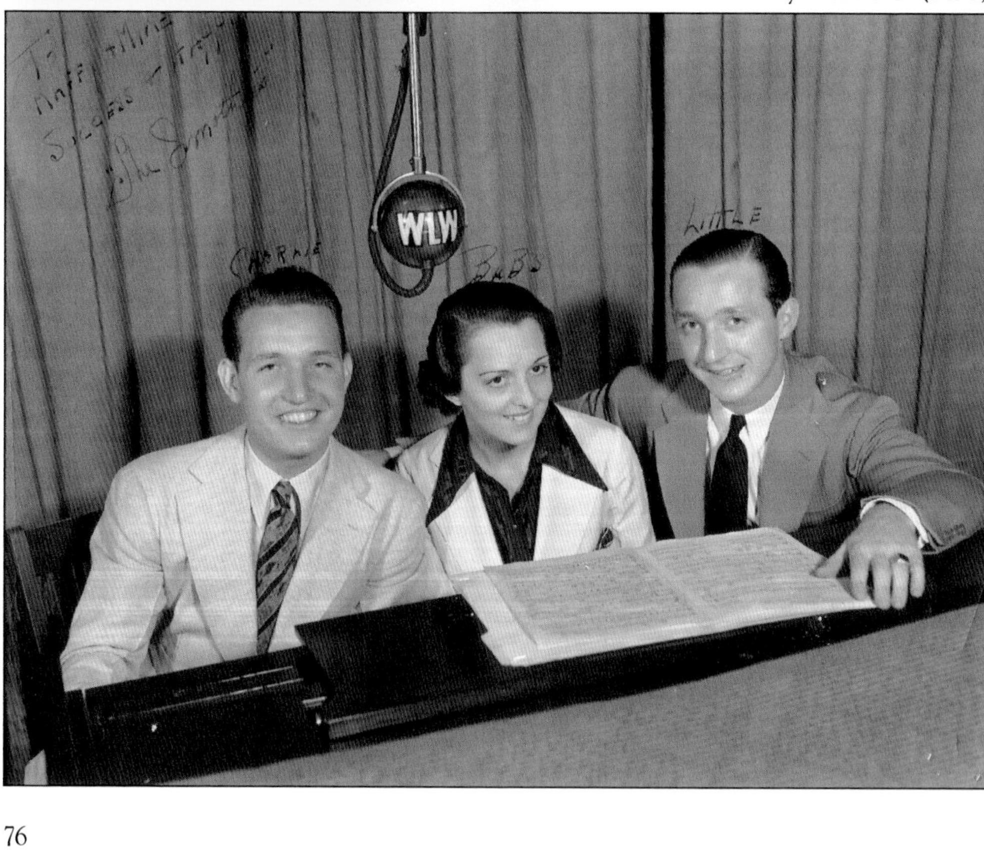

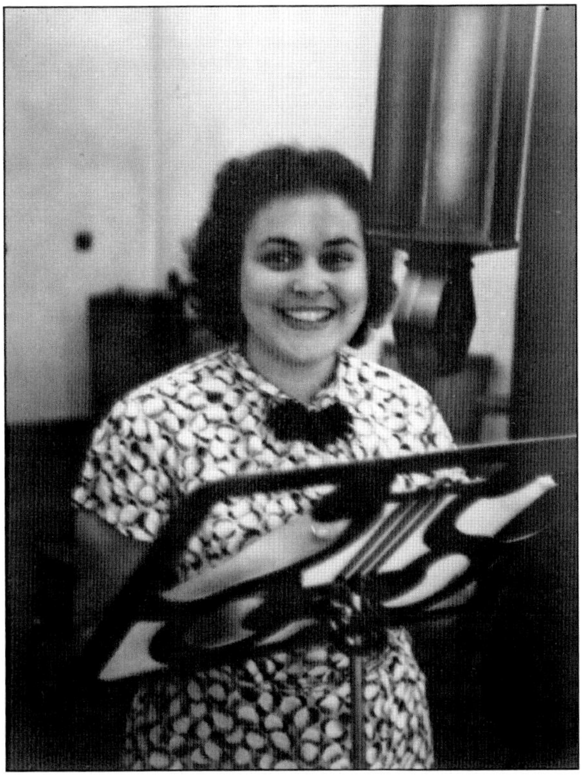

Jeannine Macy was only 18 years old when she started working as a vocalist at WLW in 1934. The New York–born blues singer had been singing professionally since she was 14. Macy became a popular member of the WLW staff and left only when her new husband, WLW drummer Tom Richley, was hired by the Paul Whiteman Orchestra in 1937. Jeannine later ended up with a network radio program on CBS. (CG.)

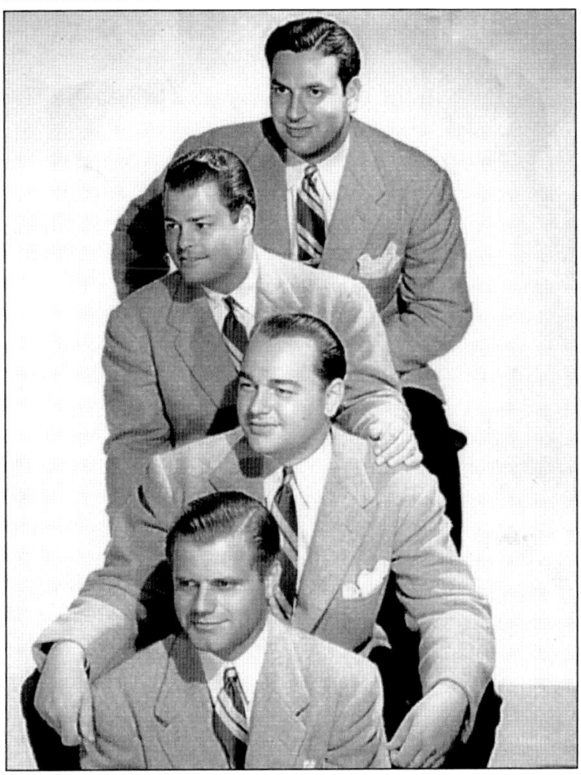

Before gaining fame as the favorite vocal ensemble of the Glenn Miller Orchestra in the 1940s, the Modernaires were a featured act on WLW and WSAI around 1938. From front to back, Bill Conway, Hal Dickenson, Ralph Brewster, and Chuck Goldstein sang on several programs, including their own show. In fact, Red Barber was their announcer on several broadcasts. Paula Kelly, aka Mrs. Dickenson, did not join the group until after they left Cincinnati. (MM.)

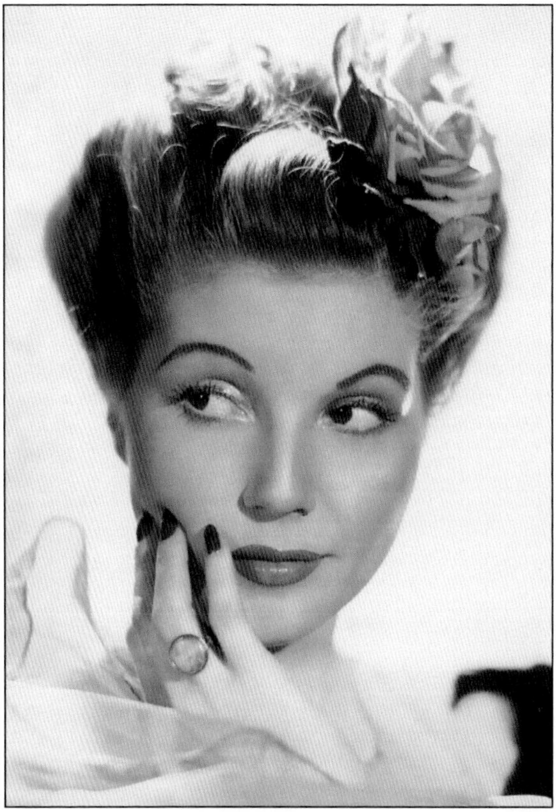

To the fans of vocalist Dorothy Janette Davis on WLW, she was simply known as "Janette." But in 1939, the popular Memphis-born singer was featured on Red Skelton's *Avalon Time*, and when the show moved production from Cincinnati to Chicago later that year, Janette went along. Eventually, she headed east and for 10 years was the featured female vocalist for Arthur Godfrey, even acting as Godfrey's producer for his final season on the network. (MM.)

Barney Rapp enjoyed a long, successful tour through the Midwest and the East with his traveling band the New Englanders. After marrying his vocalist Ruby Wright, however, there was a desire to settle down, so Rapp opened a nightclub in Bond Hill and would broadcast his band over WLW. Rapp enjoyed spending time at the radio station and often worked with the musicians and arrangers. Ruby later would become a full-time staff member in the 1950s. (MM.)

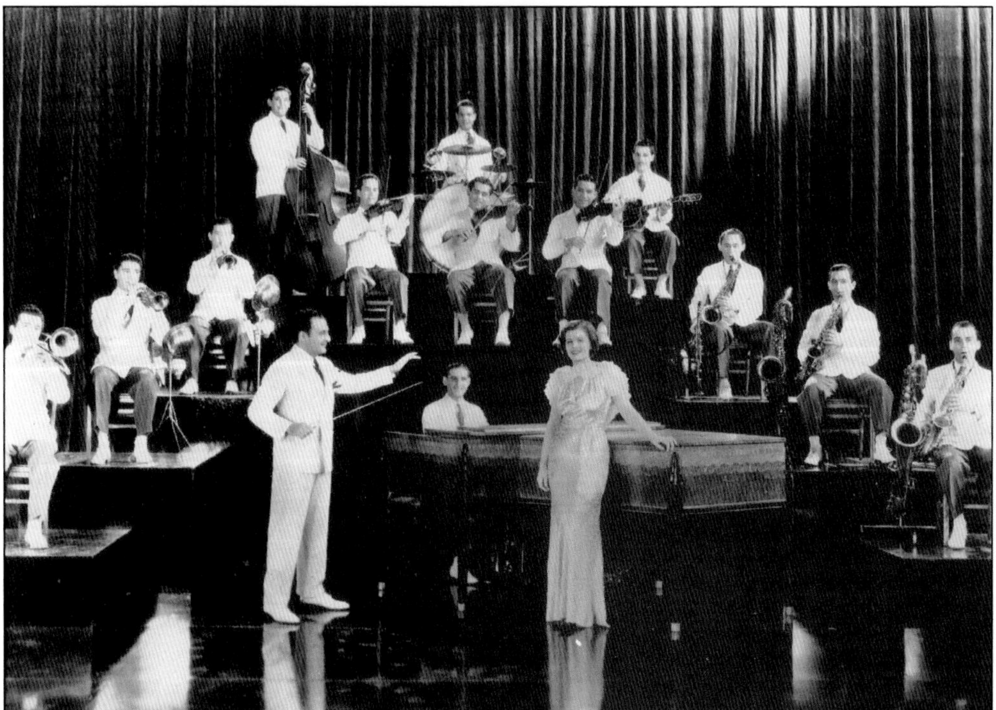

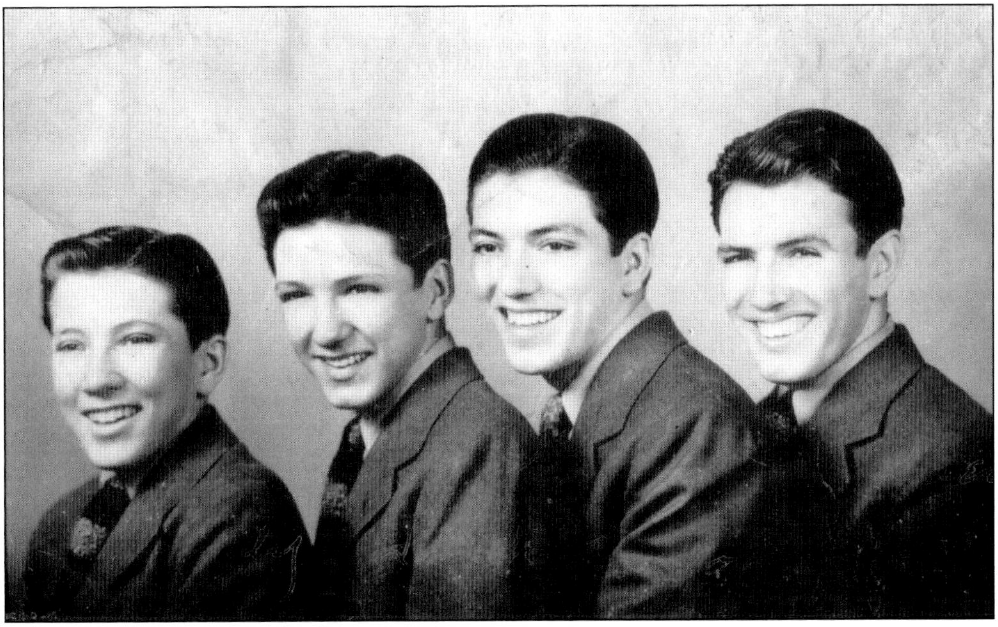

When Chicago's WLS cut back on its musical staff, the four singing Williams Brothers suddenly were out of work. Their father sent audition recordings around the country, and Andy, Dick, Don, and Bob (from left to right) were hired by WLW in 1942 to sing on several programs, including *Moon River*, *Truly American*, and even the *Boone County Jamboree*. Their main job, however, was to sing on the Griffin Shoe Polish *Time to Shine* show every morning before school. (MM.)

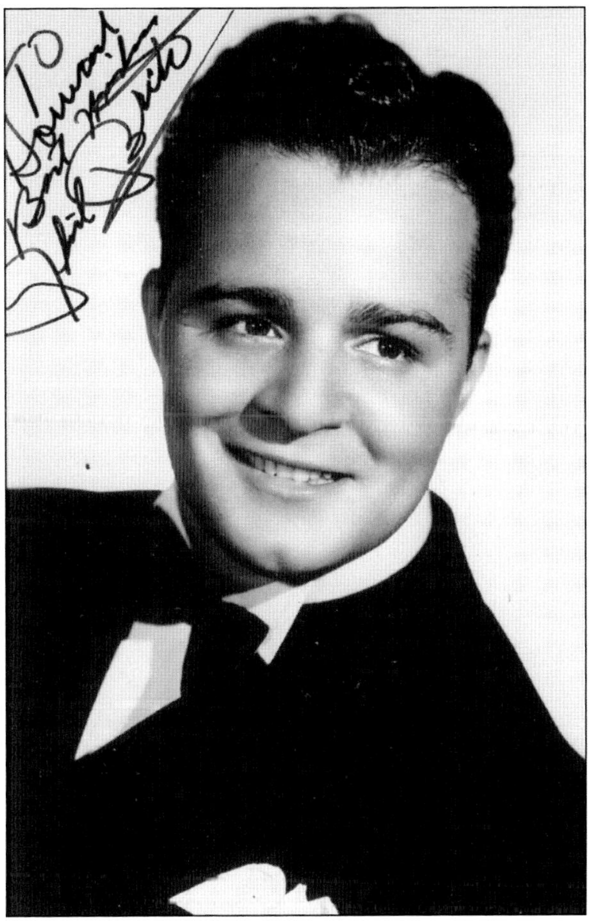

Born Phil Colombrito in West Virginia, vocalist Phil Brito came to WLW as a staff vocalist around 1942 and sang on a number of wartime programs. Not long after leaving, he introduced one of the great World War II songs "It's Been a Long, Long Time" on Bing Crosby's radio program, only to be overshadowed when Crosby recorded it himself. Brito appeared in some films and on television into the 1960s. (MM.)

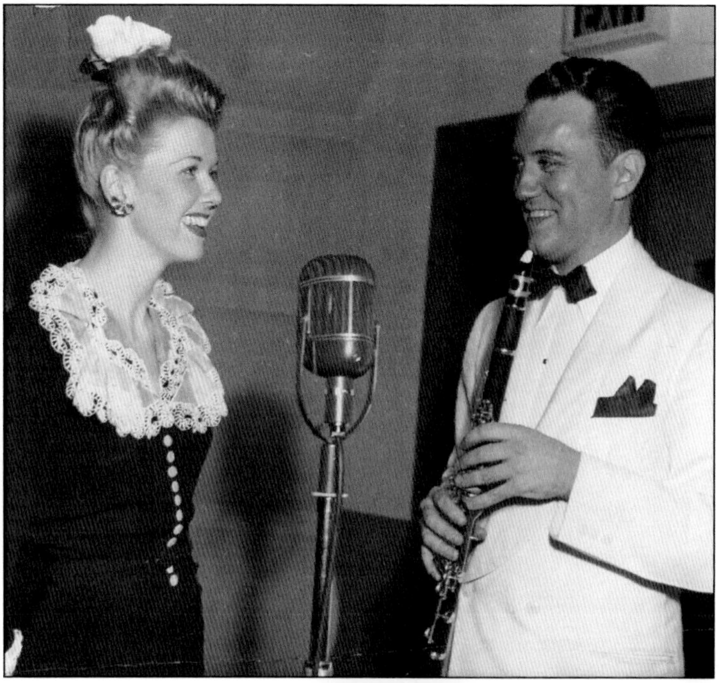

Doris Day was not a stranger to Cincinnati radio prior to her 1942 hiring by WLW, having been a vocalist on several remote broadcasts from Barney Rapp's The Sign Of The Drum nightclub. But it was for personal reasons that she returned to Cincinnati after traveling the country with Bob Crosby and Les Brown. She found a regular paycheck at WLW, singing on *Moon River* along with other appearances, including this one with WLW clarinetist and bandleader Jimmy Wilbur. (DB.)

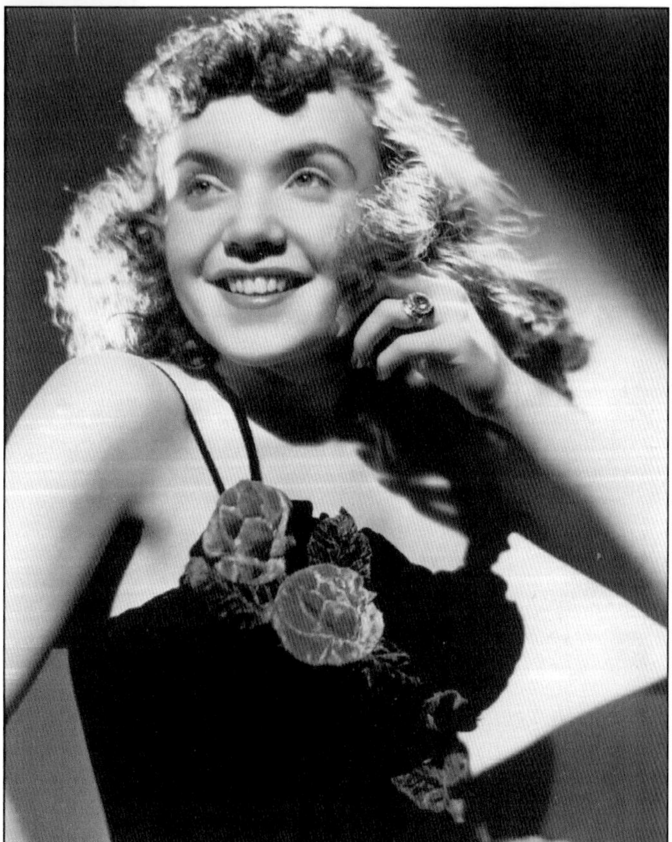

Juanita Vastine grew up in Butler, Kentucky, and in 1942, was hired as a vocalist for WLW's *Moon River* program where she performed under the name Georgia Brown. In addition to *Moon River*, she sang on Ruth Lyons' programs and as part of the trio Mary, Jean, and Betty. Later, "Sweet Georgia Brown" joined the Whippoorwills, a group led by former WLW country artist Roy Lanham, in Hollywood. (MM.)

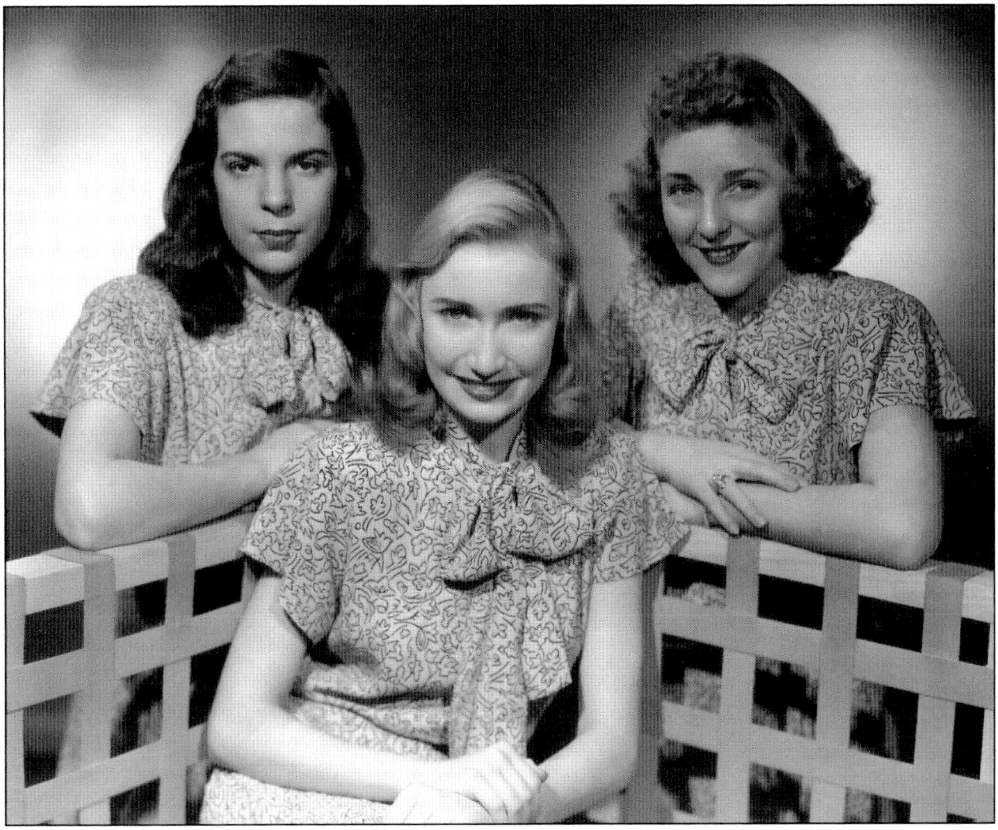

When the DeVore Sisters temporarily left radio between 1941 and 1946, WLW scrambled to find a female trio of equal talents. Vocal director Grace Raine created Mary, Jean, and Betty from among her students. Pictured from left to right are Vicky Miller, Barbara Cameron, and Shirley Theiring—one version of the trio—but the members could include other singers as well. For example, Georgia Brown acknowledged singing in the group sometimes, and would take any of the three "roles" depending on the song. (MM.)

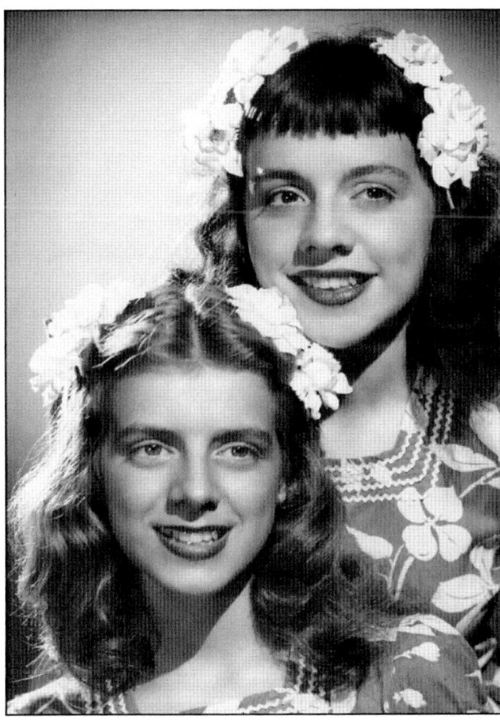

From their early childhood in Maysville, Rosemary (left) and Betty Clooney planned and schemed about a show-business career. It all started in May 1945 when the teenaged girls auditioned at WLW after school and won a job singing on *Moon River* and some other programs. By 1947, the Clooneys were on their way to fulfilling their dreams, first as vocalists for Tony Pastor and then with long careers in film, television, and radio. (DB.)

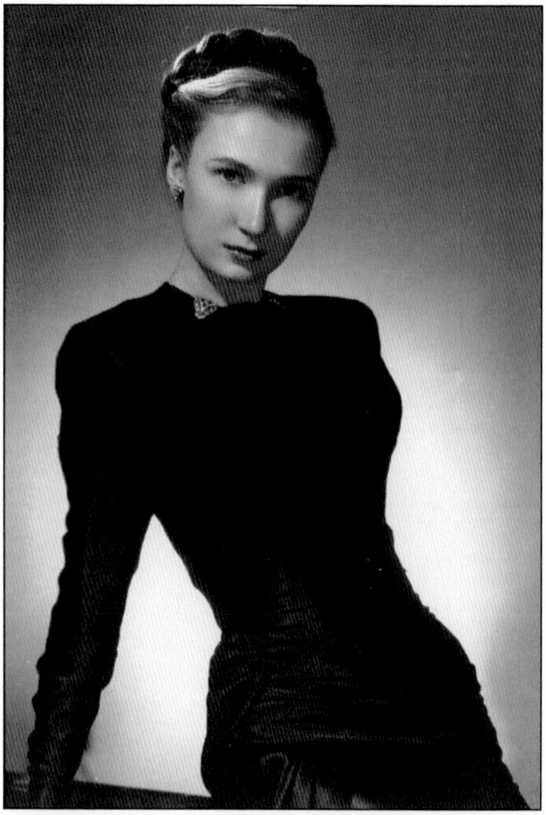

Dayton native Barbara Cameron joined WLW in 1943 after Doris Day left the station. Cameron was talented enough to appear as three different performers at the same time. She was a soloist on *Moon River*, was a member of the vocal trio Mary, Jean, and Betty, and in 1945, she replaced a married Ruth DeVore as a member of the popular DeVore Sisters. But Cameron was also a talented jingle writer and lyricist in the 1950s and after a stint at WKRC, composed and recorded the original theme for television's Road Runner cartoons for Warner Bros. (BC.)

Marian Spelman is best remembered for her work on WLWT television, but as a Crosley staffer, she was also expected to help on WLW radio. Spelman had a regular spot on some of the live WLW programs in the early 1950s and could even be heard on an occasional *Moon River*. (MS.)

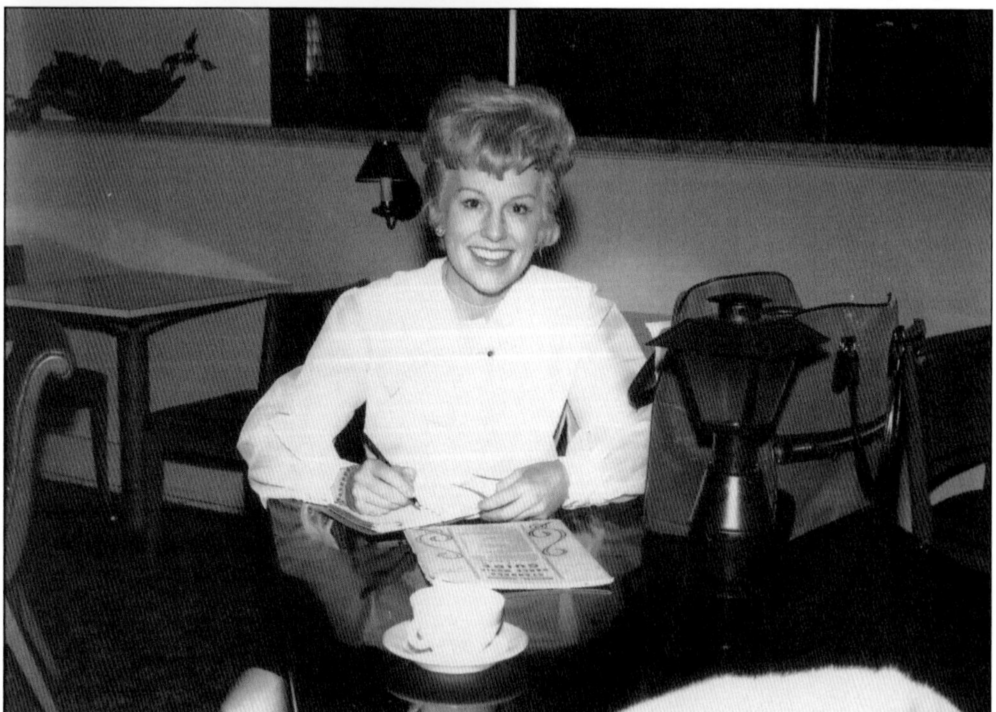

Four

Rural Radio

Broadcasting Cincinnati Sounds to the Farm Folk of the Country

There is no doubt that radio broadcasting was from its beginnings a comfort and friend to the urban dweller and city listener. Still, it can never be overestimated how incredibly important and life altering radio was to the families living in rural America. In an era when an estimated 70 percent of the population still lived on a farm, radio was able to inexpensively cut through geographic isolation like no other technology before or since. Living in a small town in the middle of a vast expanse of rural isolation with only a weekly printed news tract or occasional motion picture at the small-town "picture show" to connect with the world beyond must have been difficult. A farm family's household entertainment might be the occasional new recording for the phonograph from Sears or the latest QRS player piano roll. Cities like New York and Hollywood were exotic, almost foreign concepts, so far out of the realm of the realistic possibility of personal encounter that they might as well be named the Riviera or the Kasbah.

Then radio came magically through invisible space into the farm family's home. It entered as an invited guest whenever the dial was turned correctly and the A, B, and C batteries on the farm sets were properly charged. What was previously exotic became commonplace as friends named Jack, Edgar, Lum, Abner, Ma, Amos, Andy, and a roll call of others stopped by for weekly, or sometimes daily, visits to "sit a spell" and relax. It was not just music and laughs, either, as those invited guests could share the latest news about the drought in Oklahoma, the shortage of beef in the East, and the ramblings of some lunatic with a bad moustache raising trouble in far-off Germany.

Radio meant both revolution and relationship for rural America during the period before static caused by high-tension power lines and neon signs cut down on the coverage of the typical radio station. Even after electrification came to the farm, stations like superpower WLW saw it as their duty to provide programming for the country dweller. Some of it might have been the profit motive but, largely, there was also a sense of dedication and service that inspired these broadcasts. Because of its geographic and ideological location in the then center of the American population, Cincinnati was naturally and genuinely interested in providing the programs for farm families and dispatching "friends" who were so very welcome to stop by and visit as they passed, riding the winds to the isolated farms of America during the first half of the 20th century.

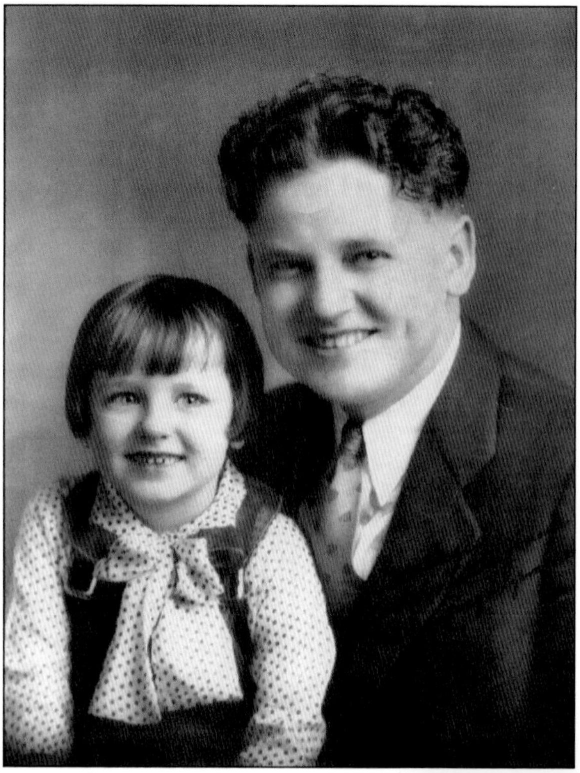

When L.B. Wilson dedicated WCKY in 1929, he eagerly welcomed a variety of acts. At that time, Kentucky native Asher Sizemore was singing on a small station with his five-year-old son Jimmie. Thus, Asher and Little Jimmie became one of Cincinnati's first country radio acts, performing at a Cincinnati theater and selling songbooks on the side. The pair later added Jimmie's younger brother Bud and spent several years on the Grand Ole Opry. (MM.)

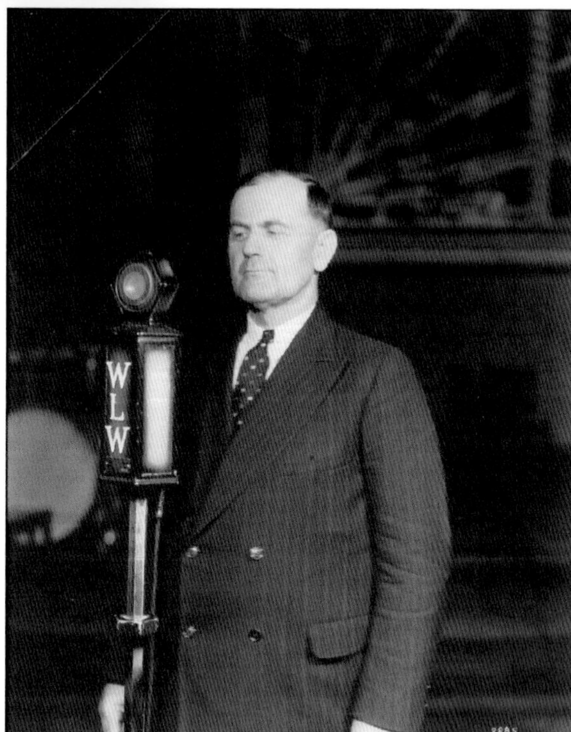

Living in rural southeastern Indiana, Maurice "Boss" Johnston met Powel Crosley Jr. through their shared interest in hunting and black-powder guns. Johnston was also a writer and storyteller, and starting in 1928, he shared weekly stories about farm life for WLW listeners well into the 1950s. Much like Garrison Keillor today, Boss might begin his narrative with, "Howdy folks, how's life on the farm? Snow fell on the rusty plow in Hogan's Valley this week." (BJ.)

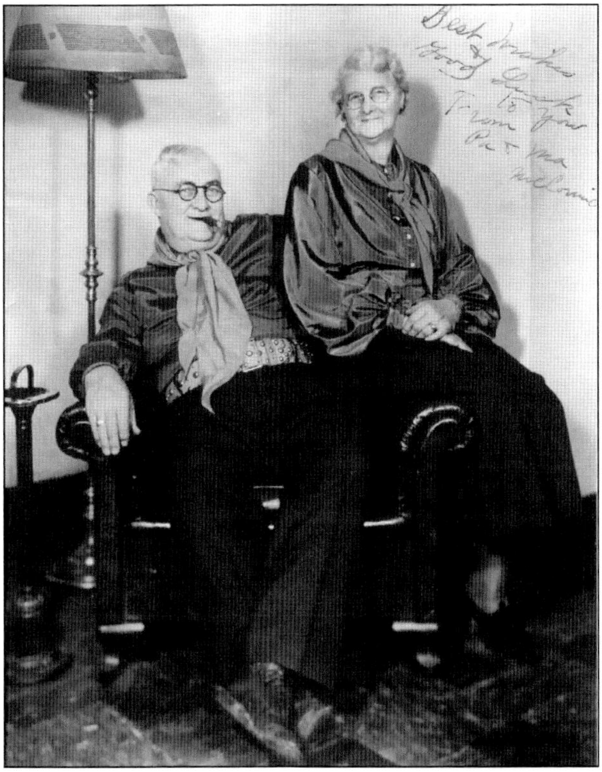

For nearly 20 years, the matriarch and patriarch of WLW were "Ma" and "Pa" McCormick. Ma and Pa were featured on many of the early country music programs, most notably the *Top O' the Morning* show and the *Boone County Jamboree*. Clarence and Alice McCormick were northern Kentucky natives who played harmonica and piano, respectively. Ma retired when Pa died unexpectedly in 1945. (MM.)

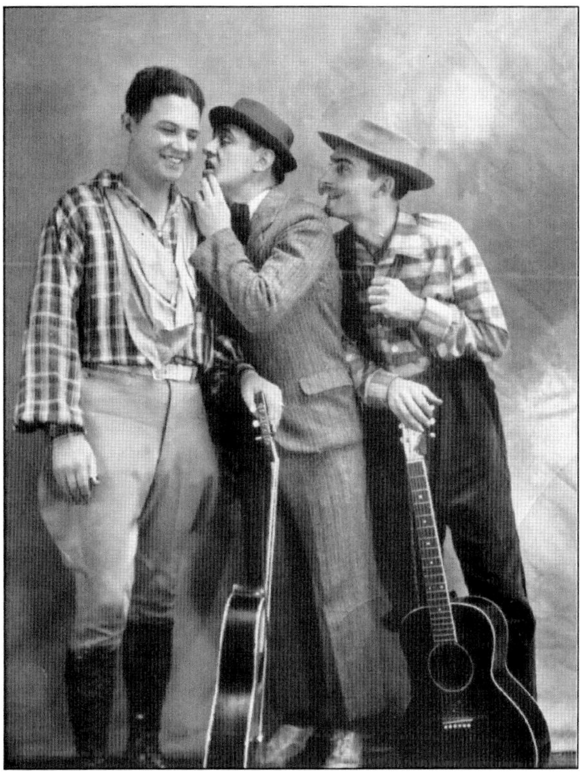

Born in rural Garrard County, Kentucky, Bradley Kincaid (left) is credited with preserving much of Appalachian culture by collecting and recording many of the area's native songs. Kincaid also published millions of songbooks, selling them at the various stations where he worked. Kincaid spent time at WLW around 1931 and returned to Cincinnati to work at WKRC in 1945. Pictured with Kincaid are Joe Troyan (center) and a young "Grandpa" Jones. (MM.)

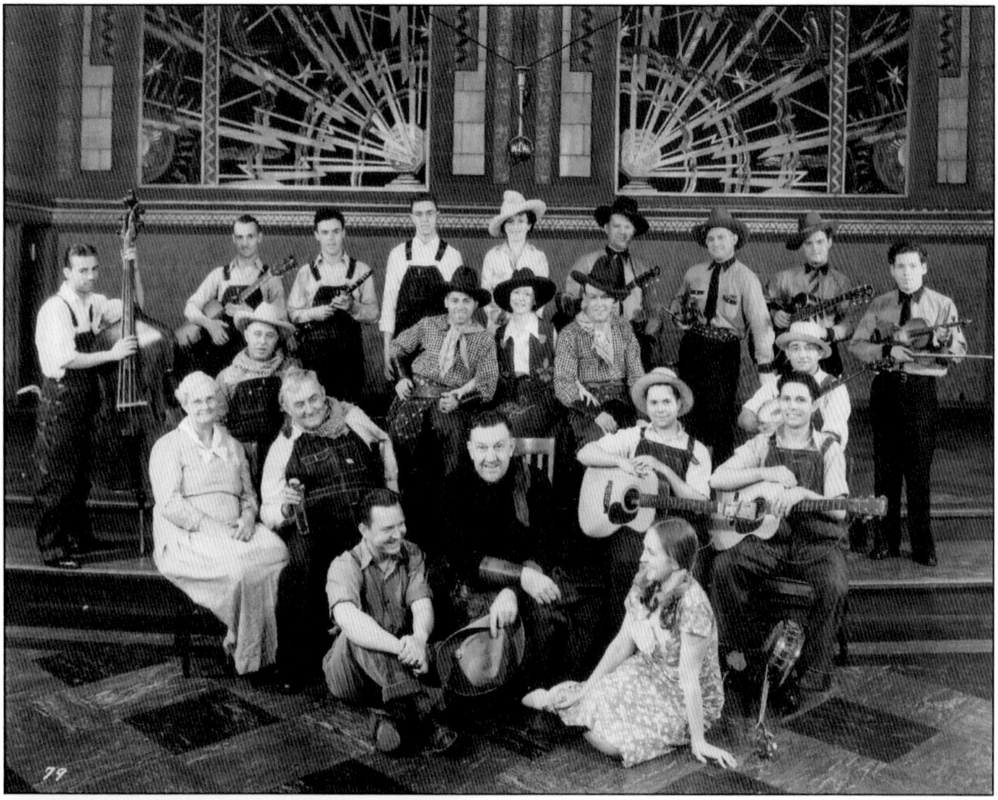

WLW's *Top O' the Morning* show began the station's program day early each morning from the late 1920s into the 1940s. At its peak around 1935, the program featured former vaudeville star Oklahoma Bob Albright, Ma and Pa McCormick, "Charlie and Sara Wayne" (in real life Charles Dameron and Minabelle Abbott), and many other talented entertainers. (MM.)

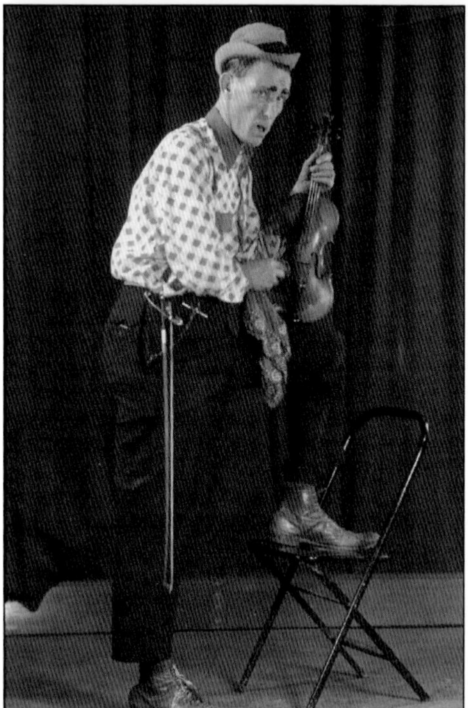

Born and raised in rural Renfro Valley in southern Kentucky, John Lair always dreamed of creating a music complex based upon his native culture. Lair aired his first country programs in Chicago but in 1937, brought those programs to Cincinnati along with his personal cast of loyal performers. Humorist and fiddler "Slim" Miller (pictured) was a member of Lair's troupe. Following his three-year stay at WLW, Lair eventually realized his dream of building his Renfro Valley entertainment area. (MM.)

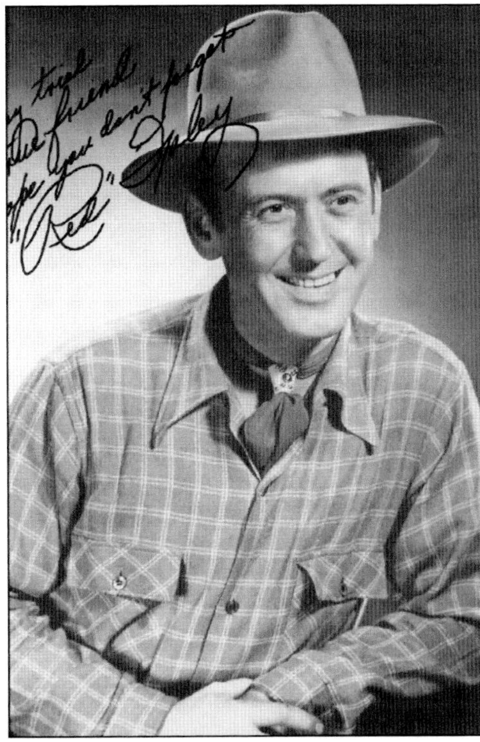

Blue Lick, Kentucky's Clyde "Red" Foley never forgot his roots, and when fellow country music entrepreneur John Lair left Chicago for WLW in 1937, Foley tagged along. In 1939, he was forced off his WLW-originated network show *Avalon Time* when another Red—Red Skelton—took over. Things worked out for Foley, though, who helped Lair dedicate his Renfro Valley entertainment complex in 1940 before enjoying a long career on the Grand Ole Opry. (MM.)

Independent producer John Lair came to Cincinnati in 1937. WLW, seeing the popularity of his *Renfro Valley Barn Dance*, scrambled to air a barn dance show that it could own outright. Thus was born the *Boone County Jamboree*, which played at the Emery Auditorium while the *Renfro Barn Dance* rented Music Hall. By 1939, Lair had moved his show to Dayton, but for one year, Cincinnati could boast of two nationally broadcast barn dance shows. (MM.)

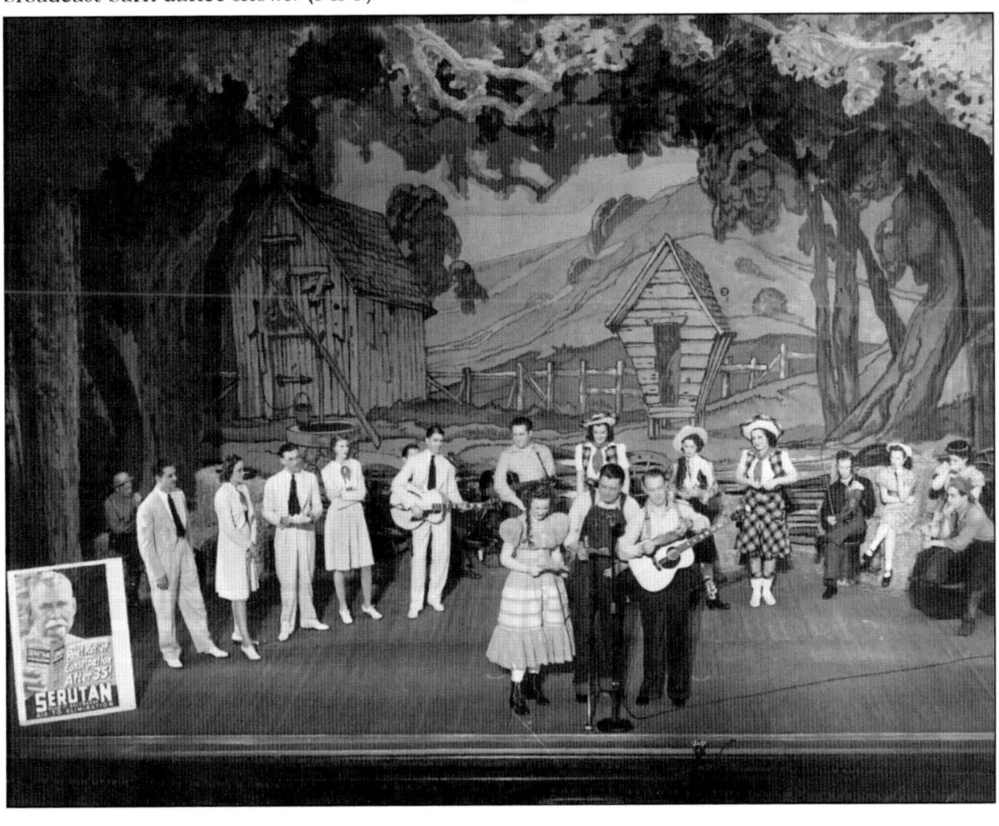

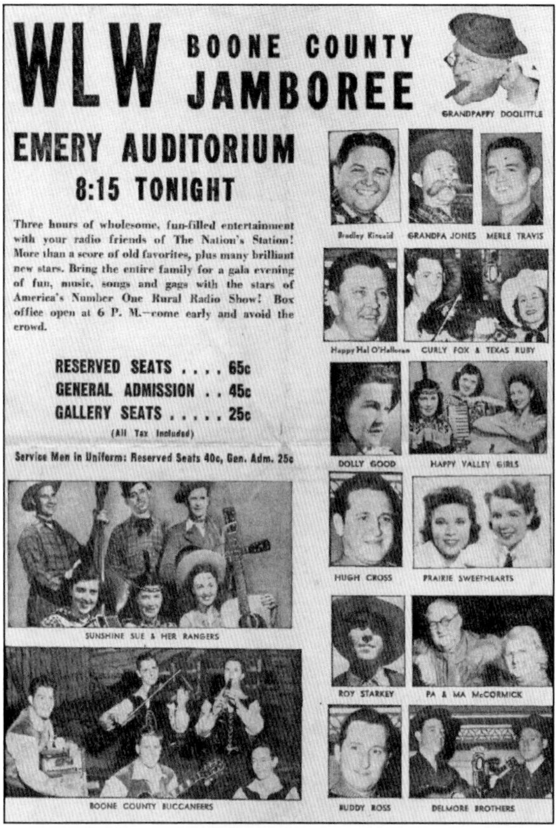

It was custom during radio's golden age to charge no admission for those who wanted to be in the audience for a live broadcast. But Chicago's *National Barn Dance* showed that country music could be quite lucrative, and when WLS's George Biggar came to WLW in 1938, he instituted a nominal admission, which helped defray costs of the *Boone County Jamboree*. Biggar eventually was named program director at the station until he left in 1945. (MM.)

After working around Indiana and Illinois for a couple of years, the Drifting Pioneers were hired in 1938 to be part of the original cast of the *Boone County Jamboree*. Shown from left to right, fiddle player and vocalist Sleepy Marlin and brothers Walt and Bill Brown provided the backdrop for their young, fleet-fingered guitarist Merle Travis. Mastering the fingerpick style of play, Travis would go on to influence Chet Atkins and millions of other guitarists. (MM.)

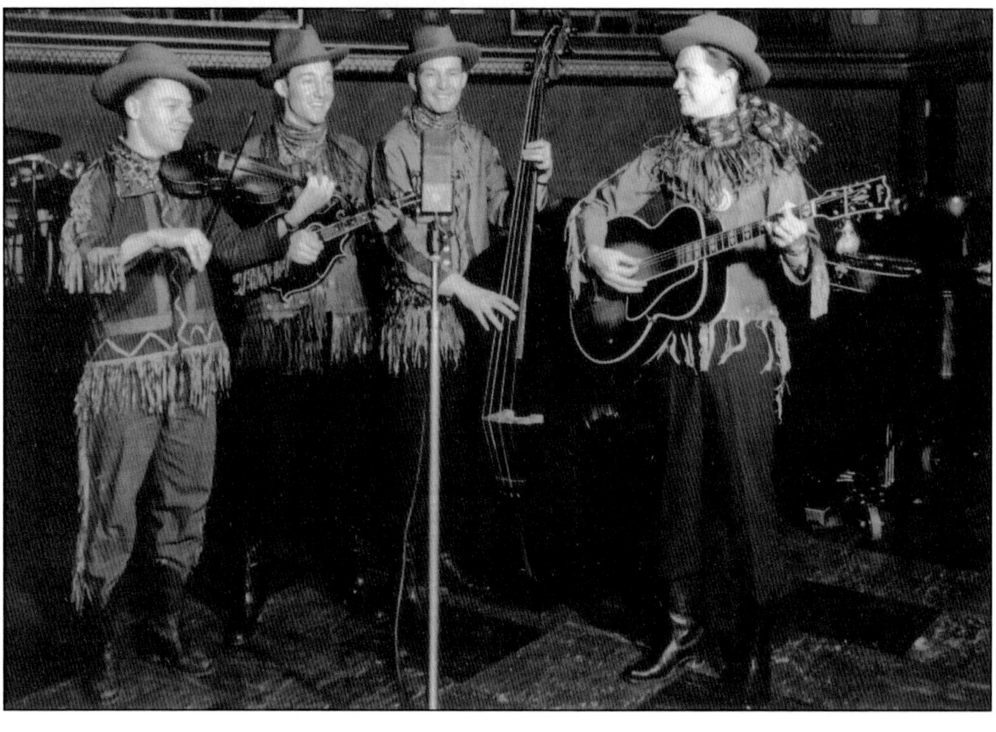

Edgar Bergen and Charlie McCarthy had nothing on Kenny Carlson and Scrappy on the *Boone County Jamboree* in 1939. The *Jamboree* was a live stage show at the Emery Auditorium, and because only a portion of the show was broadcast over the air, acts—even comedy ventriloquism acts—had to entertain the folks in the audience before and after the broadcast. Here, Kenny and Scrappy entertain Helen Diller, the Canadian Cowgirl, backstage before a WLW broadcast. (WR.)

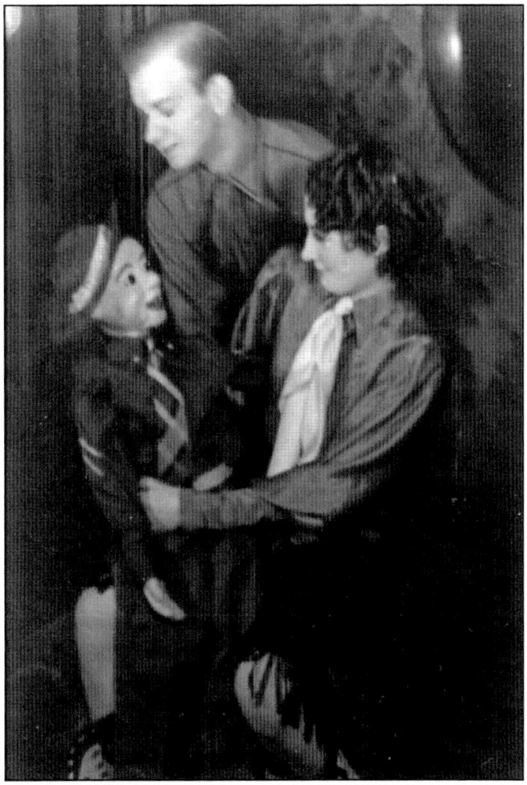

Adams County's Lloyd Estel Copas (second from right) performed on WLW in the late 1930s and on WKRC in the early 1940s. Known as "Cowboy" Copas, the singing cowboy had a band called the Arizona Boys who specialized in music of the Old West. Part of the act was fiddle player Natchee the Indian (third from left), whose real identity was Lester Vernon Storer, from Peebles, Ohio. Copas died in the same 1963 plane crash that killed Patsy Cline and Hawkshaw Hawkins. (MM.)

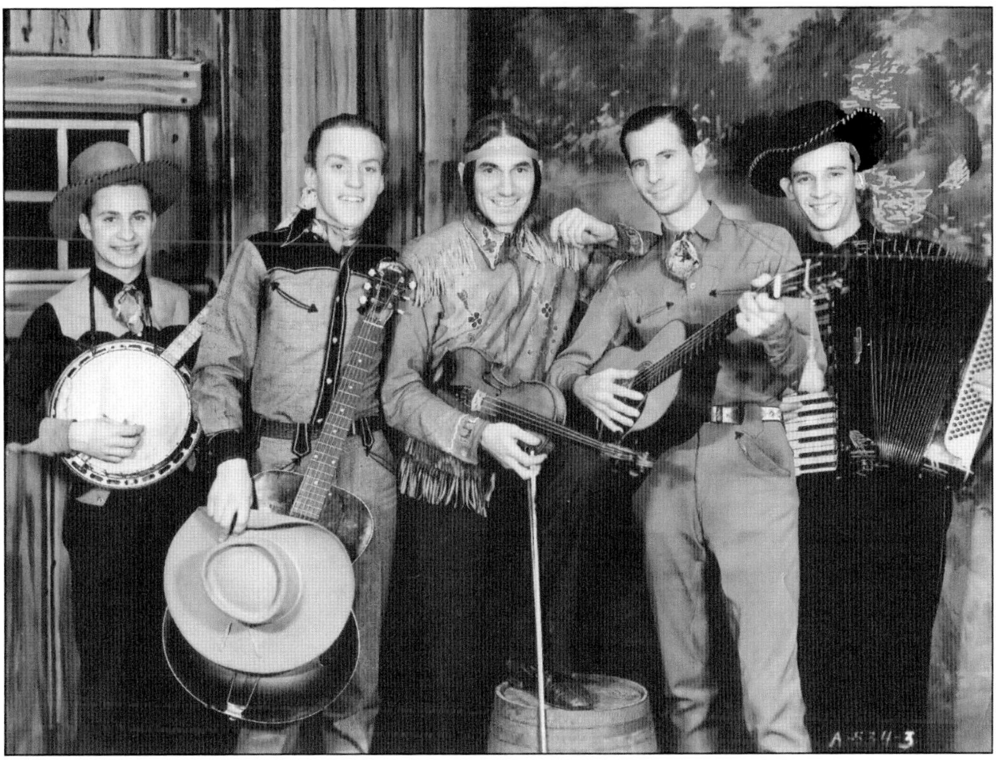

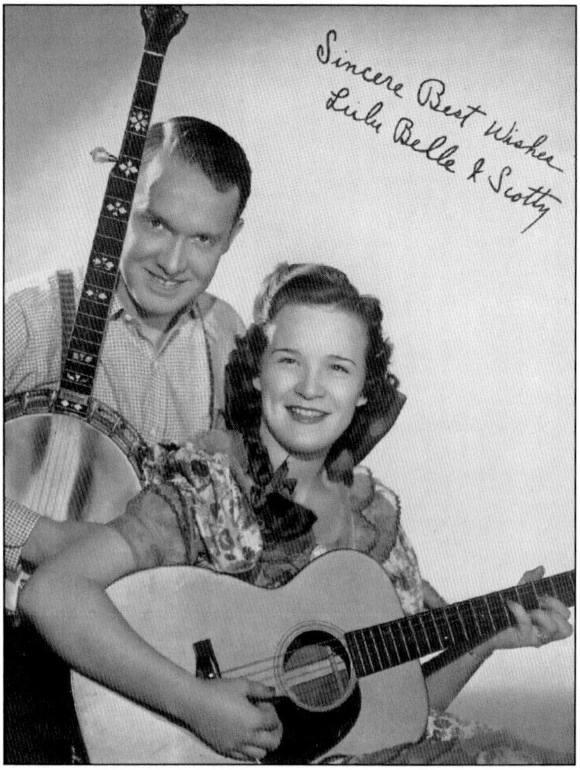

Securing the services of Lulu Belle and Skyland Scotty was a major coup for WLW's George Biggar in 1939. Among the major stars of Chicago's *National Barn Dance*, Lulu Belle twice was voted the nation's favorite female radio artist in the mid-1930s. Husband Scotty Wiseman was a composer as well, and as the story goes, he composed his biggest hit, "Have I Told You Lately That I Love You," while driving to work on Colerain Avenue. (MM.)

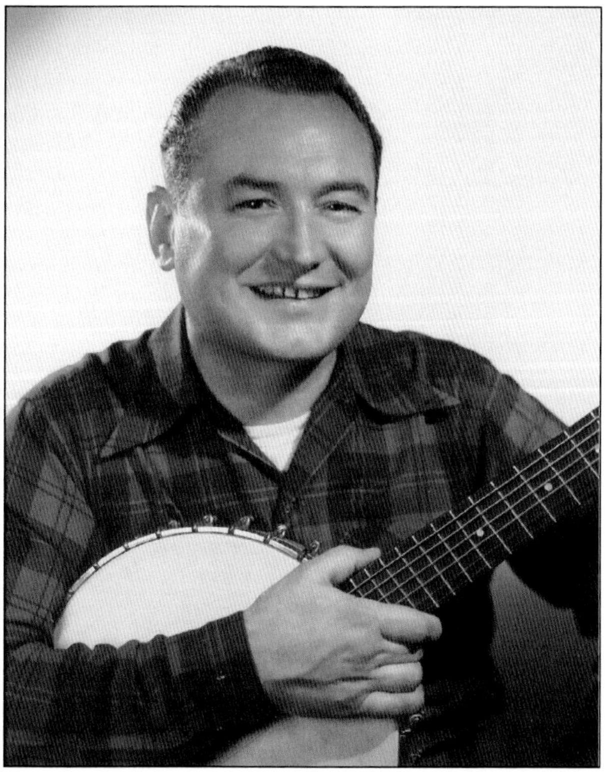

Lazy Jim Day was one of many comedians who passed through Cincinnati radio's country music scene, first appearing on WLW's *Boone County Jamboree* in 1938 and reappearing on its successor the *Midwestern Hayride* in the 1950s. Lazy Jim's most popular routine was his singing news. Among the many other WLW comedians were Lafe Harkness, Whitey Ford, Aunt Idy, and Denny Slofoot. (MM.)

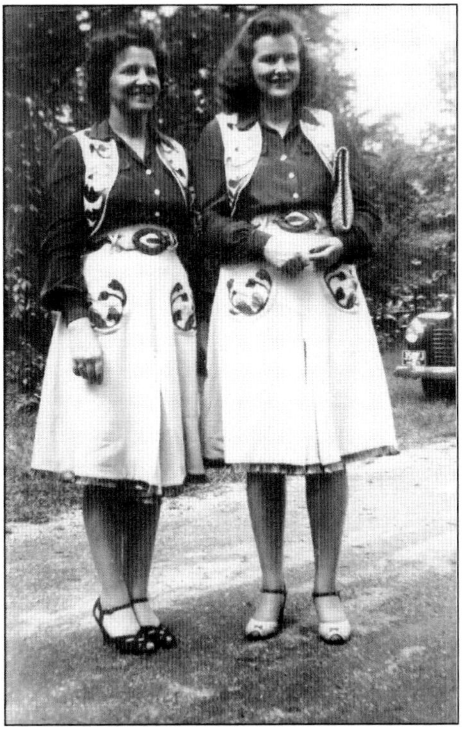

The Girls of the Golden West, sisters Millie (right) and Dolly Good, were big stars in Chicago prior to coming to WLW in 1939. Western yodelers the Good Girls were idolized by many young female country acts. Dollie married WMOH's Ray Motley, and Millie became the wife of WLW's promotion director Bill McCluskey. (JPS.)

Alton and Rabon Delmore brought their unique blend of rural rhythm to Cincinnati on several occasions. During one stretch at WLW in 1945, the Delmores sang on the *Boone County Jamboree* and teamed with Merle Travis and Grandpa Jones to form the *Brown's Ferry Four*, one of the early groups featured on King Records. (DD.)

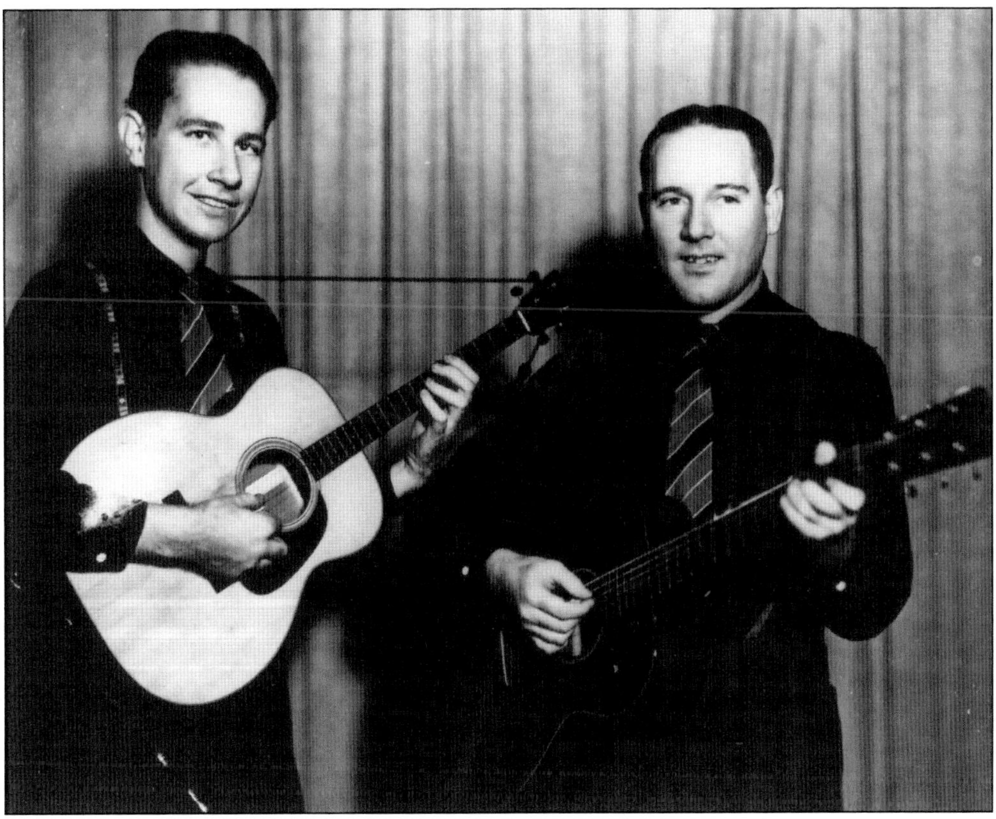

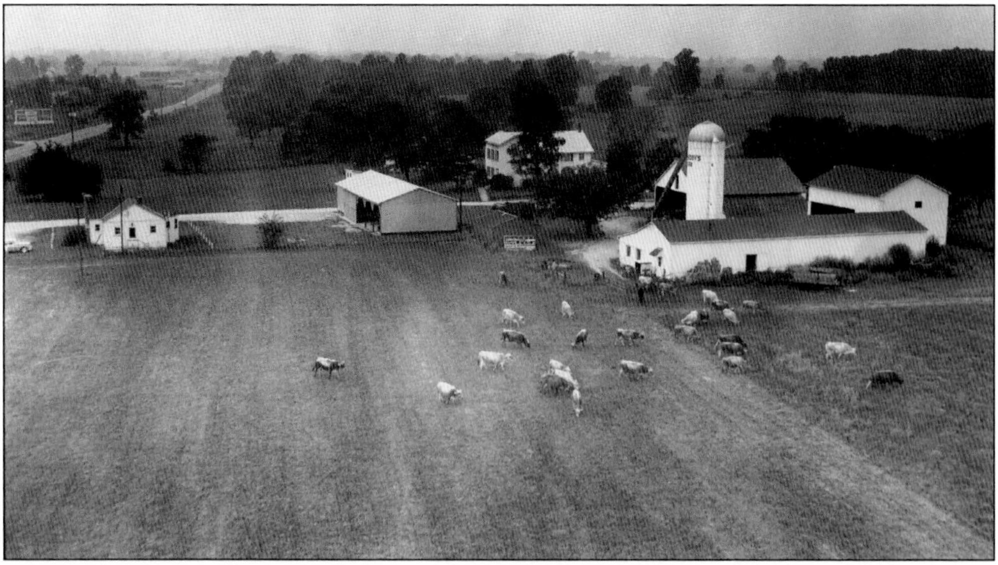

WLW's Everybody's Farm was unique in radio. Unlike other rural radio stations that would occasionally broadcast agricultural reports from farms, Everybody's Farm was an actual full-time, working farm that, under the guidance of the station's Farm Department, introduced new farming methods, hybrids, seeds, techniques, and equipment to loyal listeners. On weekends, it hosted giant cookouts and concerts for visitors. (RDM.)

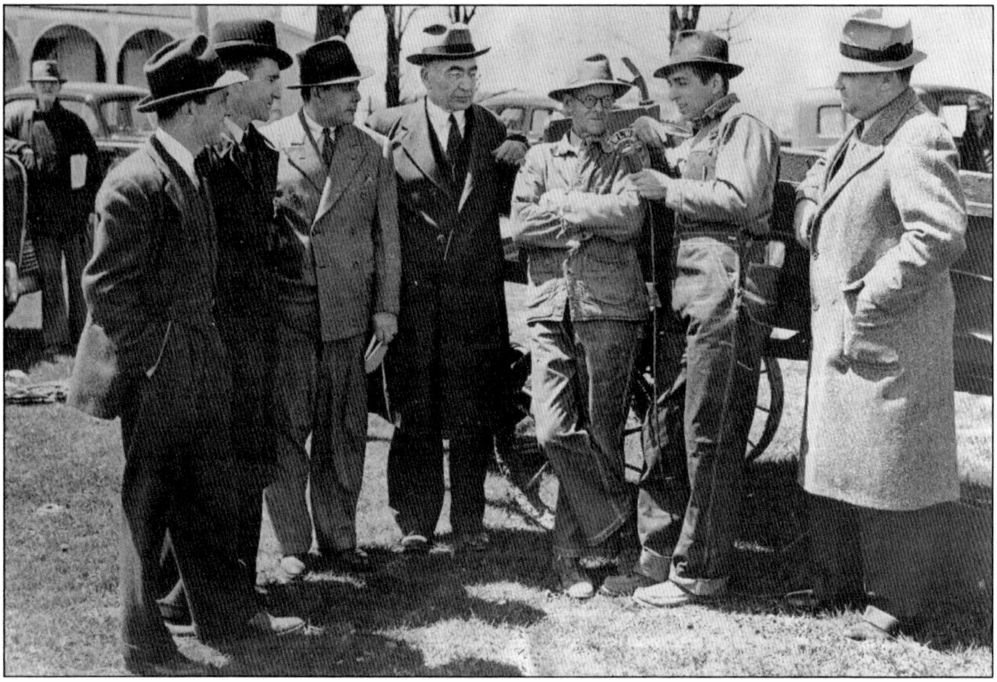

Originations from Everybody's Farm began on April 24, 1941, after dedication ceremonies featuring WLW's Robert Dunville (third from left) and program director George Biggar (right), among others. Ed Mason (holding microphone) was the original director of farm programming, and Earl Neal (third from right) was the tenant farmer who lived on the property. Broadcasts from Everybody's Farm continued for the next quarter century. (RDM.)

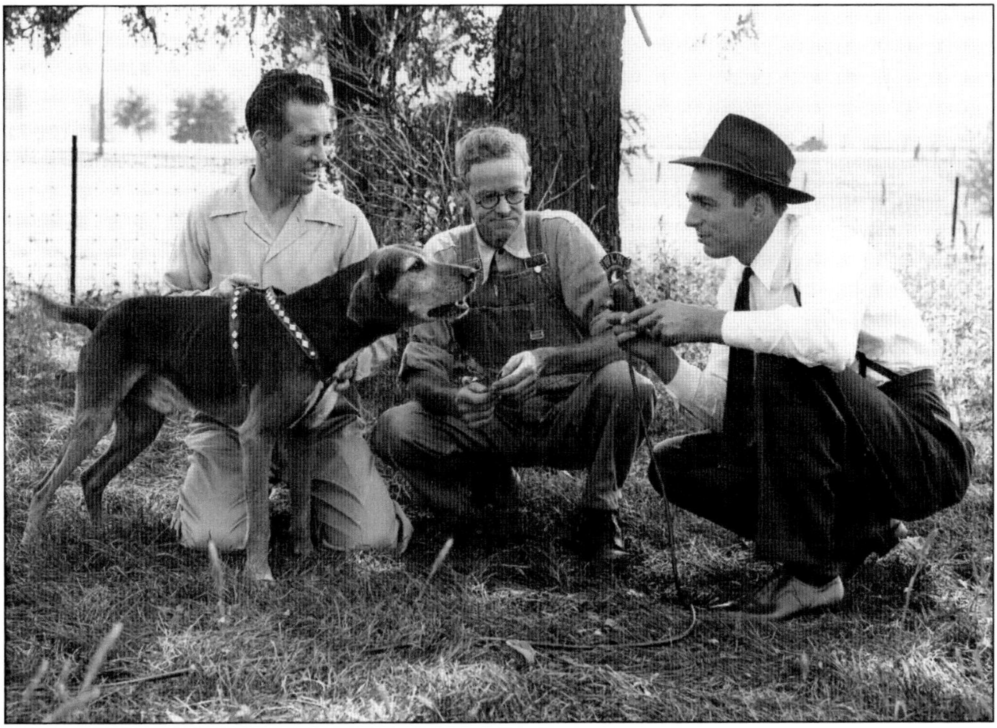

Part of the charm of Everybody's Farm was the fact that an actual farm family, not trained broadcasters, lived in the house on the farm and participated in the programs. The original family consisted of Earl (center) and Mayme Neal, a traditional farm family that was sometimes skeptical about "modern" innovations. Farm director Ed Mason (right) came from an agricultural radio station in Missouri and later, after leaving WLW in 1945, owned his own rural radio station. (RDM.)

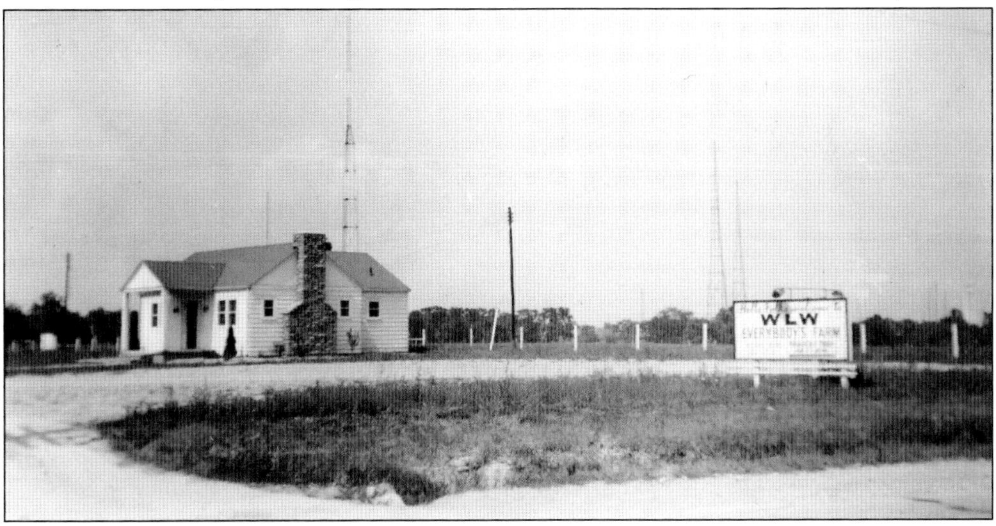

The focal point of WLW's Everybody's Farm was the Little White Studio, a modest outbuilding complete with a cozy stone fireplace. From this building came many of the interviews and demonstrations, although audio lines were strung to other buildings on the farm, including the main house and the dairy barn. On weekends, visitors would be granted access to anywhere except the upstairs living quarters of the main house. (RDM.)

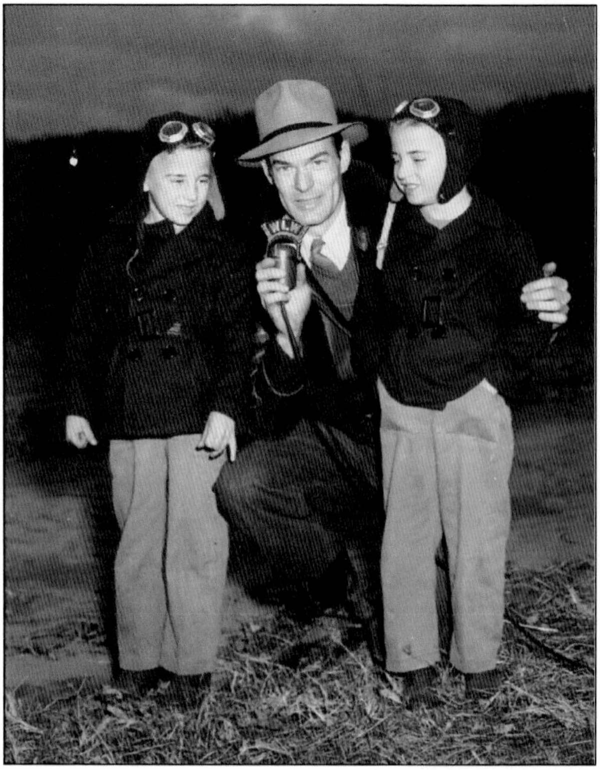

As a county extension agent, Roy Battles (pictured) found himself being interviewed for various agricultural programs on WLW. So when the station opened Everybody's Farm in 1941 to expand its rural programming, Battles was hired to help Ed Mason conduct the daily farm programs. After Mason left, Battles was promoted to director of the Farm Department and later, in the 1950s, worked for the Agriculture Department in Washington. (RDM.)

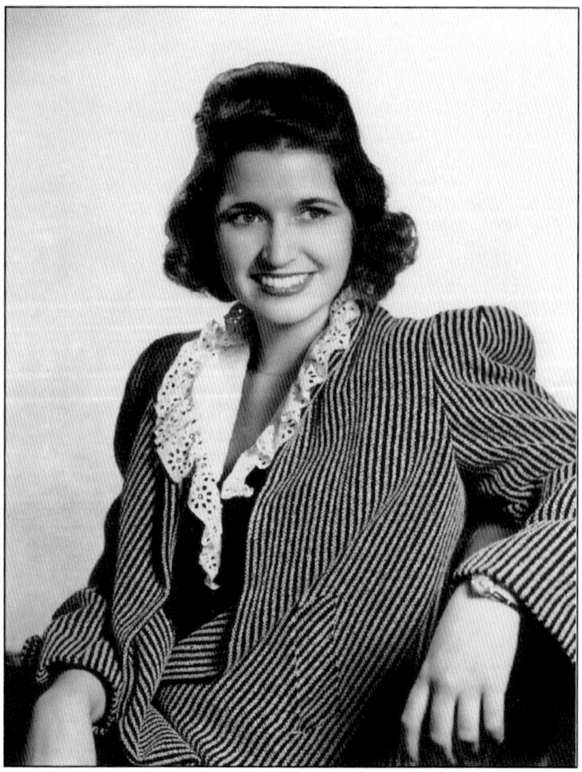

Farm life is not necessarily a "man's job," and WLW hired lovely Carrol McConaha as an announcer and hostess. McConaha grew up on a farm near Richmond, Indiana, and had no problem milking cows and describing the produce-canning process for radio listeners. A popular addition to the Farm Department, only marriage to a World War II serviceman prompted a move away from the farm to California. (CMR.)

Hand feeding visitors was not the duty of announcers at Everybody's Farm; instead, this image shows the then famous "ear-of-corn" microphone. WLW technicians hollowed out an actual ear of hybrid corn, cast it in metal, and inserted a salt-shaker-style microphone. (RDM.)

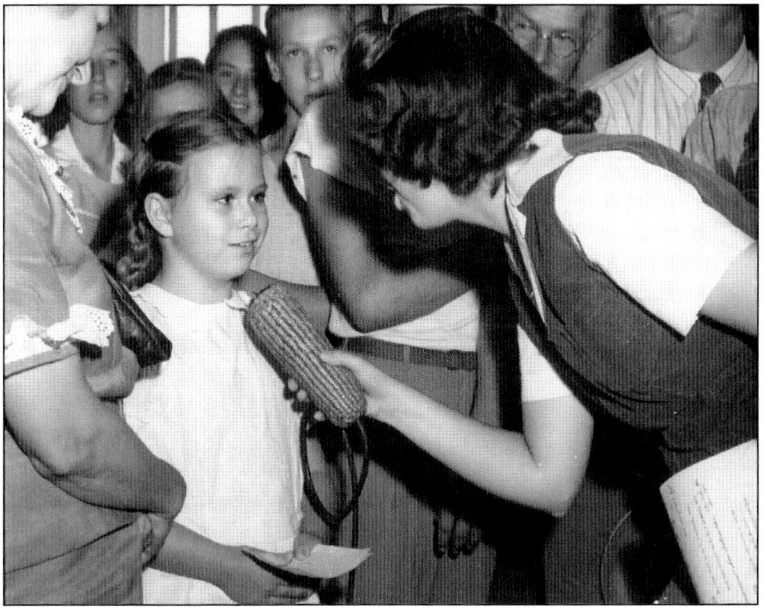

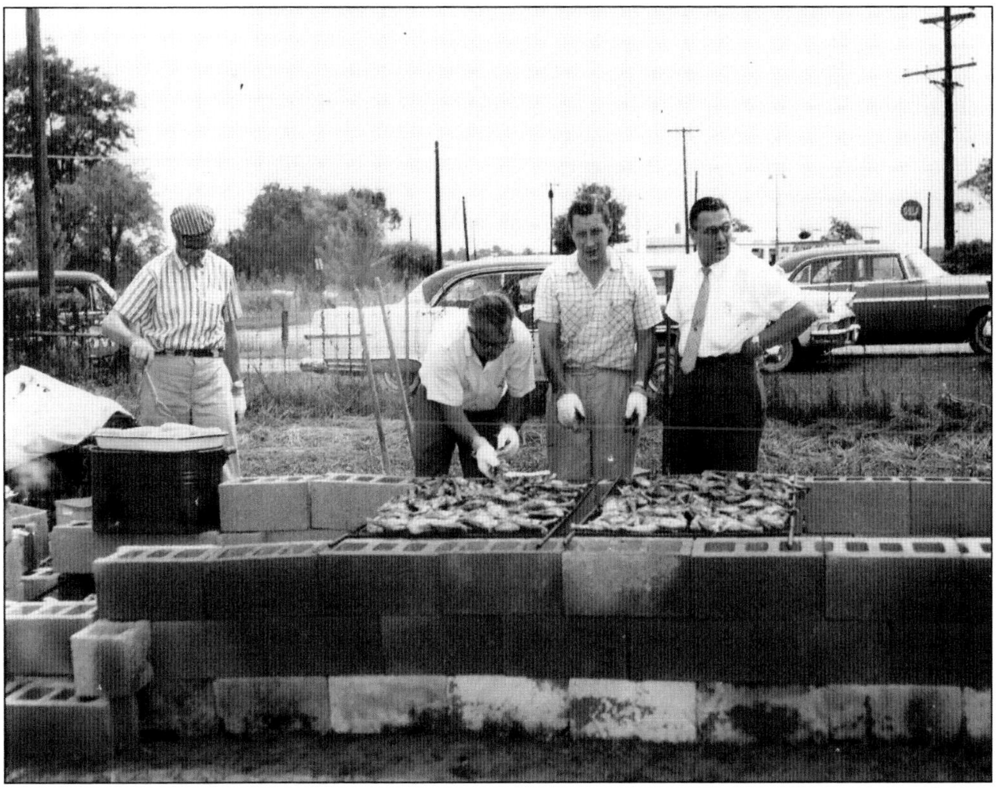

Real food could also be found at Everybody's Farm as well as some activity nearly every day during the growing season. In addition to the daily reports and broadcasts, on most weekends, many of the country music acts would come out to perform. Community groups often would sponsor large barbeque cookouts, and listeners would respond by the thousands, jamming nearby country roads to enjoy the fresh food, country music, and tours of the farm buildings. (RDM.)

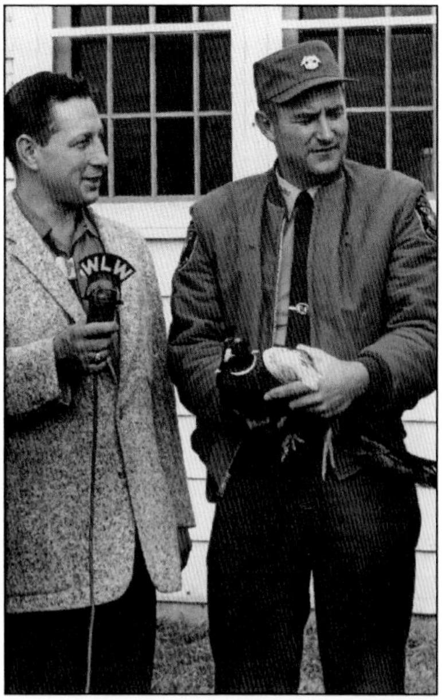

After announcer Ed Mason left the station in 1945, WLW brought in Bob Miller (left) to help Roy Battles with the announcing chores at Everybody's Farm. Eventually, Miller was promoted to farm director and became a great advocate of the educational and service-oriented responsibilities of radio for rural listeners. Miller met presidents, toured the world producing Peace Corps radio reports, and kept the station's Farm Department alive until the 1980s. (RDM.)

After the Neal family departed Everybody's Farm, WLW welcomed Jack and Jean Conner and their children Mike, Margaret, and Johnny, from rural New York. Jack Conner was an expert in breeding Brown Swiss dairy cows, and the entire family, even the children, actively participated in the daily farm chores and broadcasts. Also pictured, at left in the second row next to farm director Bob Miller (second from left), is assistant farm director George Logan, who was heard regularly on the farm broadcasts. (RDM.)

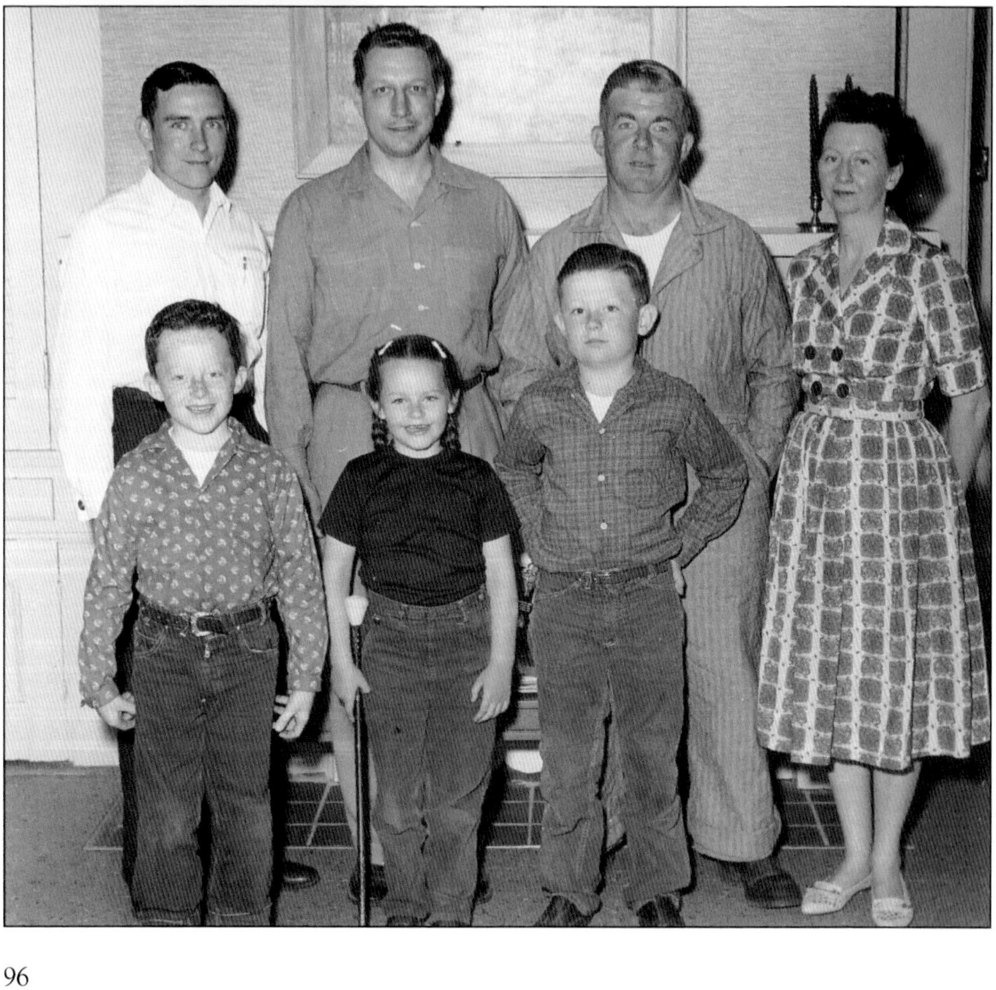

Oddly enough, Chester Atkins arrived at WLW as a fiddle player but quickly switched to and mastered the guitar after watching the fingerpick style of fellow WLW musician Merle Travis. A consummate workaholic, Chet Atkins spent every waking hour practicing new guitar licks, according to his wife, Leona, who was, along with her twin sister Lois, a WLW singer as one of the Johnson Twins. (MM.)

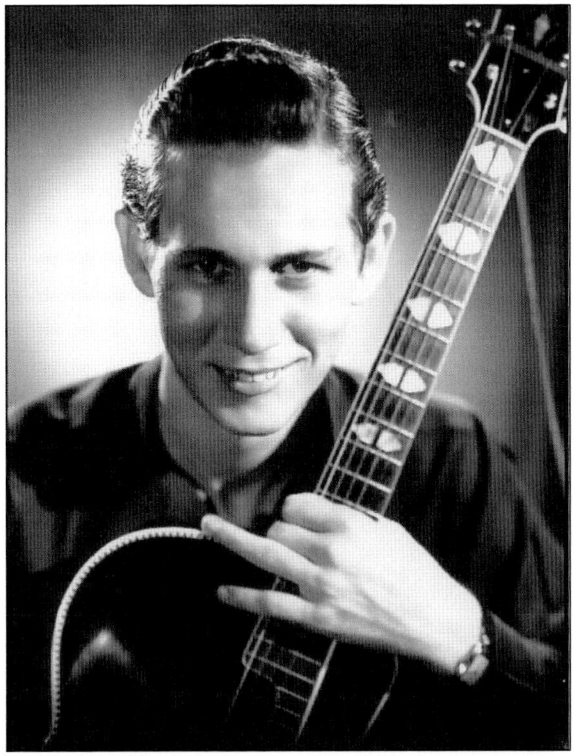

At four feet, 11 inches, Little Jimmy Dickens has been a member of the Grand Ole Opry in Nashville for over 60 years. However, one of his first professional stops was at WLW in 1944 when he was known as "Jimmy the Kid." Pictured with Leona and Lois, the Johnson Twins, Dickens enjoyed his time spent at WLW working the early-morning shows and playing regional country fairs as part of Bill McCluskey's road show. (LA.)

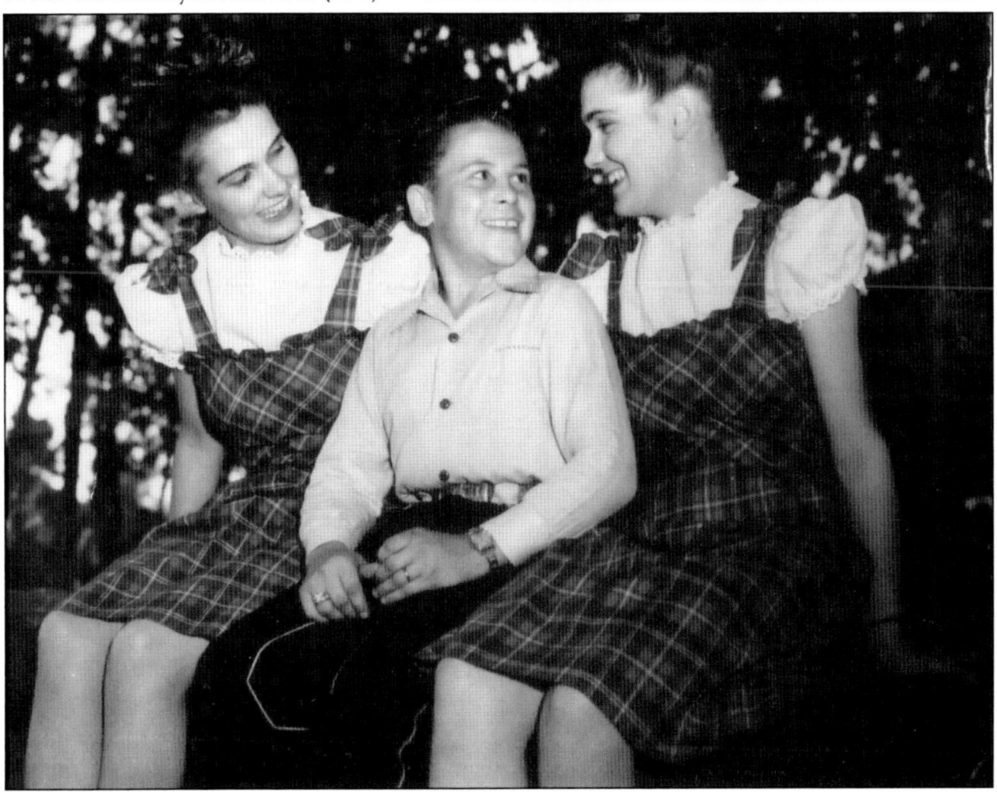

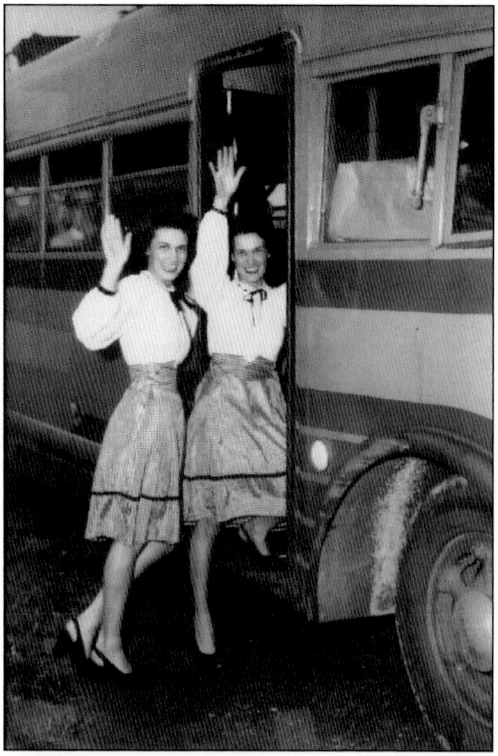

In addition to their radio performances, WLW promotions director Bill McCluskey kept performers—particularly the country acts—busy with a series of personal appearances at county fairs and small-town theaters. Riding an old Studebaker bus dubbed the "Old Gray Goose," McCluskey's acts would travel throughout Ohio, Indiana, Kentucky, and West Virginia several nights a week, only to be driven home by dawn in time for the sleepy performers to appear on the morning radio shows. (LA.)

The popularity of the Hoosier Hotshots in the 1930s led to the creation of similar novelty bands around the country. At WLW, a 1939 contest provided the name for the Boone County Buccaneers. "Captain Stubby" Fouts (first row, left) led the band with his ability to play the washboard, car horns, and slide whistle. Curley Myers and Tiny Stokes (second row, center) also appeared in the original group, which was disbanded during World War II and later regrouped with slightly different personnel. (BJ.)

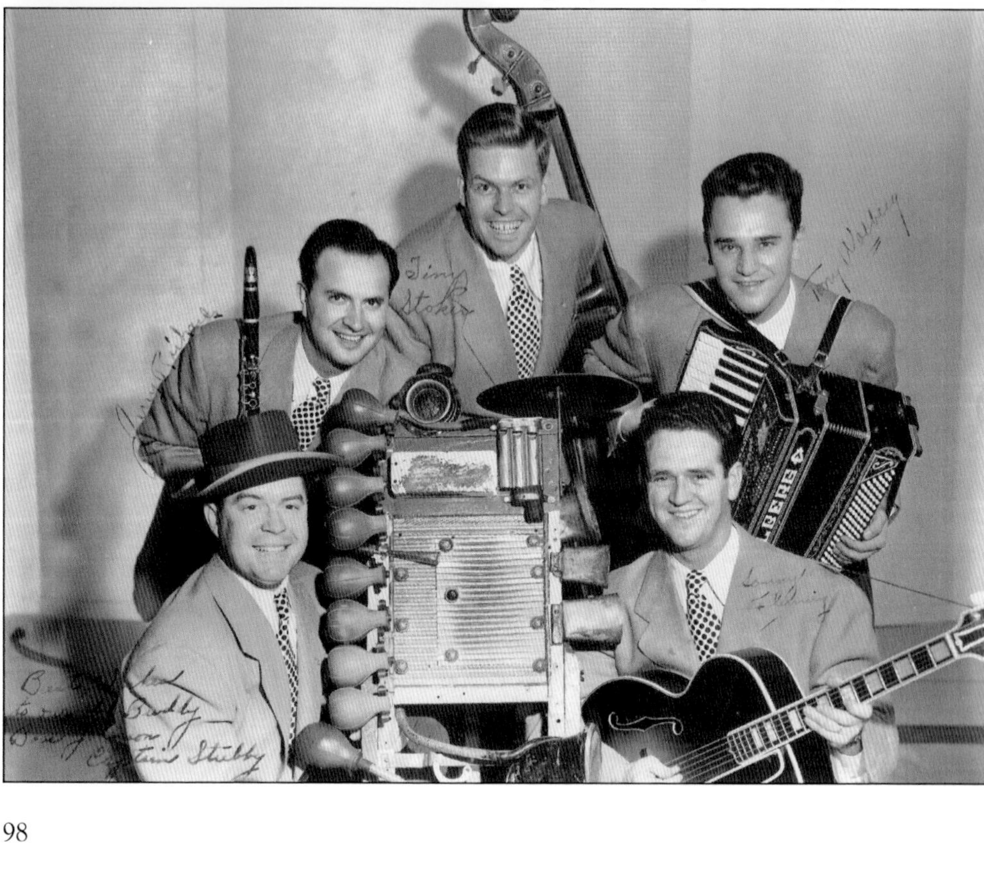

Bradley Kincaid supposedly gave Louis Marshall "Grandpa" Jones his nickname, after the 20-year-old banjo player complained about getting up in the morning during his early radio days. Indeed, Jones was hardly a grandpa when he first donned his fake moustache. At WLW, Grandpa enjoyed performing on the *Boone County Jamboree* and on other programs, but after returning from World War II in 1946, he found that the station had changed, and his friends had moved on. Eventually, Grandpa Jones would "act his age" as a founding cast member of television's *Hee Haw* program. (MM.)

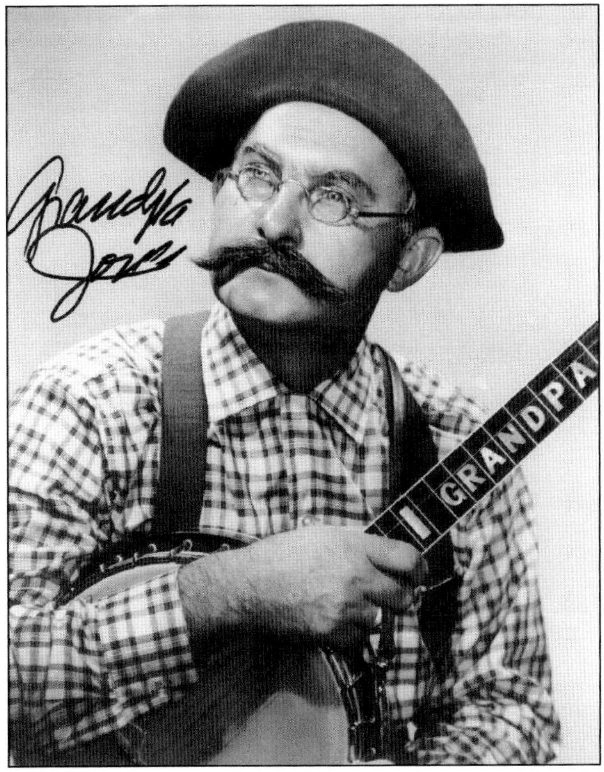

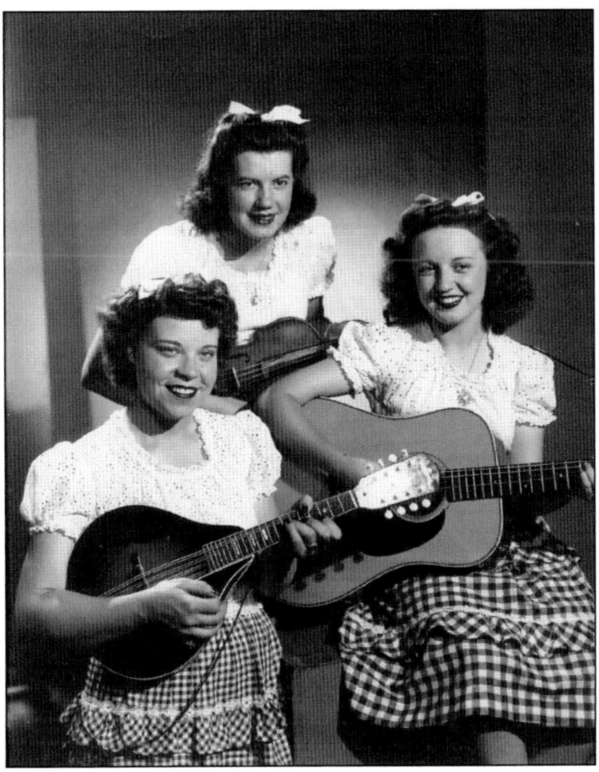

Many country acts passed through Cincinnati radio studios in the 1940s, some staying just a brief time before moving on. Often, performers intertwined to create new groups. The Happy Valley Girls consisted of, from left to right, Irene Martin, Ramona Riggens, and Jane Allen. Riggens and Allen also sang with Sunshine Sue, and while at WLW, Riggens met and married Grandpa Jones. (MM.)

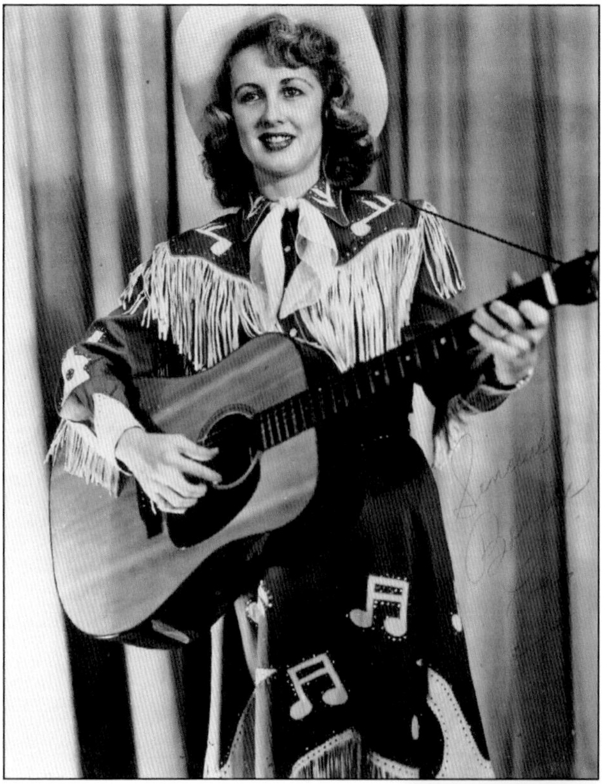

At a radio station in Kansas City, she was Sally Carson, but after successfully auditioning for WLW promotions director Bill McCluskey in early 1945, the more Irish-sounding Bonnie Lou moniker was chosen for their new yodeling country star. Bonnie Lou would go on to become a country and rockabilly icon on radio, television, and for Cincinnati's King Records, working with Ruth Lyons, Paul Dixon, and on the *Midwestern Hayride*. (MM)

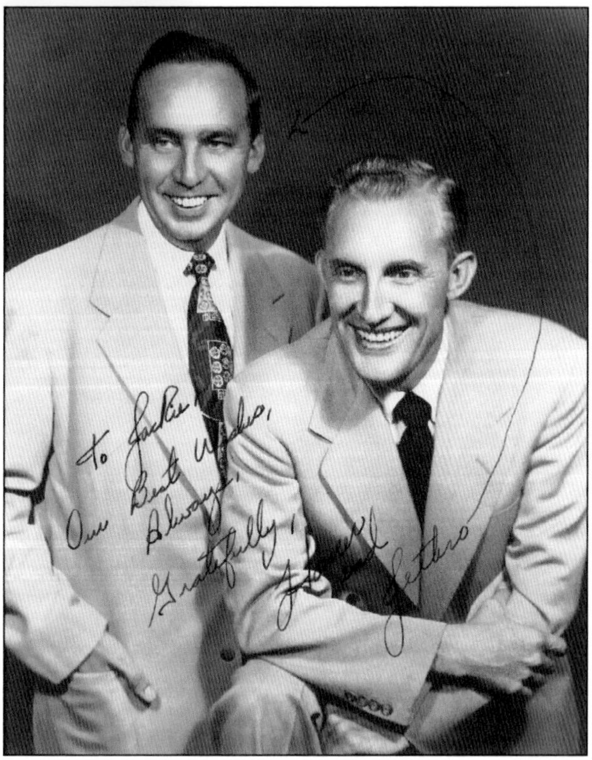

Combining clever comedy and skilled playing, Homer and Jethro (left) entertained audiences on WLW's *Renfro Valley Barn Dance*, *Midwestern Hayride*, and other programs. Henry "Homer" Haynes and Kenneth "Jethro" Burns recorded several albums during a long career that lasted until Haynes's death in 1971. Burns's mandolin skills enjoyed a revival in popularity in the 1980s. (MM.)

Husband and wife Dean Richards (left) and Penny West, along with guitarist Billy Keith (center), brought their Lucky Penny Trio to WLW in the mid-1940s. Penny, barely 5 feet tall, hauled around a string bass that surpassed her own height. Once, the trio offered a Lucky Penny token during a broadcast and was overwhelmed with the response. Later, Dean was the master of ceremonies of the *Midwestern Hayride* when it was on television. (MM.)

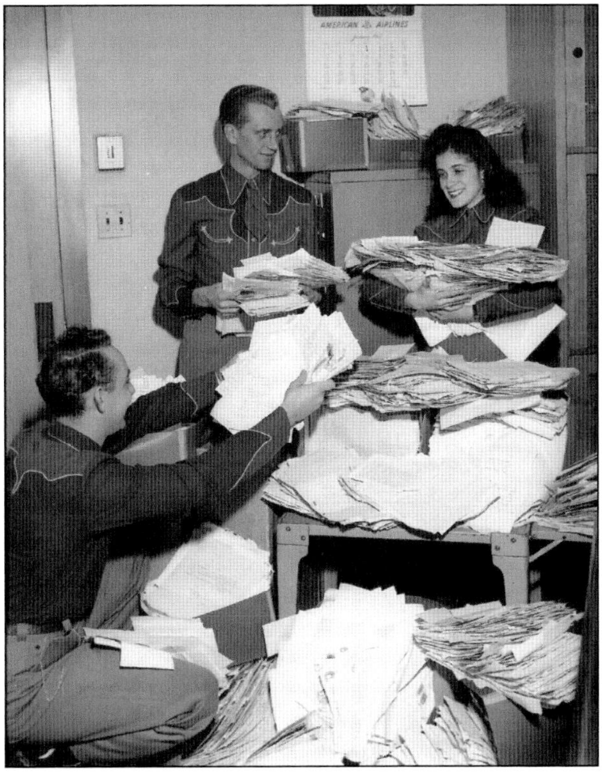

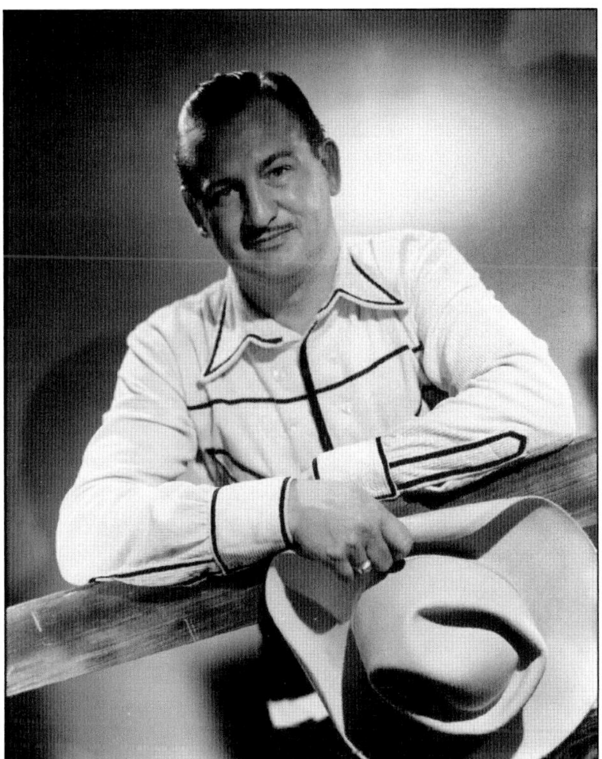

There was nothing in the delivery and speech of WCKY's *Make Believe Ballroom* announcer Nelson King in the 1940s to indicate his eventual dominance as a country music disc jockey in the 1950s. Voted the nation's top hillbilly DJ, King's highly lucrative nightly *Jamboree* program sold everything from baby chicks to tombstones as WCKY's nighttime signal blanketed the South. (MM.)

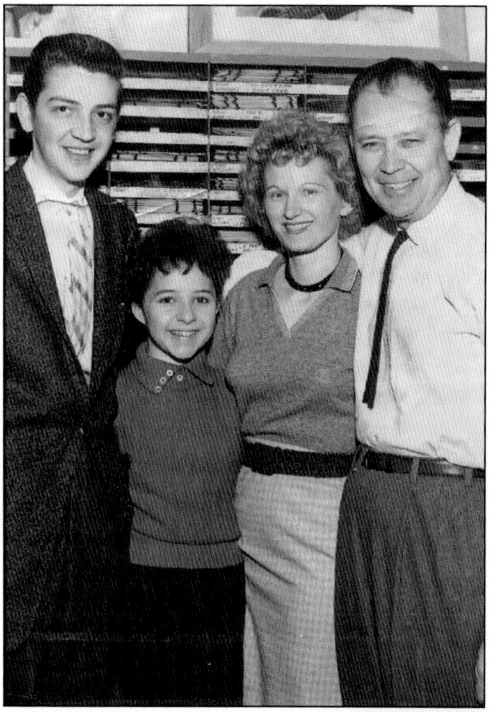

Country music entertainer and composer Jimmy Skinner (far right) was an established star when he opened a record shop in downtown Cincinnati. His Saturday program *Jimmy Skinner's Music Shop* was carried over from WNOP in the 1950s. In addition to attracting customers from around the country for his rare recordings, Skinner also introduced the public to young, up-and-coming stars like, from left to right, rockabilly guitarist Rusty York, vocalist Brenda Lee, and country songwriter Connie Hall. (MM.)

July 17, 1967, marked a symbolic end of an era. Mason firefighters were given the buildings at Everybody's Farm to utilize as training tools in a controlled practice burn. With the amount of farm service programming in decline at the station and elsewhere, WLW felt it no longer could justify the expense of operating the farm. The property was later redeveloped, and the Mason Post Office is among the businesses and homes now occupying the site. (RDM.)

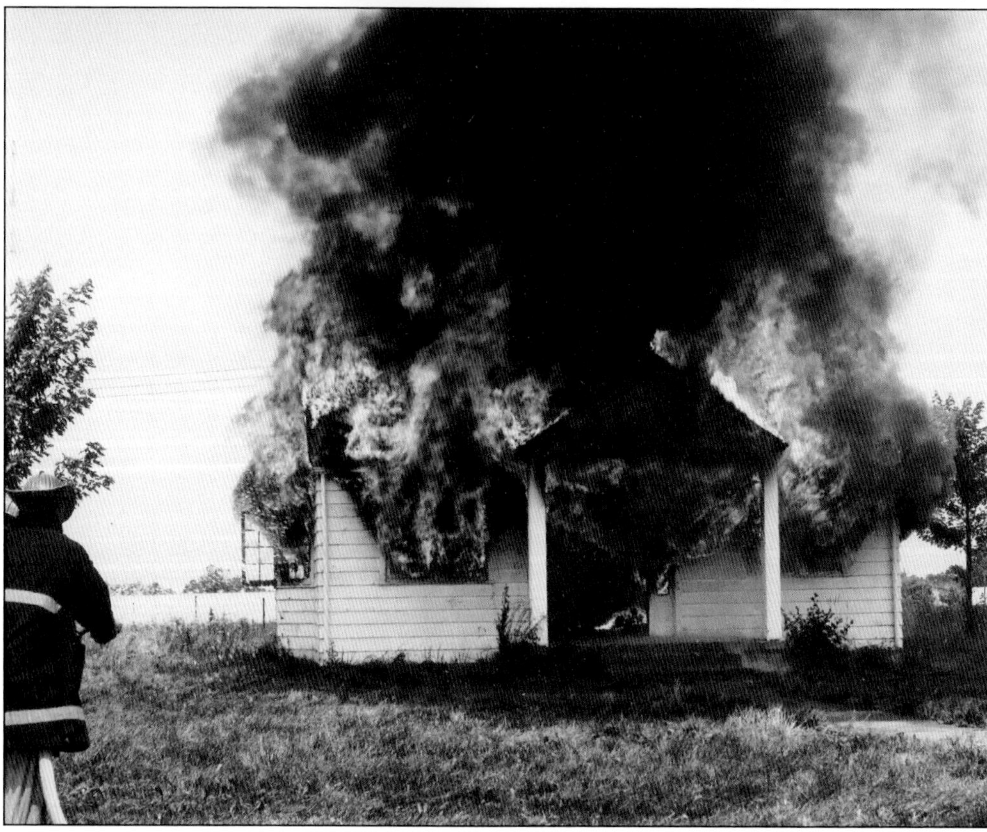

Five

Radio Reinvents Itself
World War II and the Postwar Era of Cincinnati Radio

It can be argued that radio's halcyon days, locally and nationally, occurred during World War II. Shedding the growing pains of a childlike, 1930s industry, broadcasting grew up quickly, gathered its moxie, and helped the Allies whip the Axis, all the while keeping an increasingly worried nation, almost afraid to open the daily newspaper, calmed and informed. Some of the greatest radio broadcasts in terms of pacing, flow, and style occurred during the 1940s. Whatever maturity was attained during the decade, though, quickly became nostalgia as television rose—and rose quickly—in prominence and importance. The radio business, dominant and strong in 1950, suddenly found itself on the defensive, desperately clinging to its cultural throne. Seemingly overnight, radio ceded to its baby sibling its well-earned birthright as the household entertainer, news provider, and social trendsetter. Like a dog banished to the garage, radio yielded its gains inside the living room and was forced to look elsewhere to reinvent itself. But what could radio still do best?

Despite the ever-advancing abilities of the distracted driver, radio quickly reminded itself that it would forever dominate the automobile. Whether music or news, the relationship between car and radio is cemented, and the concept of "drive time" replaced "prime time" in the radio programmer's office. Furthermore, radio could still provide a pinpointed message to a specific audience in a way that only recent satellite television and its thousands of channels could hope to match. Beginning with what was known then as "race radio" and "Top 40" in the 1950s, the concept of the radio format developed. Instead of trying to be all things to all people, radio stations did research and discovered that the nation's listeners could be divided into niches based upon specific likes and dislikes. Admittedly, the fragmentation has taken nearly ridiculous sub- and sub-sub-partitioning over the years; still, it was the shift into some degree of formatting that probably again saved radio from obsolescence. Finally, radio can, and always did, have the freedom to be taken practically anywhere—from the beach to the old North Woods. News-talk, shopping, nostalgia, digital, satellite, Internet streaming . . . even now, radio continues to reinvent itself every day, every week, and every year.

Obviously, change can be painful. In 1953, WLW had a rather large layoff of its radio musicians as it began the shift to disc jockey programs. WLW was actually one of the last holdouts—the Williams Brothers came to WLW in 1942 because they were laid off when WLS in Chicago went "all DJ." WCKY's Nelson King proved to all that not only could a disc jockey show be profitable, it could be staggeringly so. In the latter decades of its first half century, radio adjusted, and out of the dust appeared an amazing array of talented personalities who came to Cincinnati and then moved on to bigger markets or perhaps hung around a few decades to become an important part of the local community fabric.

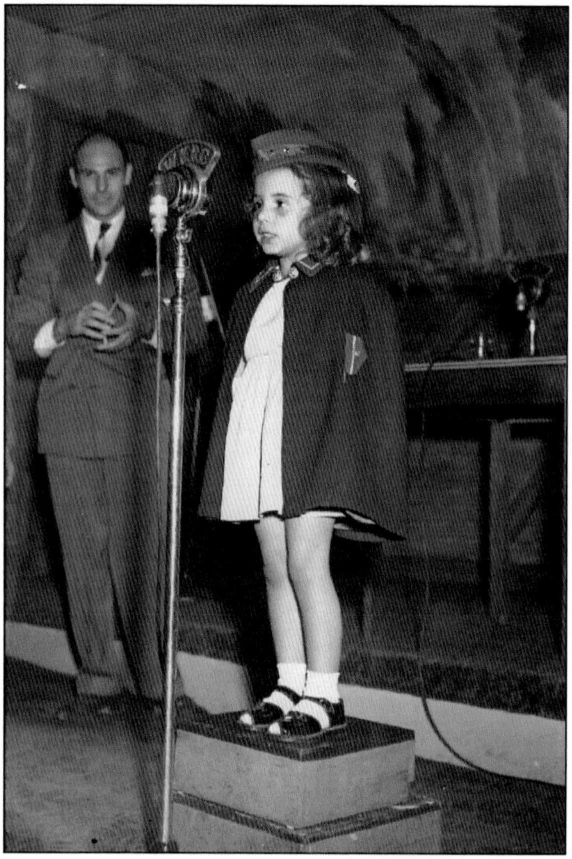

World War II catapulted radio into its halcyon years. Never before or since was America's radio broadcasting so vital in its contributions in terms of news, information, public service, home-front entertainment, comfort, pride, motivation, and ultimately victory. From reporting at a military induction center, to the simple, patriotic song of a small girl over WKRC, fortunately, radio was there. (MM.)

From the earliest years, Powel Crosley's engineers experimented with shortwave broadcasting. In 1939, experimental W8XAL became WLWO, one of the first commercial shortwave stations. Beamed primarily to Latin America and Europe, WLWO had its own separate staff of Spanish-speaking announcers and entertainers as well as German and Austrian broadcasts. During World War II, WLWO was incorporated into the Voice of America's broadcast facility, which Crosley also operated. (MM.)

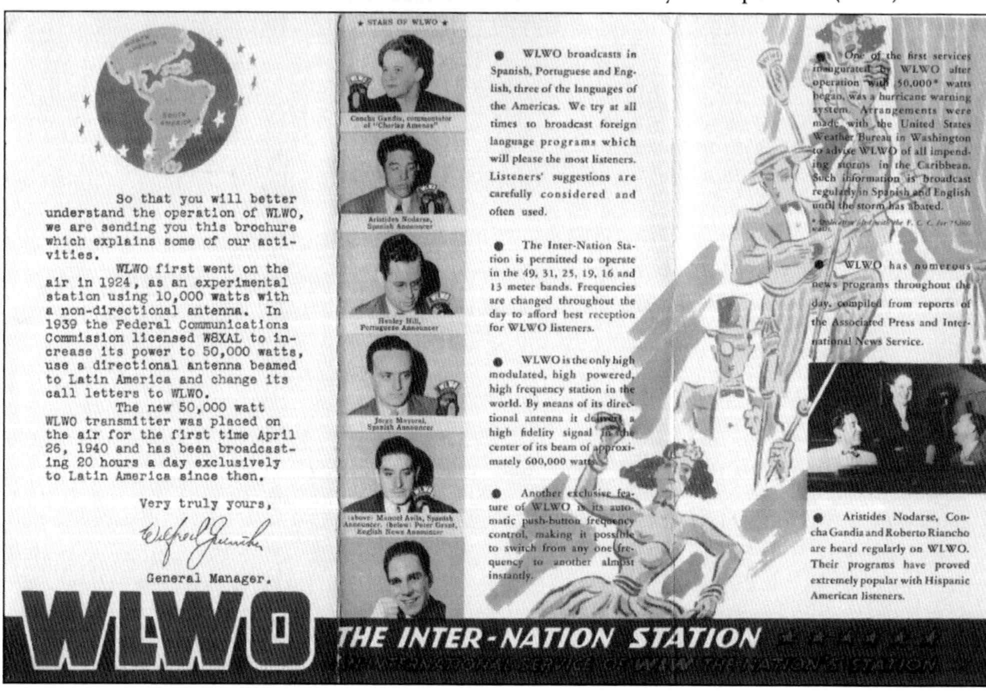

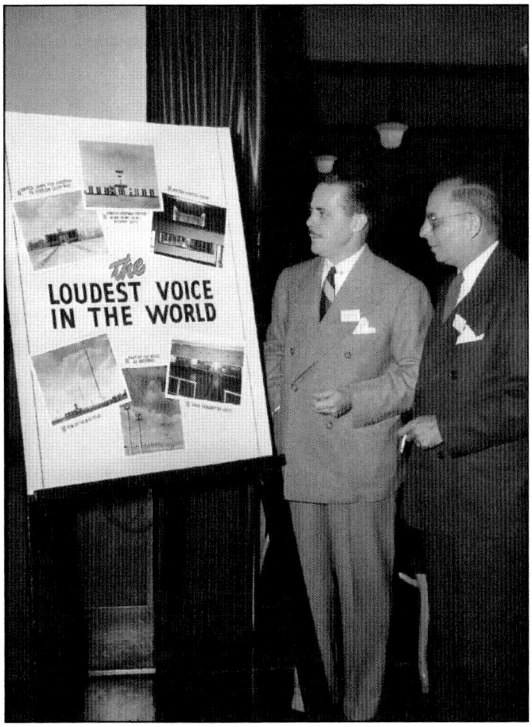

Crosley's experience in the development of commercial shortwave radio broadcasting gave the company an advantage when, after meeting with government officials in 1942, they were awarded a contract to build the most powerful shortwave transmitting station. Crosley chose vacant land in Bethany about a mile from their Mason transmitter and within a year, had designed and built six of the world's first 200,000-watt shortwave transmitters. (EDCH.)

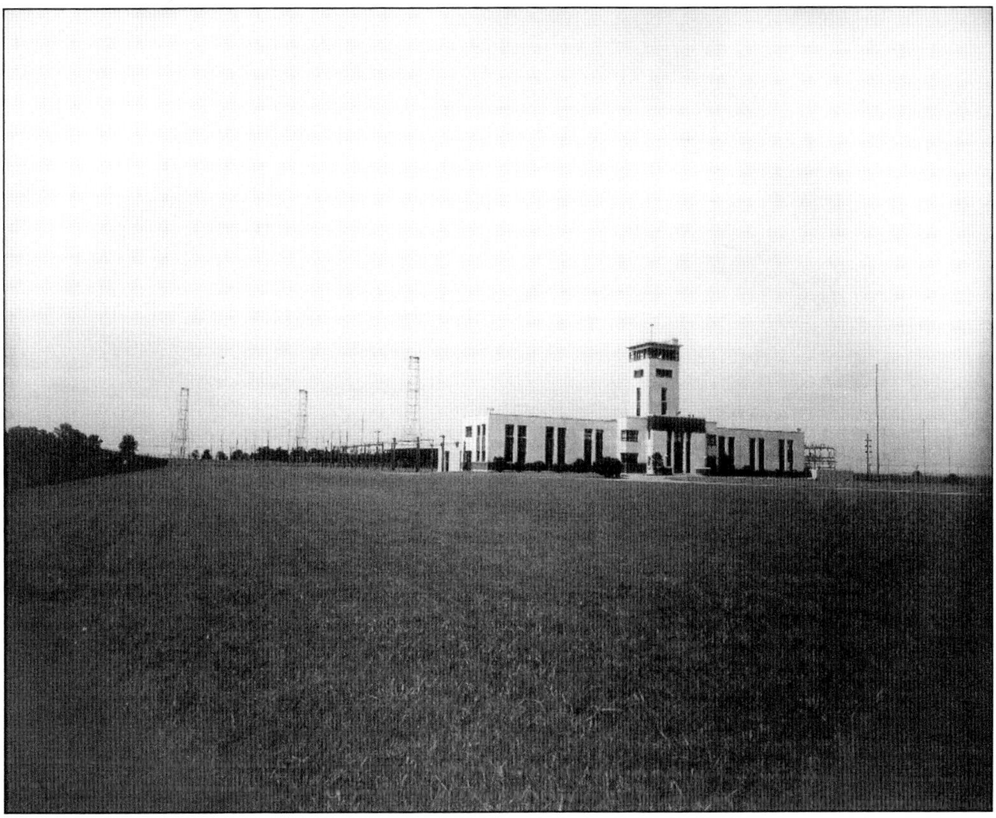

The Crosley-built Bethany transmission facility became one of the world's prime sources for the Voice of America, an independent provider of unbiased news and information during World War II and into the Cold War era. From this plant, shortwave signals were beamed around the globe utilizing the earth's reflective ionosphere. Because of its importance, its level of security rivaled that of a military installation. (EDCH.)

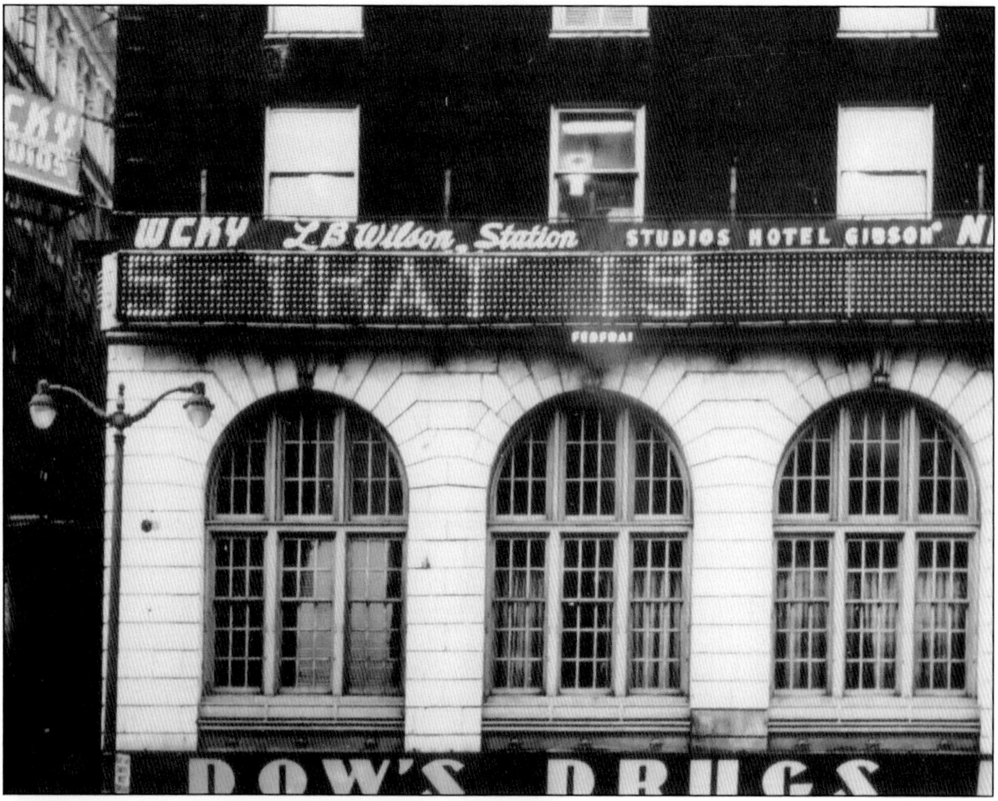

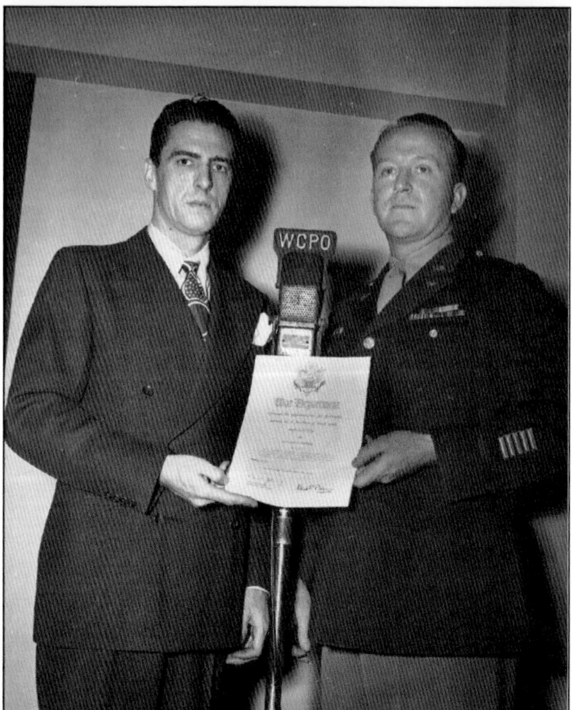

WCKY owner L.B. Wilson loved the show-business excitement of New York, so he brought a little of that to downtown Cincinnati when he had a large Motogram sign installed on the east corner of the Hotel Gibson facing the fountain esplanade. In fact, one of longtime Cincinnati Reds stadium announcer Paul Sommerkamp's early jobs was to place large letter plates on an interior conveyor belt to activate the sign. (MH.)

The switch to emphasis on news paid off for WCPO, which saw its ratings rise steadily during World War II despite its weaker signal. In addition to better ratings, WCPO rose in prestige as private and public entities recognized the station's contributions to the war effort. Station manager Mort Watters (left) accepted many awards both during and immediately after the war. (MM.)

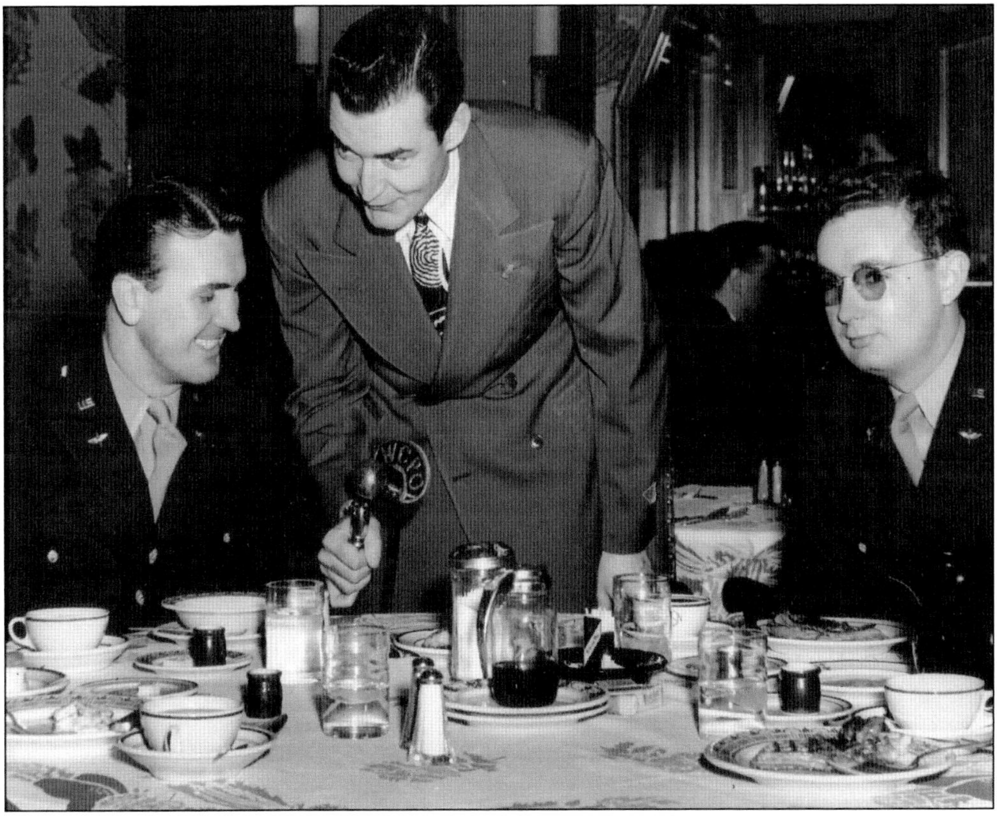

In 1945, WCPO radio general manager Mort Watters hired Chicago announcer Paul Dixon (center) as a newsman, but Dixon lobbied long and hard to achieve his goal to be a radio disc jockey. Gradually, Dixon shifted away from news and toward entertainment, but not before hosting a breakfast interview program at the Netherland Plaza Hotel's sandwich shop. Later, Dixon employed all his skills on television on WCPO-TV and WLWT. (MM.)

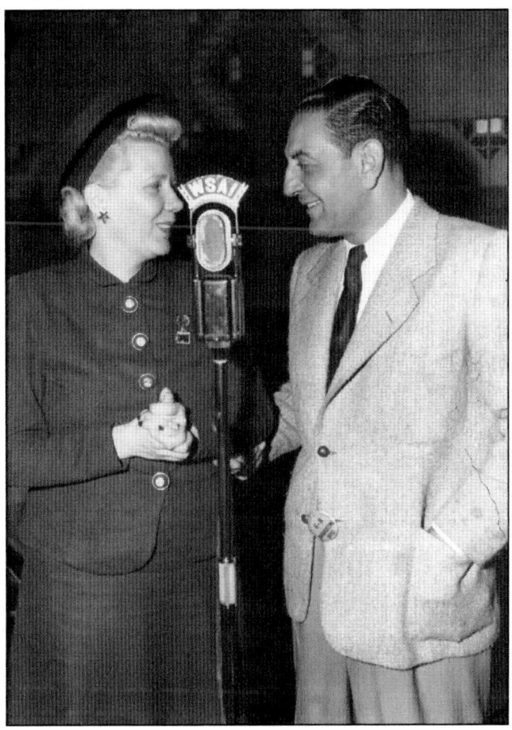

In 1942, WLW pulled off a deal that would benefit the company for the next quarter century. Luring away an unhappy Ruth Lyons from WKRC, they acquired the city's most popular women's radio host, who later would dominate regional television. As a foreshadowing of her later *50-50 Club*, Ruth had several shows early on, including *Petticoat Partyline* on WSAI, where she interviewed celebrities like Guy Lombardo, and *Morning Matinee* on WLW. (MM.)

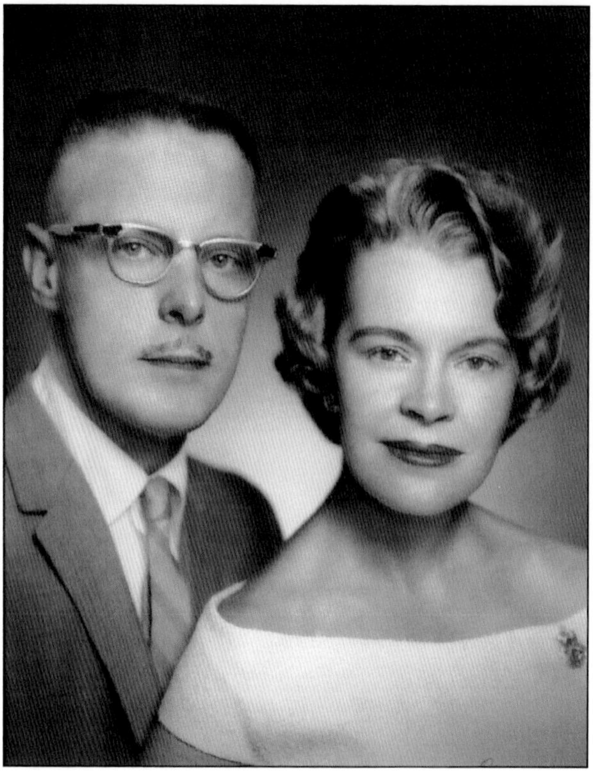

As descendant of one of Cincinnati's wealthy pioneer families, Jack Strader, who successfully could have pursued any career, chose radio. Strader worked at WLW as an actor and at WCPO, WCKY, and WKRC as an announcer. Jack and his wife, Joan, also started Cincinnati's first independently owned FM radio station, WVAW, above the Cheviot Theater in Cheviot in 1947. But Cincinnati was not yet ready for FM, and the station folded after one year. In later years, both Jack and Joan became leaders in the preservation of local broadcast history. (MM.)

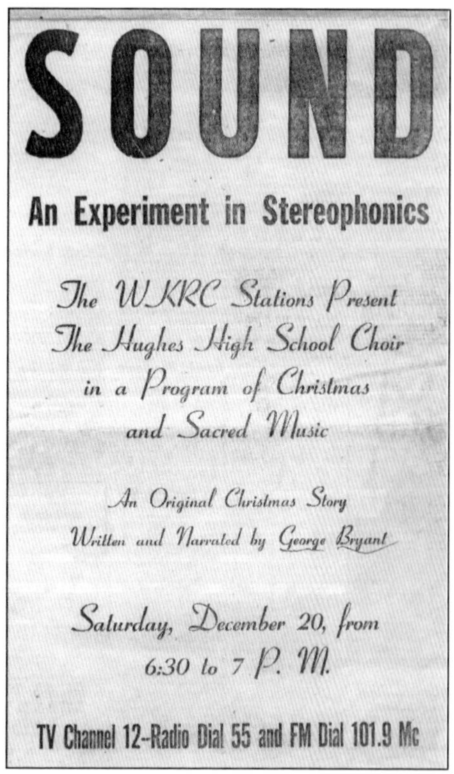

Around 1945–1946, WLW and WKRC began applying for licenses on the new FM radio band. WLWA appeared in July 1947 and was mostly filled with music and arts from local college students. In April 1948, months after it went on the air, WKRC attempted to turn its FM station, WCTS (for *Cincinnati Times-Star*), into a profitable collaboration with the local transit system when WCTS was broadcast over speakers in the city's buses. Later, as WKRC-FM, the station was part of experimental stereo broadcasts using AM radio on one channel and FM and television on the other—a sort of early surround sound. (GB.)

When Crosley was forced to sell WLW's sister station WSAI in 1945, the staff basically could choose to stay or go with new owner Marshall Field. Announcer Jon Arthur decided to go with WSAI and created Sparkie, an imaginary elf—Arthur's voice sped up—for his disc jockey show. Eventually, the concept became the children's show *The Adventures of Big Jon and Sparkie*, which was carried daily over ABC and was Cincinnati's last network contribution during radio's golden age. (MM.)

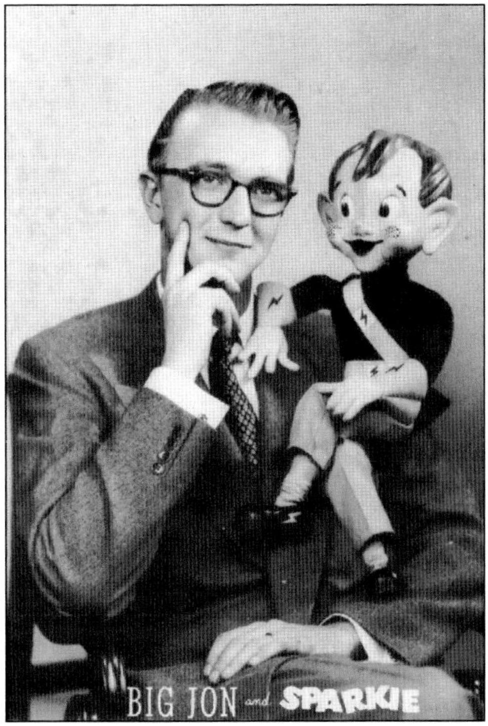

After the war, the government opened the radio spectrum a bit to allow more smaller radio stations. The first of three new stations to appear in Greater Cincinnati was WZIP on October 5, 1947. As part owner, WCKY chief engineer Charles Topmiller helped put WZIP on the air in the former WCKY Covington studios. Its broadcast tower, which still stands along Interstate 75 near Mainstrasse Village, once belonged to WSAI in 1936 when it was situated in Clifton Heights. (LB.)

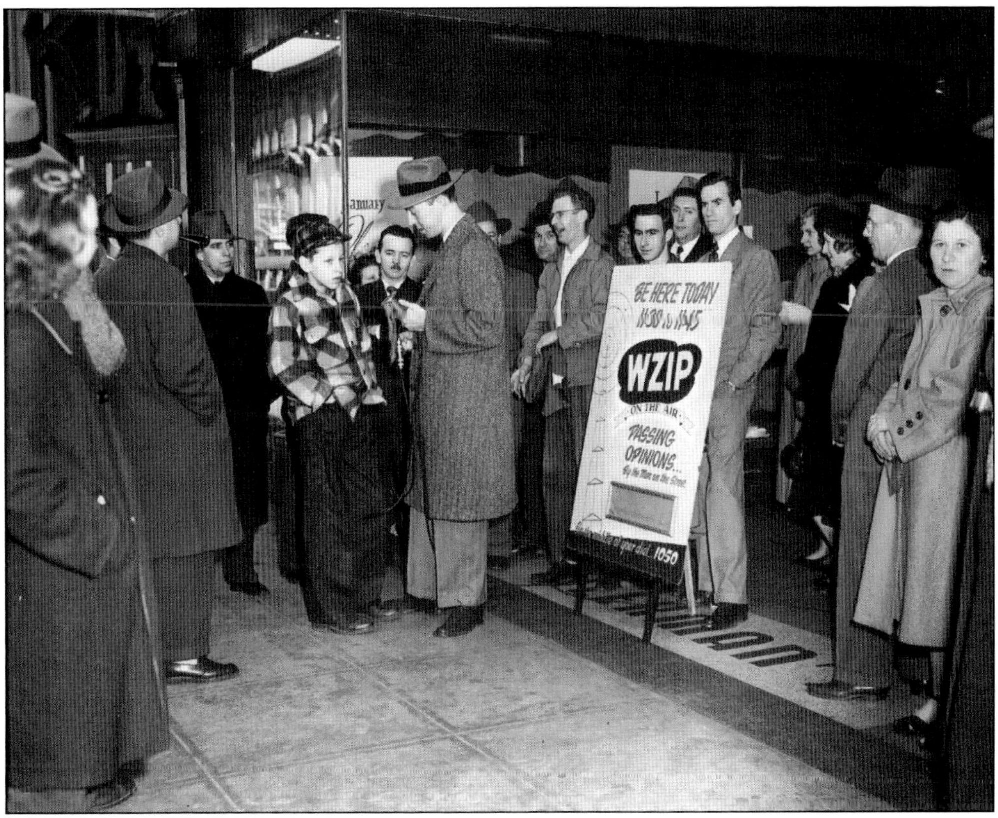

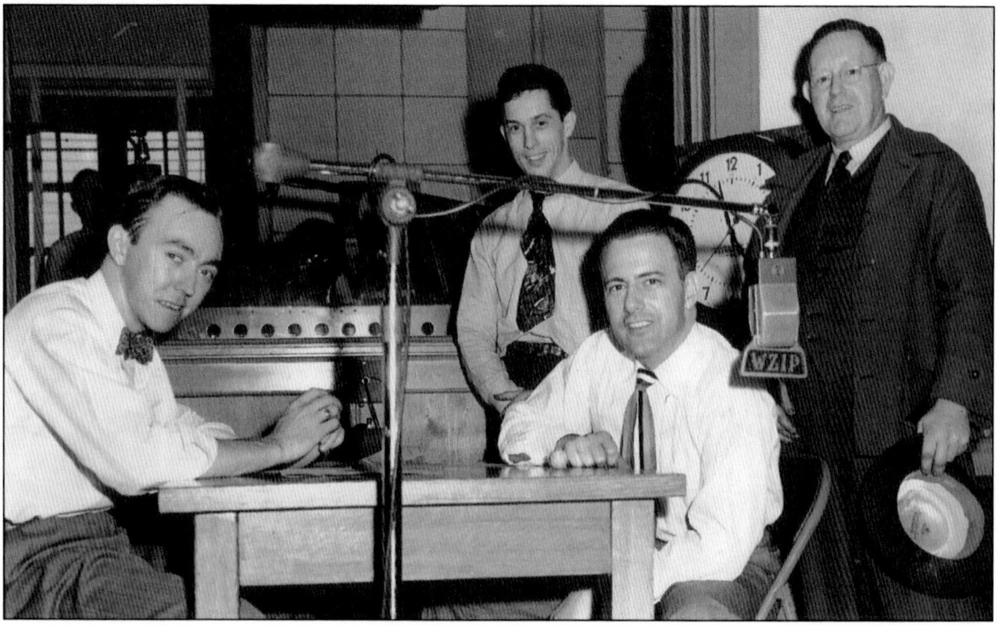

Covington's WZIP quickly gained a reputation as the local station that would do things the other stations would not. In addition to offering straight jazz, blues, and hillbilly music, it provided a home for not one, but two, pioneer African American announcers: Ernie Waits and Bill Fields. Operated by Art and Carmen Eilerman, WZIP also had a keen news-and-information staff featuring Steve Crane (seated left) and Lloyd Baldwin (seated right). (LB.)

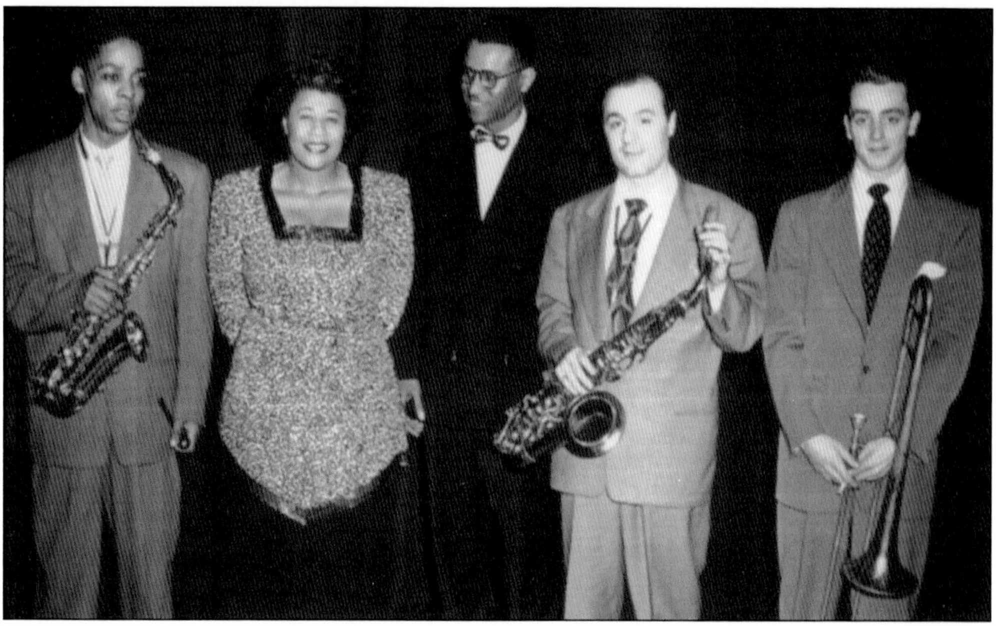

As Greater Cincinnati's pioneer black disc jockey, Ernie Waits (center) had to break several barriers along the way during his lengthy career. Waits literally had to find his own sponsors to buy airtime on his first station, WNOP. On WZIP, Waits brought jazz programming to the eclectic station, introducing his audience to several acts not typically featured in Cincinnati, like Ella Fitzgerald (second from left). (MM.)

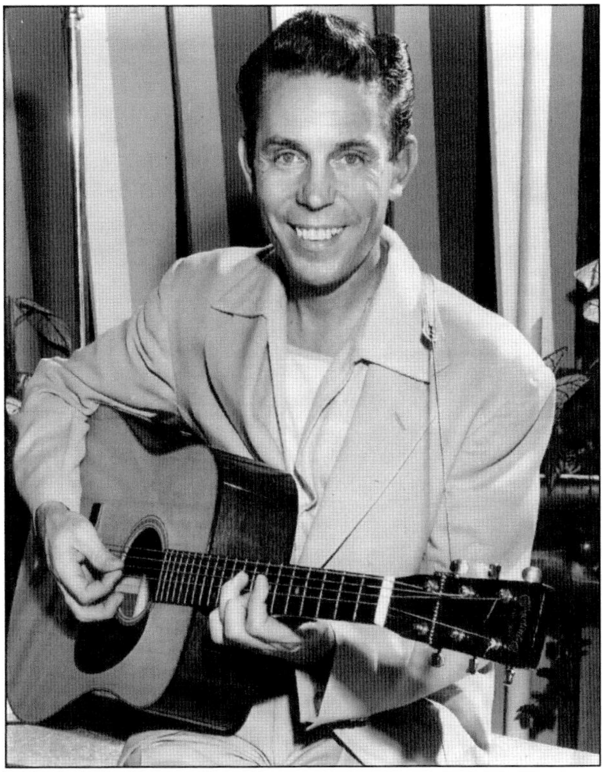

WNOP went on the air August 21, 1948, in Newport, Kentucky. During the 1950s, the station played several styles of music, including jazz and pop, but was largely a country music station. One of its first disc jockeys was singer Ray Scott. Newport was notorious for its gambling in the 1950s, and WNOP was not excluded. Regular broadcasts, even in the middle of a song, could be interrupted with the results of any horse race around the country. (MM.)

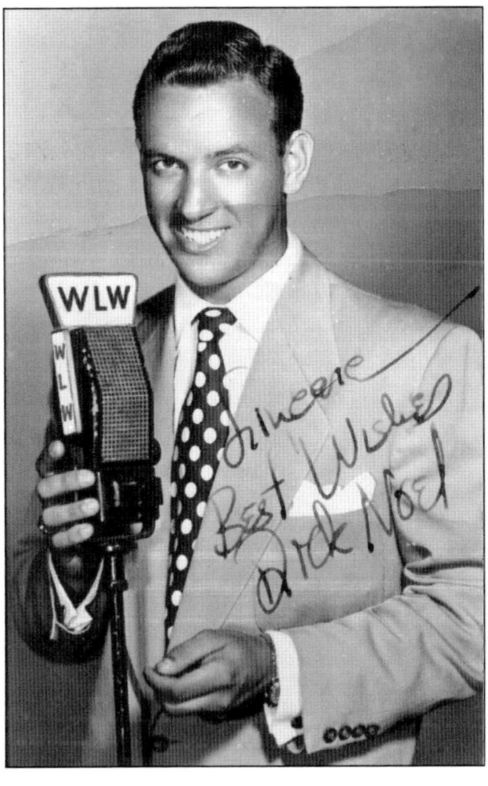

Vocalist Dick Noel filled a vacancy at WLW as a smooth baritone who could handle any genre of music, including *Moon River*. Noel also appeared on WLWT television and in his spare time, cofounded Cincinnati's Fraternity Records. His Dick Noel Singers sang backup on dozens of recordings before Noel moved to Chicago and *Don McNeill's Breakfast Club* and later to Hollywood to work as a jingle writer and producer. (MM.)

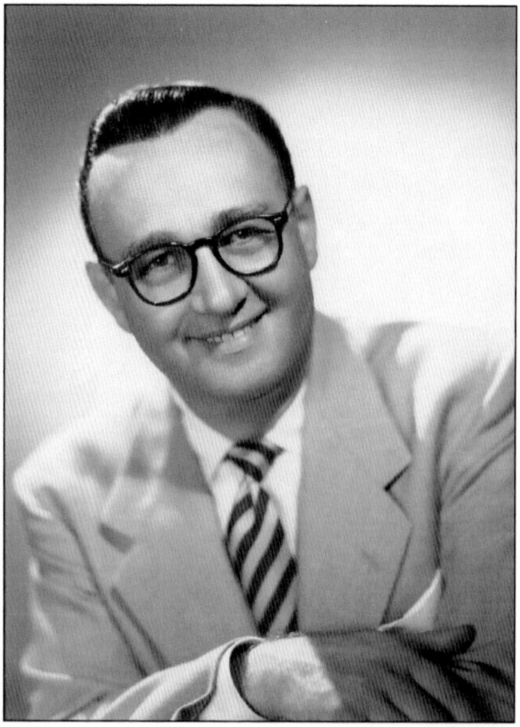

His real name was George Blumenthal, but as Willie Thall, this talented performer excelled as comedian, musician, master of ceremonies, announcer, and sidekick. Thall came to WLW in 1943 to perform with Dolly Good and the Buccaneers country band. Before long, he was starring on radio and television as host and later still, Ruth Lyons's sidekick. In the 1960s, he moved to WKRC-TV where he hosted his own program and became a commercial pitchman. (MM.)

He is best remembered today for his classic film A *Christmas Story* and for his years on New York radio, but author and storyteller Jean Shepherd was hired and fired by three Cincinnati radio stations—WKRC, WCKY, and WSAI—later working at WLW radio and television. Shepherd also did remote broadcasts from Lunken Airport's Sky Galley and from Shuller's Wigwam restaurant, seen here around 1951. (MM.)

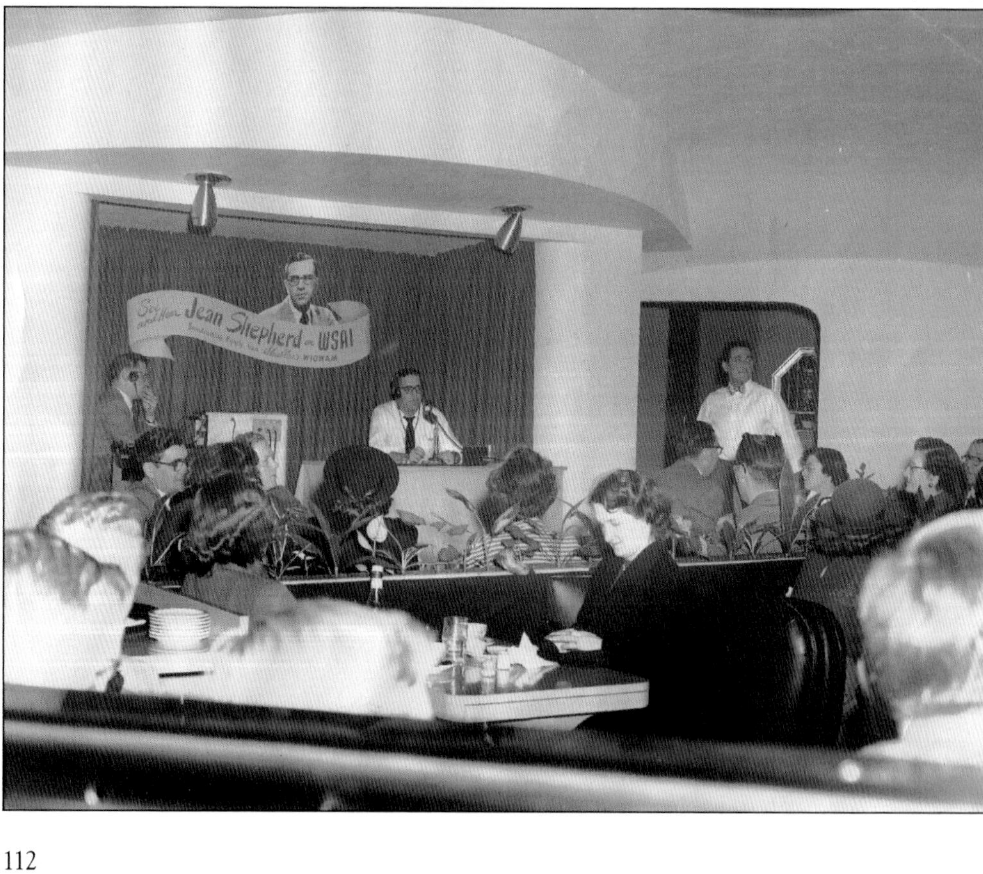

Following World War II, several talented people came to Cincinnati colleges on the GI Bill to study broadcasting. Earl Hamner was a College of Music student, writer, and actor hired by WLW in 1946 to help edit their newsletter and give tours. He also wrote and acted in several school-sponsored radio dramas on WLW and its sister station WLWA before joining their continuity department. Hamner left Cincinnati by 1949 and is best known today as creator of television's *The Waltons* and *Falcon Crest*. (MM.)

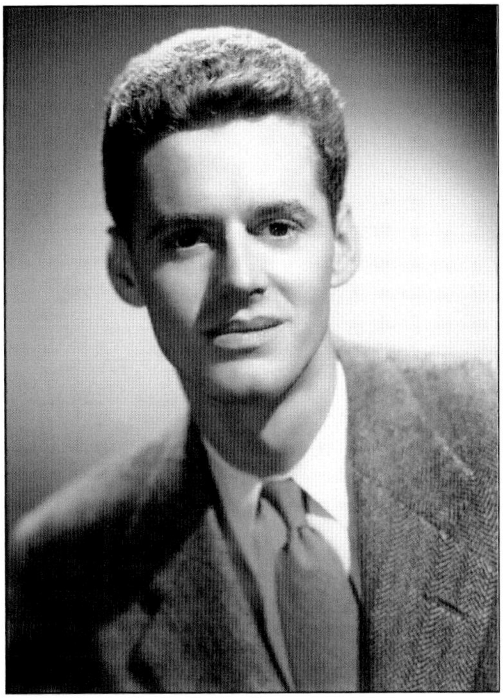

Charles "Buggs" Scruggs (left) was a pioneer disc jockey at WCIN, Cincinnati's first African American radio station. WCIN went on the air October 31, 1953, and Scruggs was an immediate hit with young listeners of all races with his patter, "Buggs Scruggs, the man with the plugs." He is pictured in 1955 with car-dealer sponsor Frank Spampinata. The car, by the way, is a 1923 Star. (MM.)

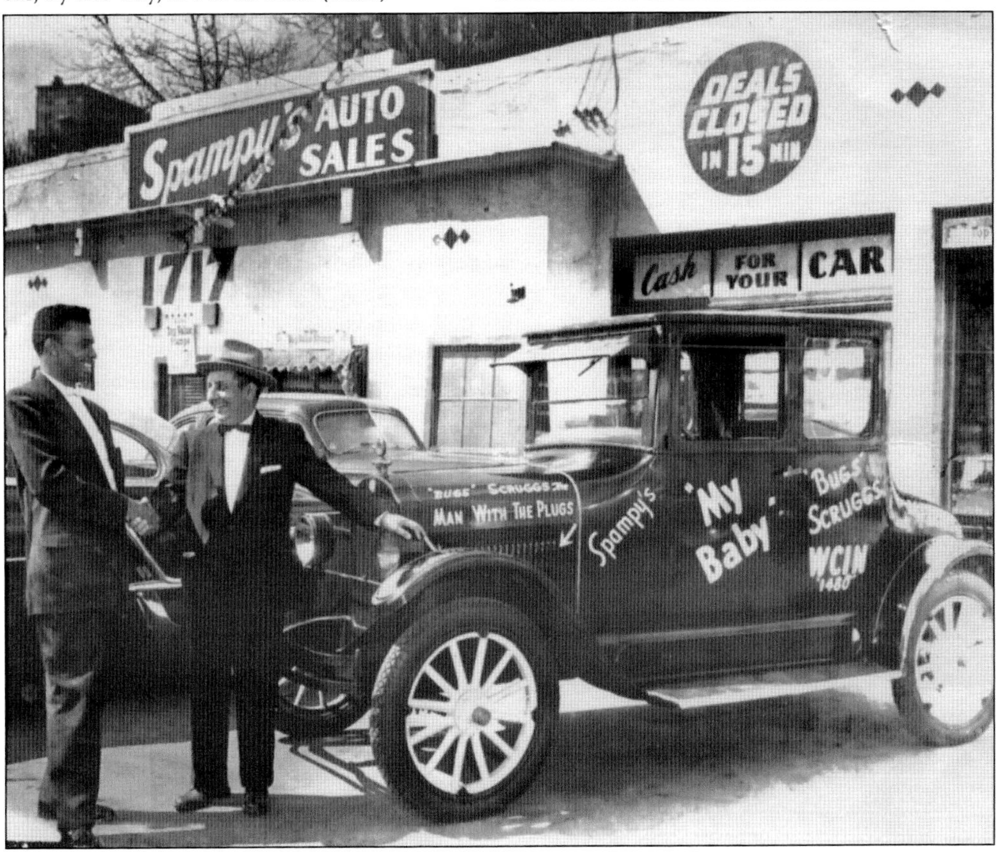

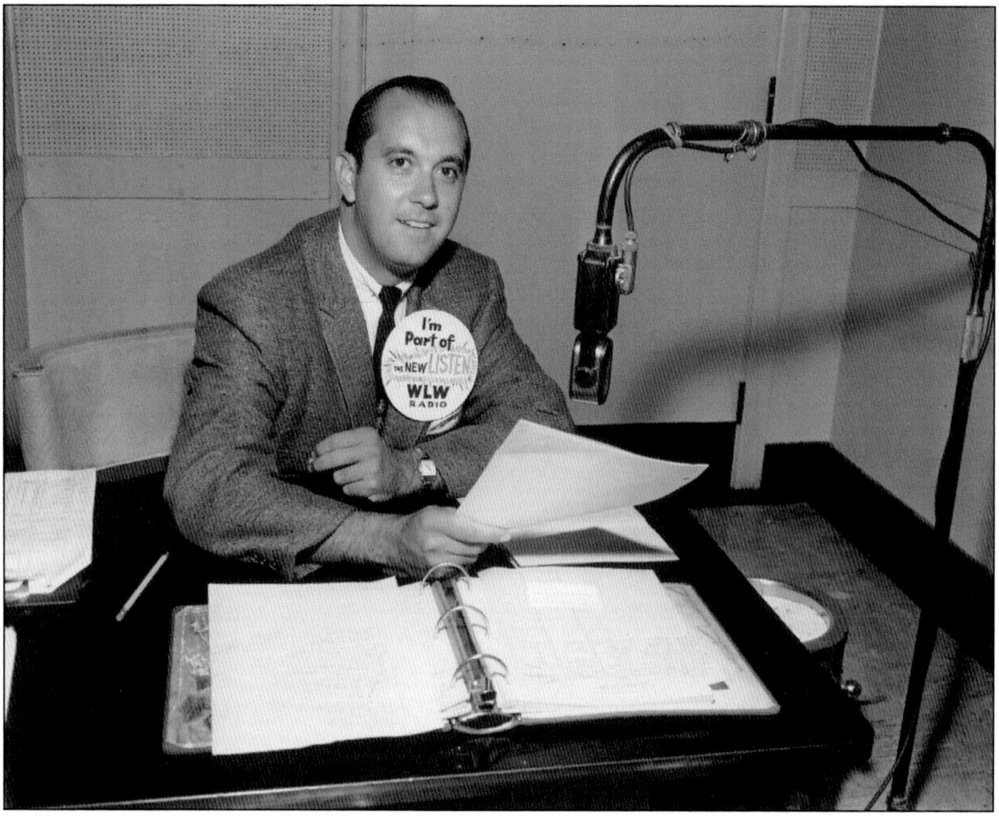

Portsmouth-born Walter Phillips came to Cincinnati radio in 1947 to work at WSAI and in 1948, on WCPO. Around 1950, he was hired away by WLW where he became a major radio and television star. In 1956, Crosley vice president Ward Quaal left to head WGN in Chicago, and he took along Phillips and fellow announcer Bob Bell. Phillips enjoyed a hall-of-fame career at WGN, and Bell became Bozo the Clown. (MM.)

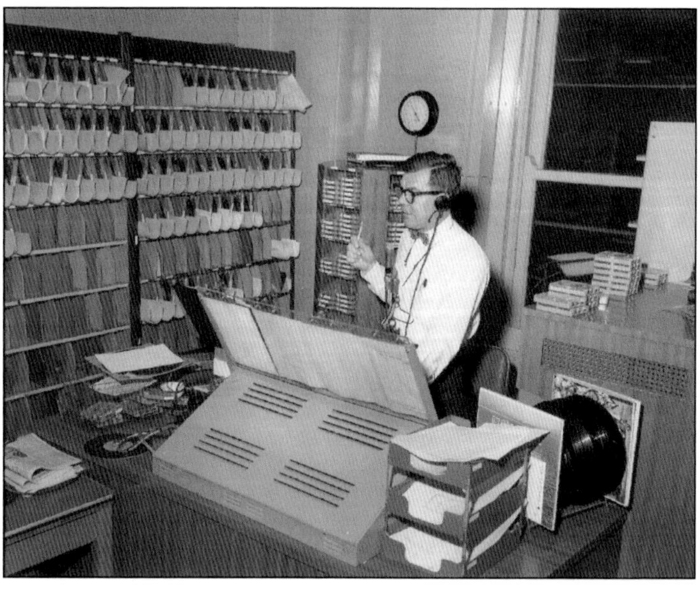

Dating from the late 1930s, WCKY occupied the mezzanine level of the downtown Hotel Gibson. The studios and offices were located in former guest rooms, which made for an unusual layout that would not pass muster in today's high-security world. In this mid-1950s image, disc jockey Gil Shepherd conducts a broadcast featuring traditional discs and the newly invented "cartridge," the mainstay of radio into the 1990s. (LB.)

In 1961, WNOP switched from a wide-ranging format that included many styles of music to a mostly jazz format. From this point on, WNOP gained a cult following despite its weak nighttime signal. Ray Scott, Dick Pike, Oscar Treadwell, and—above all—morning man and resident curmudgeon Leo Underhill, attracted a loyal following who could only snicker when in 1972, the station relocated to a set of refurbished oil drums bobbing in the Ohio River just off the Newport riverbank. David Ziegler, manager, is shown. (KCL.)

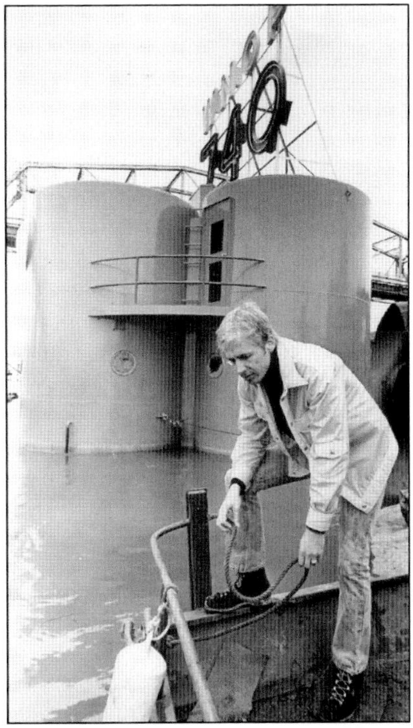

WCKY owner L.B. Wilson was a vaudeville showman in his youth, and that mindset continued through his life. From the Hotel Gibson Motogram sign to the Studio Plane mobile studio, Wilson poured his showmanship into everything he did. Although he died in 1954, his fingerprints were on the order for four new Isetta Turismo three-wheeled cars for his staff. WCKY's Lloyd Baldwin is pictured here with the news car. (LB.)

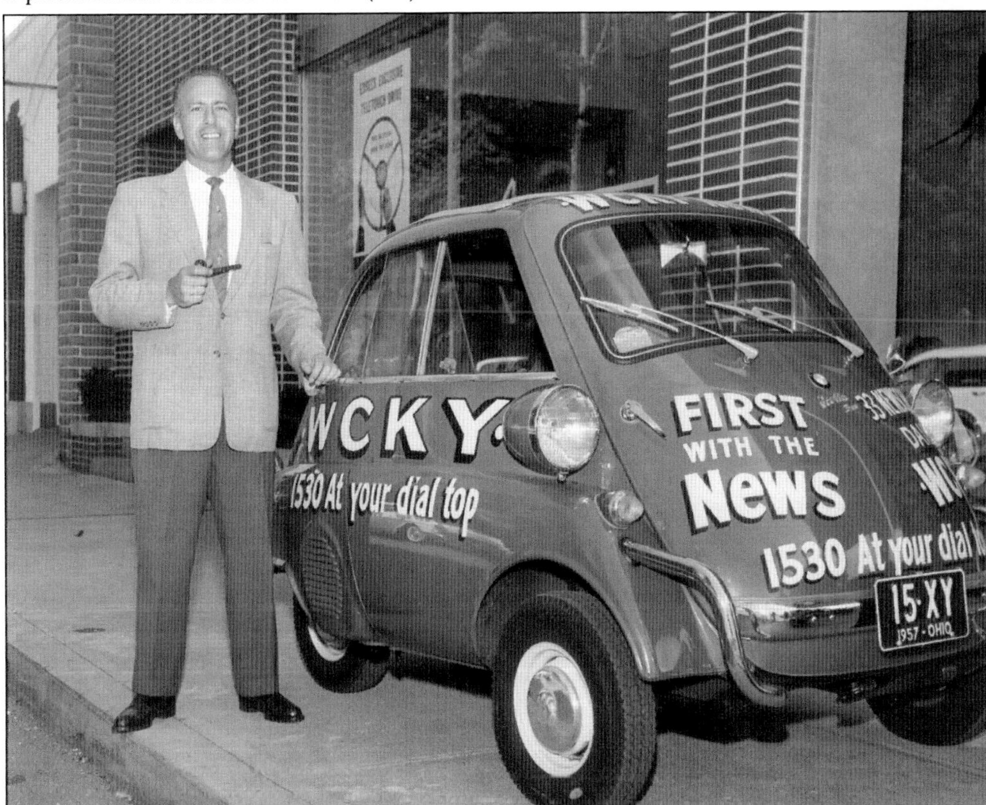

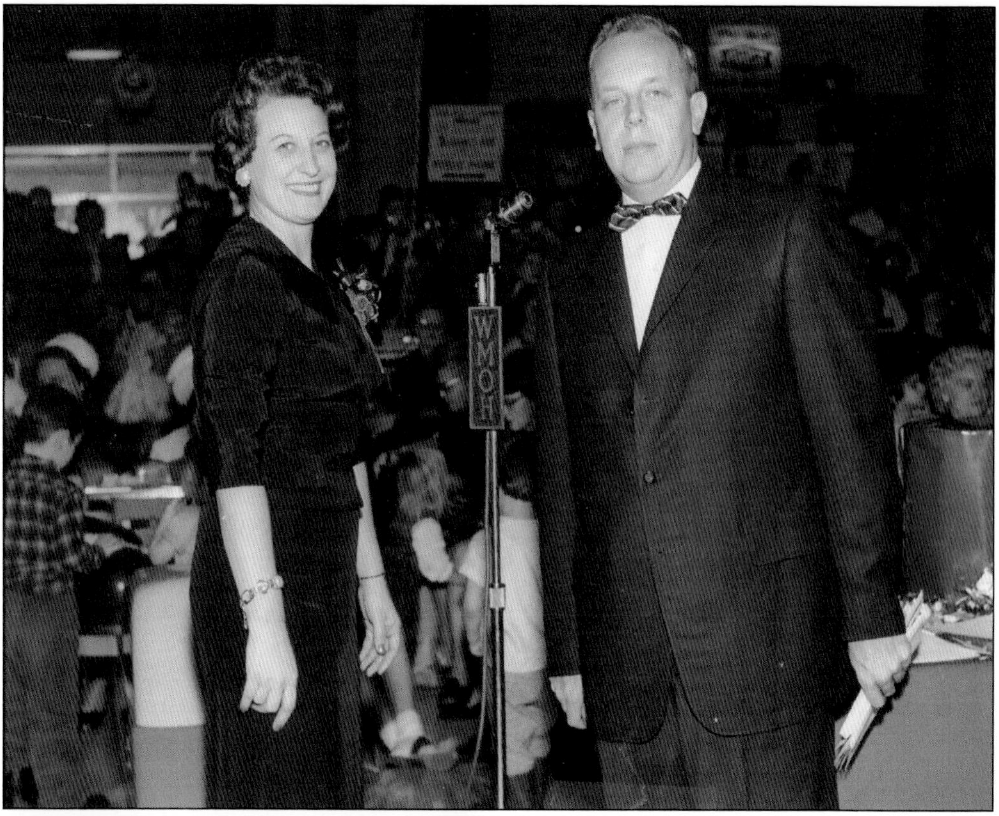

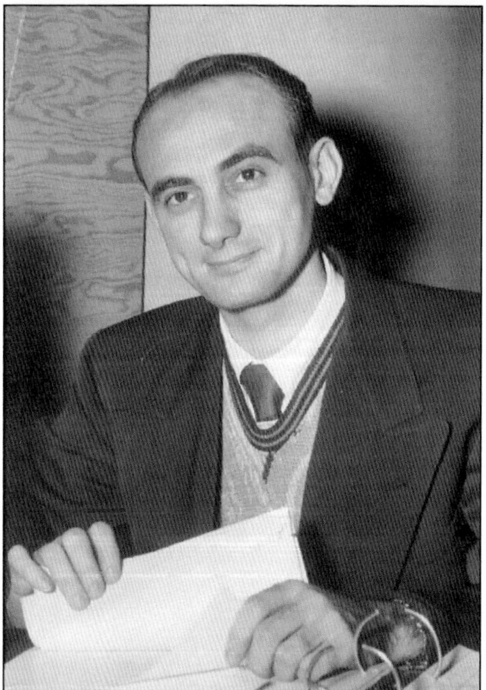

On August 15, 1944, fourteen years after its predecessor WRK went silent, radio returned to Hamilton when John Slade put WMOH on the air. WMOH, for "Middletown, Oxford, and Hamilton," was truly a community station, broadcasting in and around Hamilton and featuring such personalities as Ted Richardson and Ray Motley. Judy Perkins and Norm Keller are seen broadcasting here from Columbia Lanes in 1962. Perkins was a longtime vocalist and hostess, who also worked at WKRC and WLW as well as on television on WLWT. (JPS.)

Greater Cincinnati's first public radio station went on the air in late 1950 when Miami University dedicated WMUB-FM to replace its carrier-current AM station. Don Leshner, a student attending Miami on the GI Bill who was active on the student station, was one of its founders. Leshner enjoyed a long career in Cincinnati broadcasting and advertising while WMUB remained active as an important local station until it was turned into a "repeater" station in 2009. (GB.)

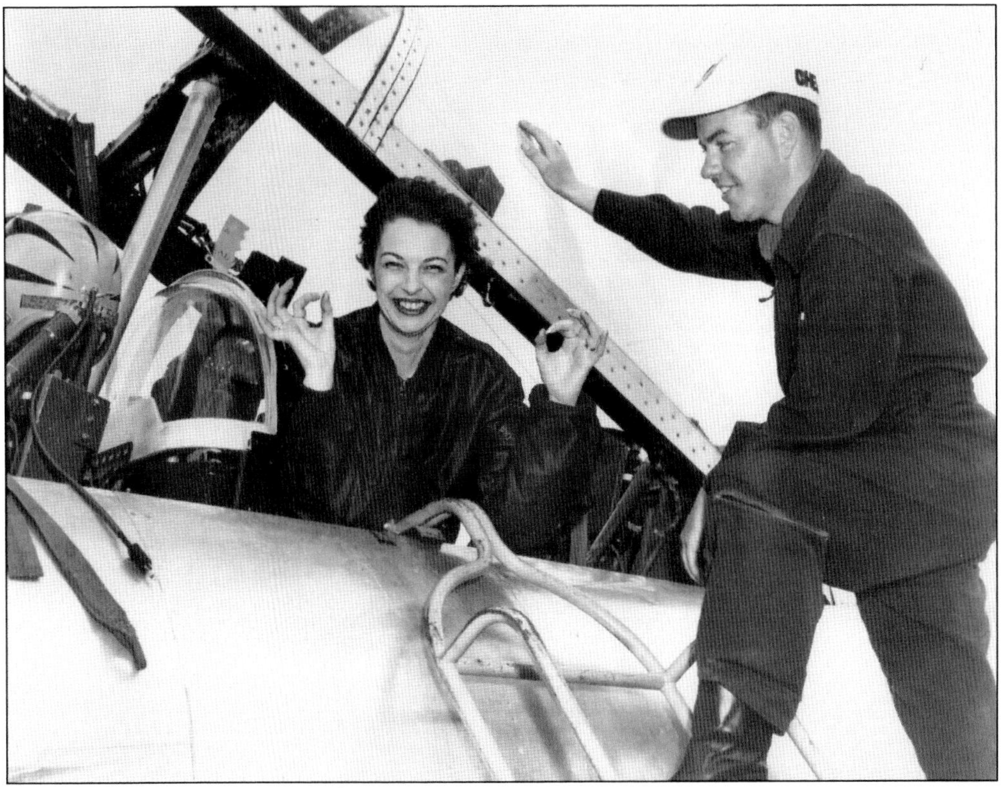

WCKY women's programming director and hostess Delvina Wheeldon certainly received her share of "airtime" when she became the first female reporter to fly faster than the speed of sound in the mid-1950s. Wheeldon followed up this daredevil act by spending several seconds in weightlessness on a different Air Force–sponsored flight. In the 1960s, she became simply "Delvina" and spent her remaining years as a lecturer on aviation issues. (MM.)

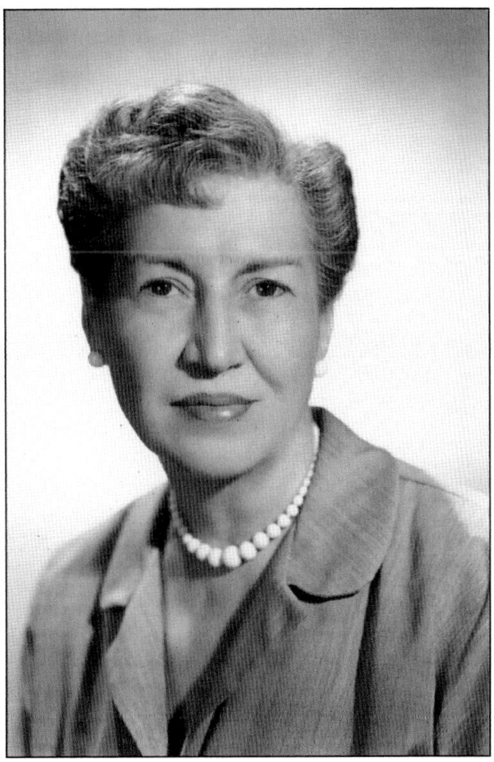

Proving that turnabout is fair play, after WLW secured the services of WKRC program director and popular host Ruth Lyons in 1942, WKRC obtained the services of the "Old-Fashioned Girl." That was the name given to vocalist Helen Nugent, who appeared on the network, in local opera, and on WLW in the 1930s. At WKRC, Nugent became program director of WCTS and was the longtime women's affairs director, a job she continued into the 1960s, much like Lyons. (MM.)

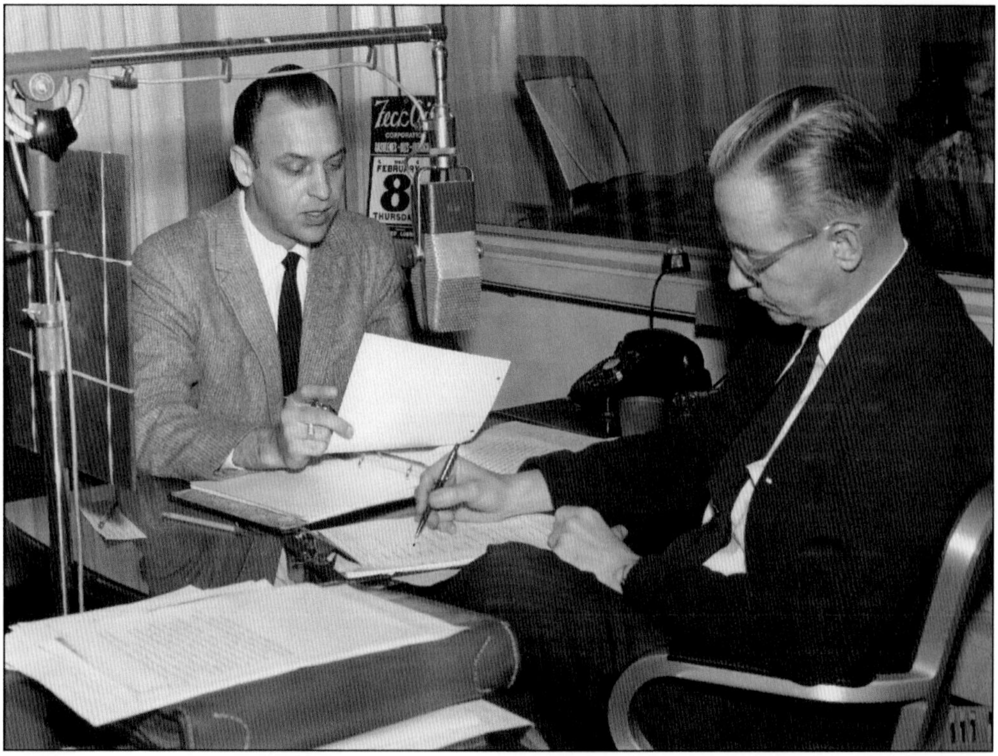

No individual Cincinnati radio broadcaster enjoyed better ratings than WKRC's Stan Matlock (right). Matlock took over WKRC's morning program when Tom McCarthy left in the mid-1950s and created the *Magazine of the Air.* A library bookworm, Matlock spent countless hours sifting through books and magazines to come up with tens of thousands of small trivia narratives, which he would sprinkle throughout his show. Matlock scored ratings well into the 50-percent range and dominated local morning radio through the 1960s. His newsman during this particular broadcast is Will Warren (left). (WW.)

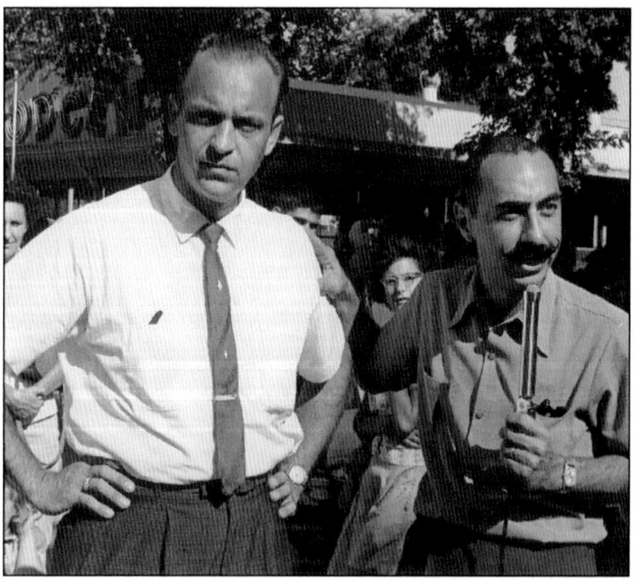

In the mid-1950s, two of the first three live, interactive radio talk shows in the country began at Cincinnati's WKRC. Station technicians developed a way to use two old tape machines to create the first "delay unit," which could allow callers on the air. In 1955, handlebar-mustachioed Ted McKay (right) was the first at WKRC with a program of general talk called *Party Line* and was followed by Will "With a Way" Warren (left), whose nightly call-in program on home repair and general around-the-house projects was a local fixture for 35 years. (WW.)

Cincinnati native Jerry Thomas began his broadcast career as an off-camera setup man at WLWT television. It was not long, however, before he found his niche in radio, first at a small station in Kentucky, and then in 1961 at WKRC. Thomas was a clever and talented disc jockey who brought youth to a station with a stodgy reputation. With inventive characters Granny, Usua Lee Wong the Chinese Weatherman, and others, Thomas remained at WKRC nearly uninterrupted for over 45 years, which is uncommon in the radio business. (JT.)

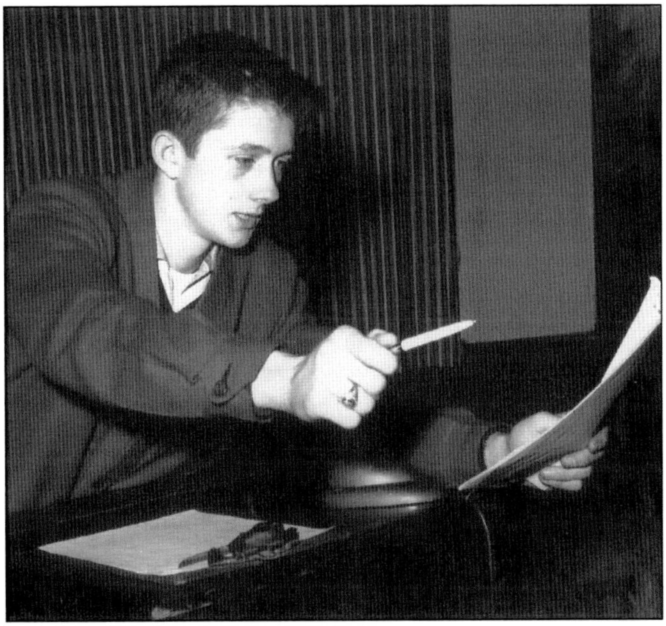

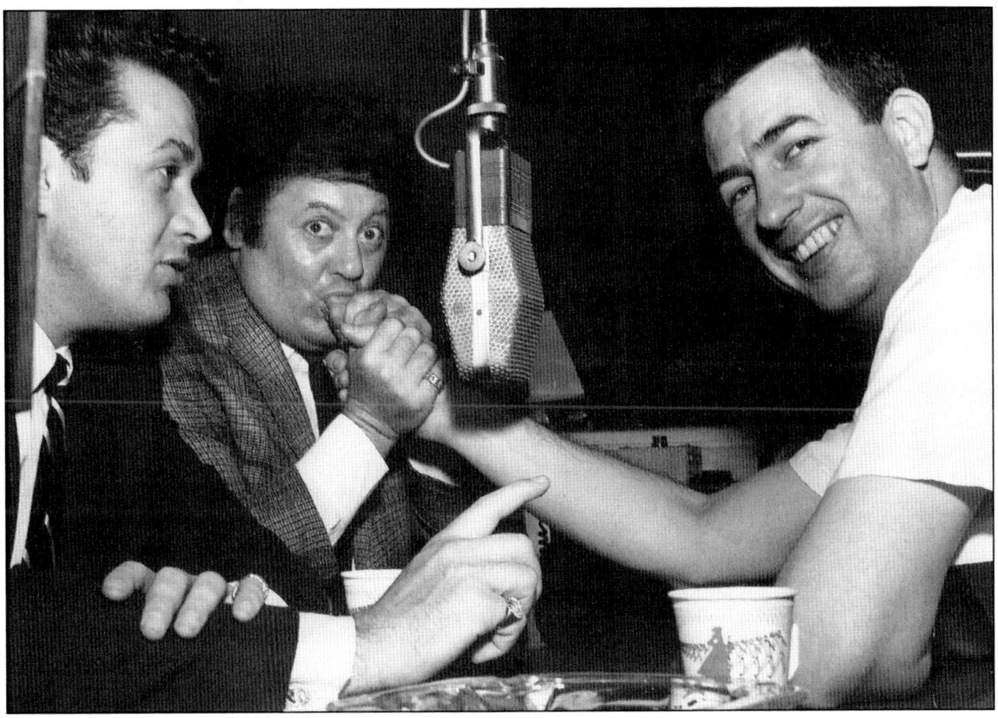

Bob Jones had two stints at WKRC: one before he entered the Navy during World War II and the other beginning in 1963. After the war, Jones became a popular radio and television personality in Baltimore, returning to WKRC to create an afternoon radio program of interviews and music called *Kaleidoscope*. Nearly every day, Jones (right) would prerecord celebrity interviews and then incorporate excerpts into the program. Jones's guests could be authors, actors, future presidents, and even comedians, like Marty Allen and Steve Rossi. Jones later moved the program to WCKY after a brief stint as a Channel 12 news anchor. (JJ.)

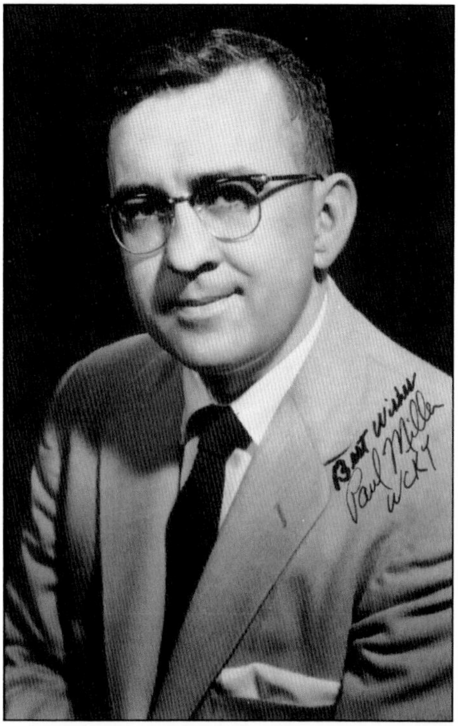

Like many in radio broadcasting, Paul Miller began at WCKY as a disc jockey and worked his way into the management of the station, first as program director and later as general manager. One of Miller's proudest moments came when he turned WCKY over to the government during the Cuban Missile Crisis. Because WCKY boomed throughout the South and even into the Caribbean, President Kennedy issued a special certificate of appreciation. (MM.)

WCKY scored a bit of a coup in 1961 when they hosted a debate between Teamsters national president James Hoffa and local union organizer James Luken. Luken was threatening to pull his dairy drivers out of the Teamsters. The debate and press conference was held at the Hotel Gibson. WCKY announcer and future manager Paul Miller is seen standing center behind the seated Hoffa. (LB.)

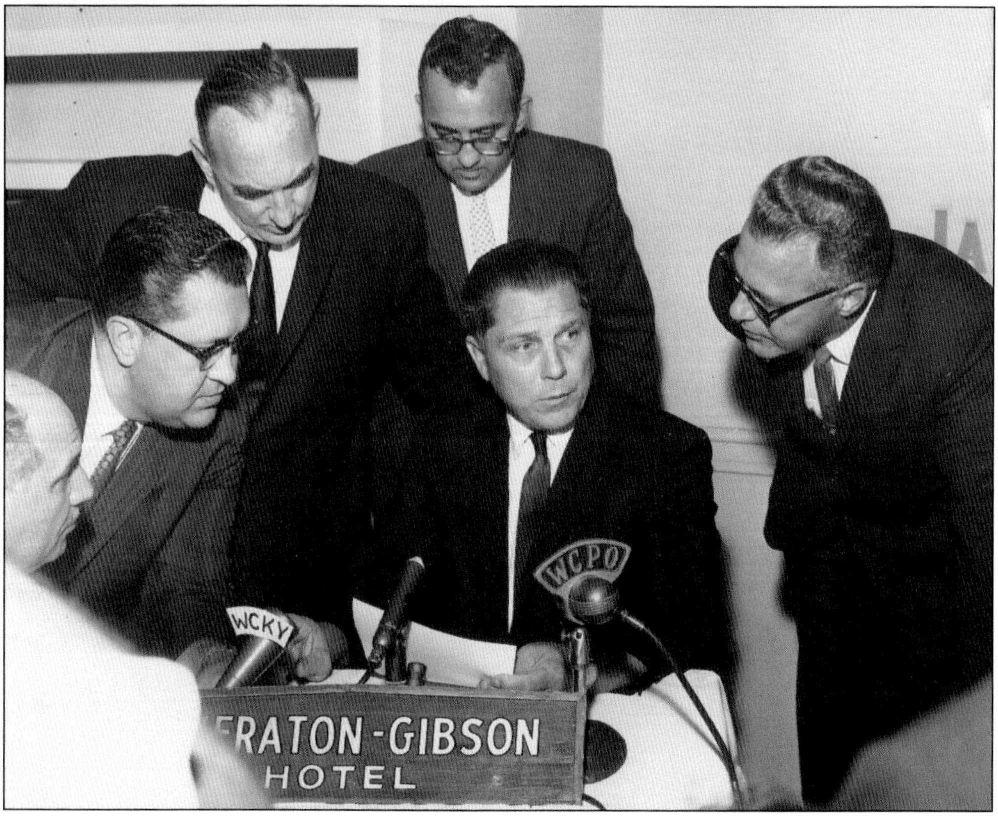

Longtime WCKY announcer Don Herman did a little of everything at the station over the years. His deep, resonant voice was heard on music programs and station announcements. Perhaps more than anything, though, Herman took pride in his news broadcasting, which he continued into the 1990s on WSAI. (MM.)

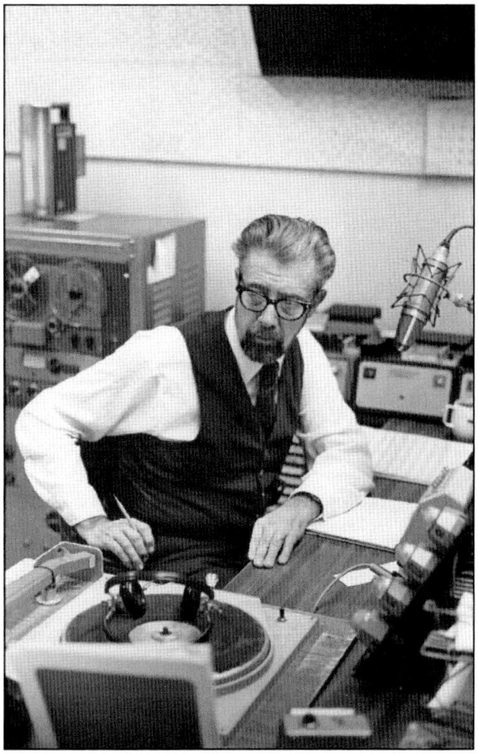

For many years, WLW—as did nearly all stations—would sign off during the overnight hours. Beginning in the 1950s, however, the concept of 24-hour-a-day service started to spread across radio, and WLW was no exception. The station was one of nine clear channel stations originating a program of soft classical music called *Music 'Til Dawn*. Sponsored by American Airlines, the program featured local hosts who were provided with identical music lists for each night's airing. Pete Matthews (shown) and Bill Myers were among the WLW local announcers. (MM.)

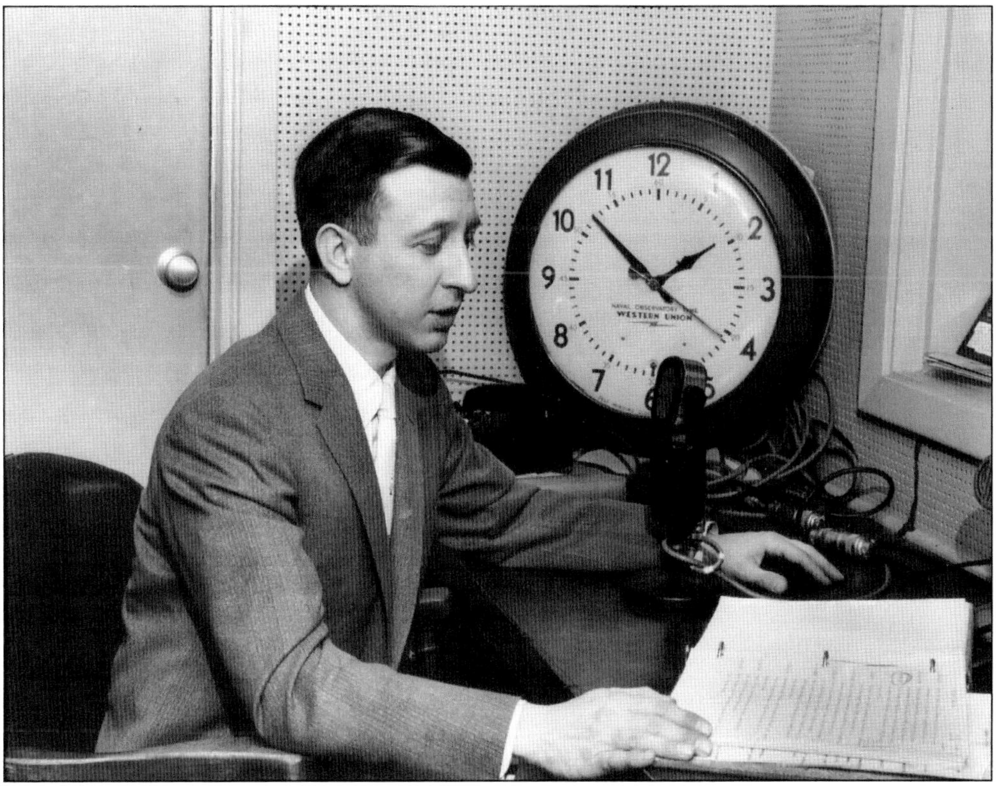

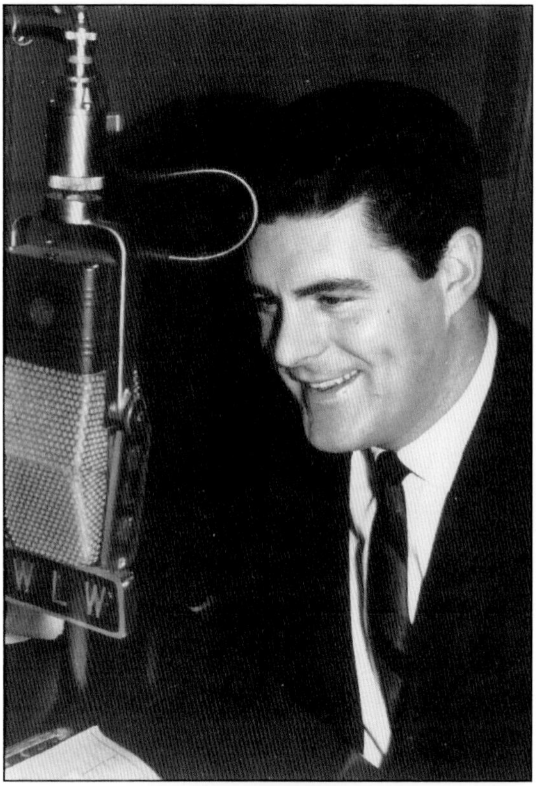

Handsome, young Bob Braun burst into local broadcasting in 1949 at WCPO but switched to WLWT after a successful appearance on Arthur Godfrey's *Talent Scouts* in January 1957. Braun appeared on television on several programs but is best remembered as star of the *Bob Braun Show*, previously known as the *50-50 Club*. He also worked on WLW radio hosting a daily disc jockey program and broadcasting from McAlpin's department store downtown. (WJB.)

After unsuccessfully trying hootenanny as a musical format in 1961, WCPO radio attempted to go head-to-head with rival WSAI by bringing in Top 40 disc jockeys from around the country. Among them, Shad O'Shea and Mike Gavin were promoted as one of the few morning DJ "teams" at that time; their comedy was so irreverent and bizarre that they developed an amazing cult following despite WCPO's puny 250-watt signal. Like Bob and Ray, few subjects escaped the attention of the *Shad and Mike Show*. (MH.)

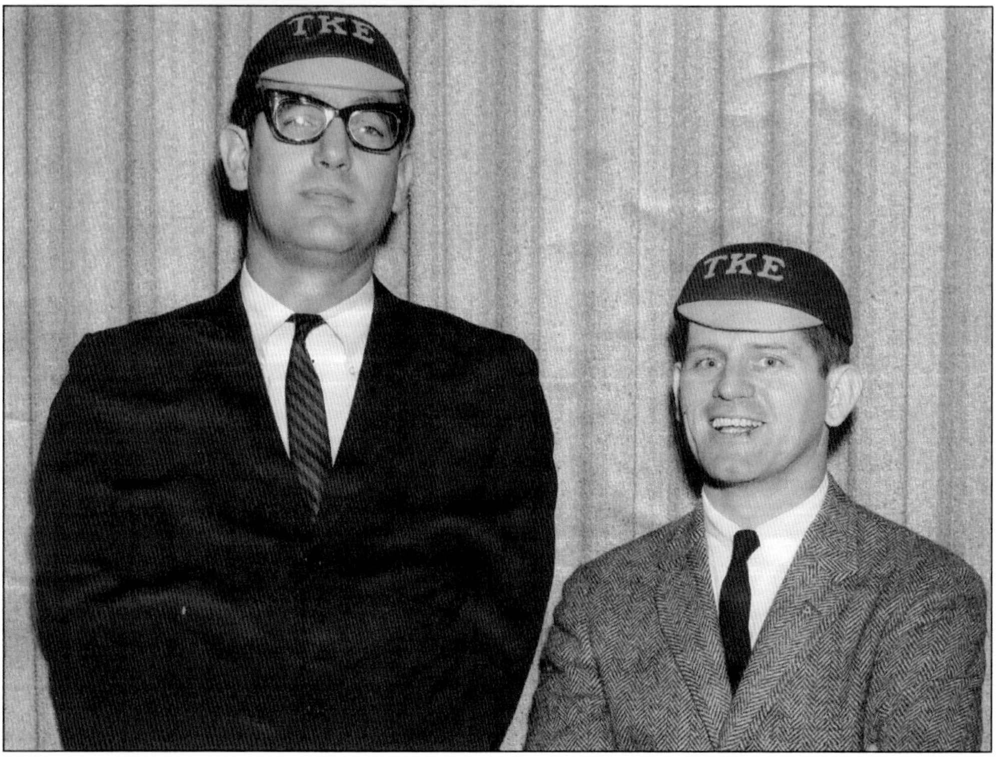

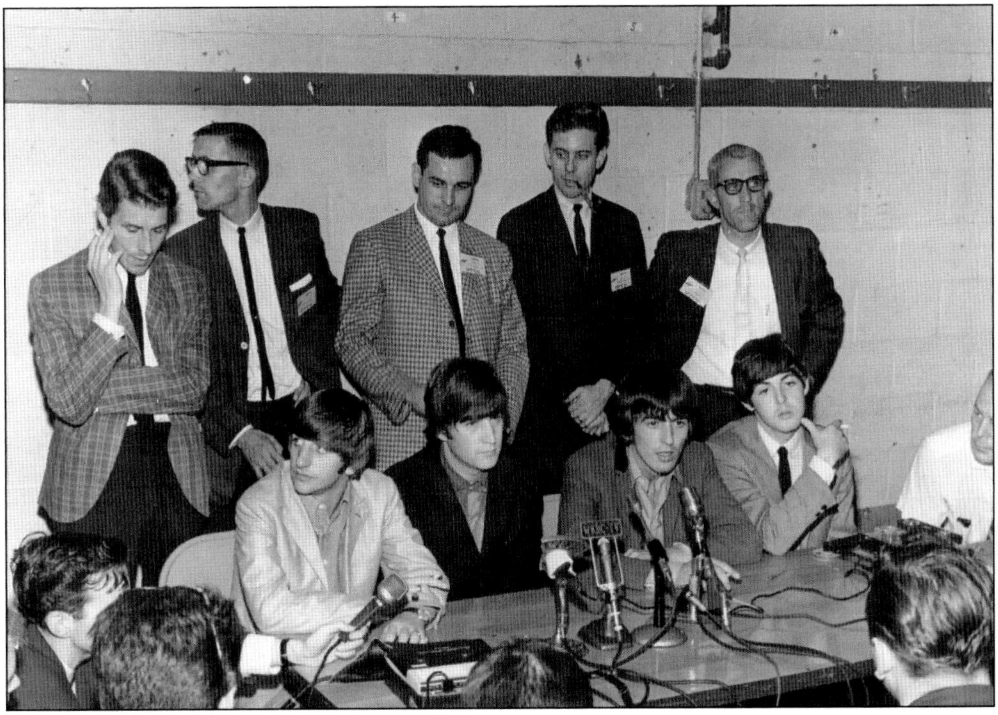

After finding success in other markets, the Top 40 radio format came to WSAI in 1961 and was an immediate hit. Younger listeners tuned in for the patter of Good Guys disc jockeys Gene Austin, Skinny Bobby Harper, Paul Purtan, Ron Britain, Steve Kirk, Mike Sherman, Dick Wagner, Dusty Rhodes, and others. In August 1964, five of the DJs—Harper, Purtan, Rhodes, Kirk, and Sherman—chipped in their own money to bring the Beatles to the Cincinnati Gardens. Harper, Purtan, Rhodes, and Kirk are pictured in the second row behind the Beatles, starting at second from left. (DR.)

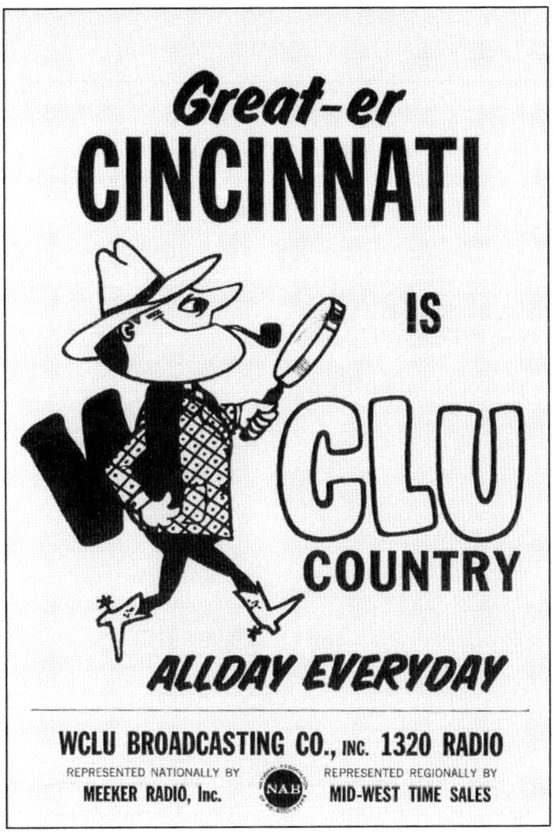

Radio changed in the 1960s when specific formats were directed at specific audiences. This fragmentation of the radio audience began with the rise of the Top 40 format but was amplified by Cincinnati's first all-country-music station, WCLU, in August 1964. Later, WCLU became WCVG, and for one year in 1988, it was actually an "all Elvis Presley" music station. (MM.)

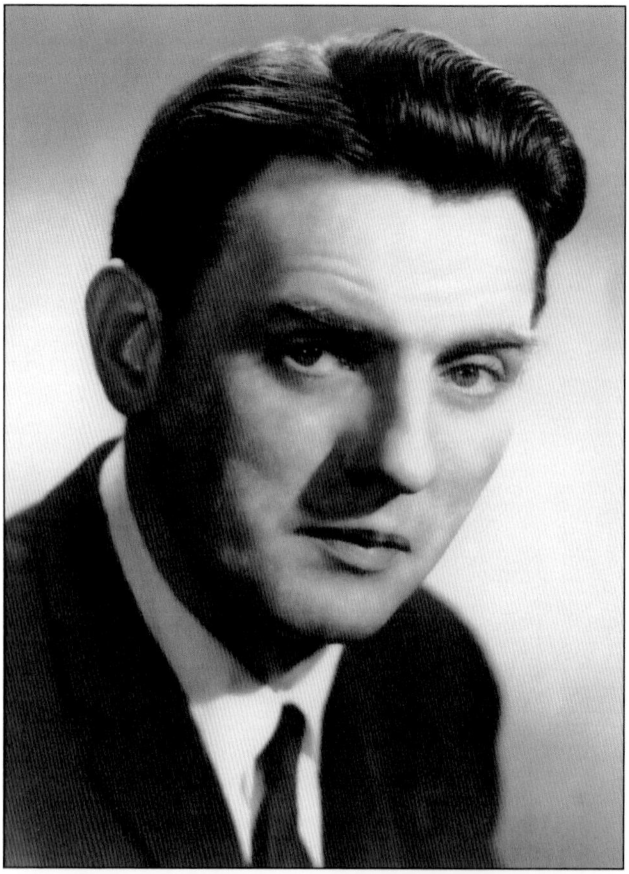

In the 1960s, WLW radio found itself the neglected older sibling of WLWT television. Crosley/Avco attempted to inject new life by hiring the team of Tyler Dunn and Max Warner in 1964. One year later, James Francis Patrick O'Neill, better remembered as JFPO, began delivering years of laughs with, among other features, his fictional comedy soap opera *As Your Stomach Turns*, which he performed live every morning. (KO.)

In addition to JFPO, WLW hired a popular St. Louis disc jockey, who for years went by the name "King Richard." At WLW, he chose the name "Rich King" and introduced Cincinnati to his own unique form of clever, witty wordplay. But unlike JFPO, the station did not keep King very long, and he later surfaced at WKRC and WCKY where he became more of a talk host. (MM.)

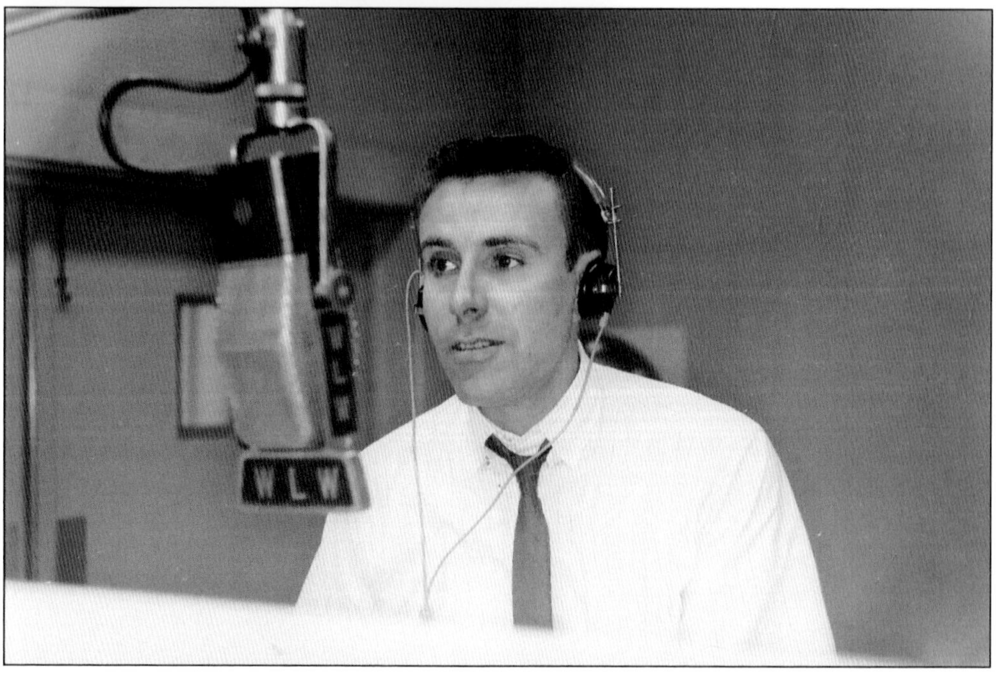

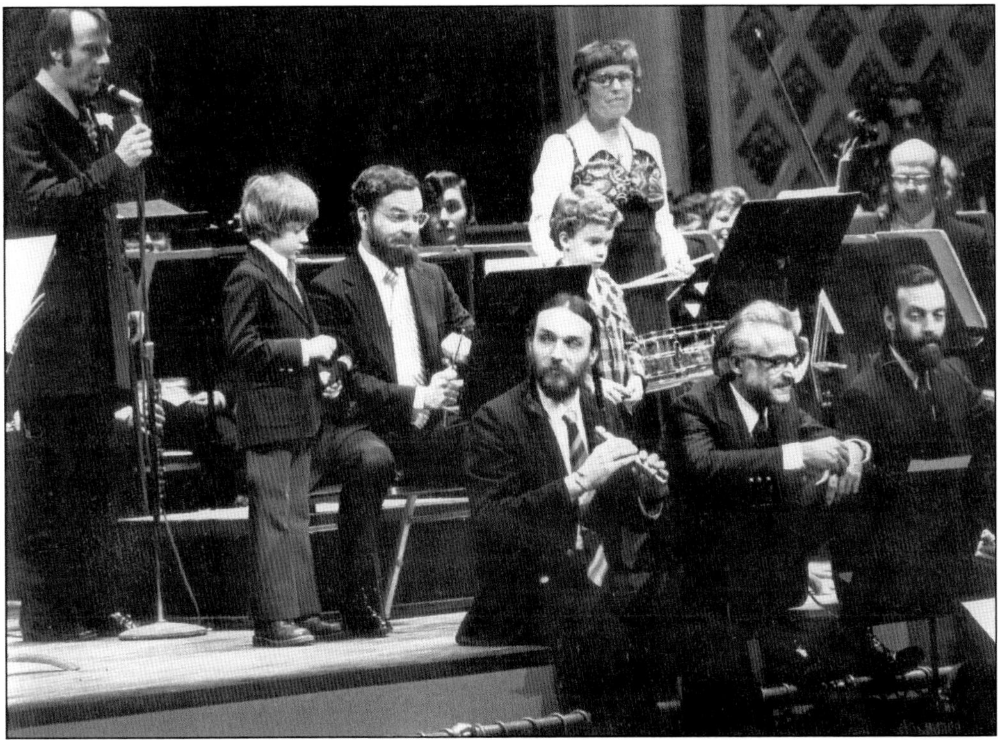

Beginning in 1960 and originally owned by the University of Cincinnati, WGUC always put fine arts and classical music front and center in its mission. Pictured here in 1968 with the Cincinnati Pops Orchestra during a broadcast of a benefit performance of a Toy Koncert for Children are a young Erich Kunzel (standing at far left), veteran WGUC hosts Andrew Jergens (second row, third from left) and Carolyn Watts (standing), and, in the first row, Gary Barton, general manager George Bryant, and Myron Bennet. (GB.)

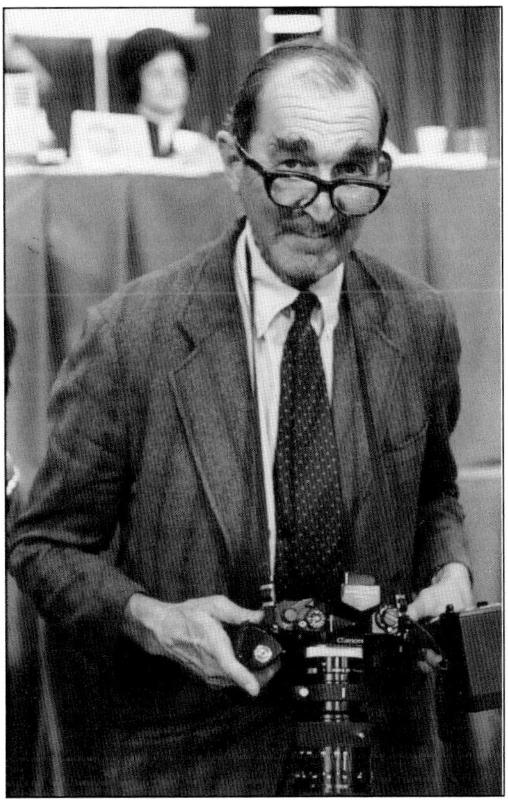

When the owners of WSAI-FM purchased the license of WJBI-FM and moved to 94.1 megahertz, their old spot on the dial at 102.7 became available. Enter lawyer, entrepreneur, photographer, and pilot Frank Wood Sr., who snapped up the license and put classical music WEBN on the air in 1967. Wood allowed his son Frank Jr. to play rock music on a Sunday-night program called *Jelly Pudding*, and it was not long before a cult following convinced the Woods that maybe rock-and-roll could be a successful FM format. (MH.)

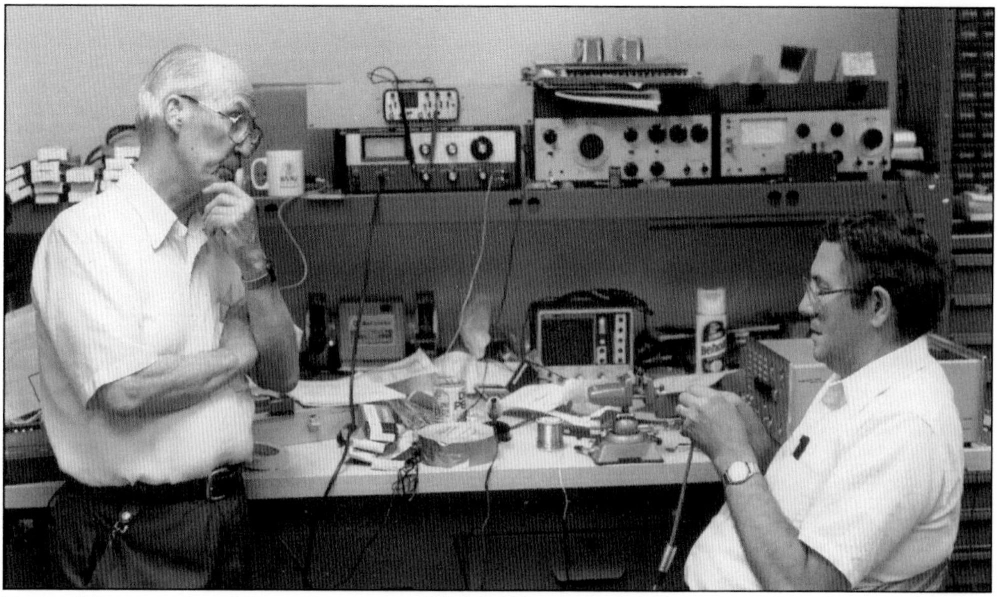

Xavier University's public radio station WVXU-FM traced its beginnings to the late 1950s as part of the ROTC program. In the 1960s, after operating as carrier-current WCXU, Fr. Lawrence Flynn (left) led the way toward an official license as WVXU in 1970. In 1976, Father Flynn hired Dr. James C. King (right) from the University of Cincinnati, and over the next two decades, he built the station into an eight-station, three-state network—the largest privately held public radio network in the country. Xavier sold the network in 2005. (MM.)

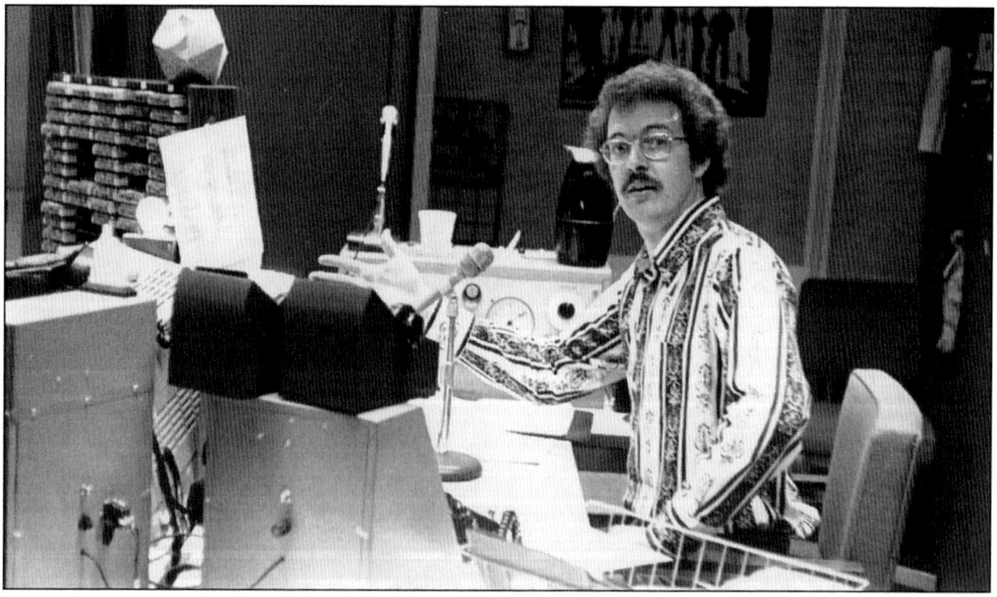

WSAI Good Guys personnel came and went during the 1960s as disc jockeys moved with the Top 40 format from city to city. Jim Scott arrived at WSAI in 1968 with the intention of moving on after a few years. But the business of radio was changing, and although Scott did leave WSAI for other stations, he later became a fixture on Cincinnati radio at WLW. It is fitting that Scott concludes this work because, as of 2011, he is the last of that pioneer era to remain an active, full-time radio host on Cincinnati radio. (JS.)

EPILOGUE

The period covered in this book is the first 50 years of Cincinnati radio, roughly 1921 until 1971. That stated, this in no way negates or minimizes the events that have occurred in the business since the early 1970s. Although perhaps not well suited photographically, the events and changes in radio during the latter decades of the previous century and first decades of the current century are both interesting and important.

The 1970s, for example, saw the rise of FM radio into its dominant place as music provider. Disc jockeys, like Jim LaBarbara, Casey Piotrowksi, Mark Sebastian, Robin Wood, and others, became teen idols.

The grappling between WEBN and Q102 for the young, 1970s rock audience is legendary among Cincinnatians who purchased inexpensive FM converters and installed them under the dashboards of their parents' cars to listen to the rivalry.

As FM stations planted their flags in the various fiefdoms of music, cunning programming innovators, like Randy Michaels, introduced the old AM band to talk radio and not only staved off obsolescence but, in the words of a Cincinnati media scribe, "taught the old lady to dance." National and regional personalities Bill Wills, Bill Cunningham, and Mike McConnell benefitted from the "reinvention" of the AM band to talk.

While "race radio" dates back to the 1950s, local African Americans really found their voice on radio in the 1980s thanks to visionaries like Lincoln Ware and Ross Love.

Public radio came into its present form in the 1980s and 1990s as college stations, like Xavier's former WVXU, grew out of being merely a training ground and into a high-quality alternative for those tired of the commercial end of the dial.

Original comedy became less obvious, but Cincinnati had one of the best last national talents in the form of Gary Burbank and his sidekick Kevin Wolfe.

National industry-wide deregulation and the rise of mega-corporations controlling thousands of radio stations, including those in Cincinnati, also helped shape the recent decades, as did the trend toward embracing technological advancements to streamline expenses and facilitate cost-effective strategies.

Even the concept of "oldies" developed as the music of parents and grandparents suddenly became whisked along in a wave of nostalgia, furthering the careers and popularity of the voices heard over the years. Bob Braun, Nick Clooney, Don Herman, Dusty Rhodes, and others were reinvigorated through an endless progression of stations whose musical goal lines were pushed along with the generations. Indeed, radio never died in Cincinnati. It was battered and beaten around at times, but it remains, despite the scars, a living and breathing and, yes, even a growing concern.

As for the future? There is little doubt that radio will have to reinvent itself again and again. The teenager who seems chained to his laptop computer downloading songs to his iTunes file and who has mastered social media, cyberspace, and Facebook is so eerily similar to the child in the back of the garage with the 1920s crystal receiver it is uncanny. Does radio even have a chance of keeping the modern, young mind stimulated? Time will tell. But in looking at the eyes and faces of the men and women seen within this book—the pioneers of Cincinnati radio—one can see that there is a mindset and mutual interest among radio broadcasters of every era to take up the challenge and fight, in every way possible, to continue to keep providing the canvas upon which the theater of the mind is painted every day in and around Cincinnati—and beyond.

Discover Thousands of Local History Books Featuring Millions of Vintage Images

Arcadia Publishing, the leading local history publisher in the United States, is committed to making history accessible and meaningful through publishing books that celebrate and preserve the heritage of America's people and places.

Find more books like this at
www.arcadiapublishing.com

Search for your hometown history, your old stomping grounds, and even your favorite sports team.

Consistent with our mission to preserve history on a local level, this book was printed in South Carolina on American-made paper and manufactured entirely in the United States. Products carrying the accredited Forest Stewardship Council (FSC) label are printed on 100 percent FSC-certified paper.

MADE IN THE USA